W9-BTP-915

Uncle Sam and You Curriculum Package

How do elections work? What does the President do all day? Who decides where stop signs go? What is Labor Day? *Uncle Sam and You* is a one-year civics course that answers these questions and many more. Designed for students in grades 5-8, this curriculum guides you on an engaging tour of American government. Learn about elected leaders and everyday citizens who have important roles to fill in making our country work.

All of the instructions for how to use the course are included in Part 1 and Part 2, so you do not need a separate teacher's manual. At the beginning of each weekly unit, an introductory page gives an overview of the unit, a list of the lessons, and a list of what additional books the student will be using while studying that particular unit. Each unit has four daily lessons, followed by a holiday lesson you choose. While this course is designed for children in grades 5-8, younger children can listen to the lessons and participate in the family activities.

The lessons are richly illustrated with full-color photographs and historic illustrations. At the end of each regular (non-holiday) lesson is a list of several supplemental activities. You may choose which activities to assign. Depending on how many activities you assign, most students will need 45-90 minutes to complete one lesson. One special family activity is assigned each week that corresponds with the holiday lesson you choose for that unit. These activities include craft and art projects, themed meals, and other multi-age activities.

The full curriculum package includes:

- *Uncle Sam and You Part 1*
- *Uncle Sam and You Part 2*
- *The Citizen's Handbook*
- *Uncle Sam and You Answer Key*

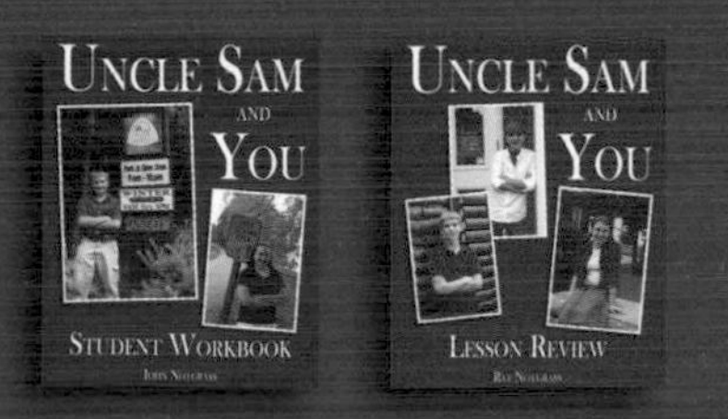

Eight works of literature are assigned in the *Uncle Sam and You* curriculum to give your child a richer perspective on the various topics studied. Two optional additional resources are the *Student Workbook* and *Lesson Review,* each of which provides a way to review material in each lesson. The *Answer Key* that comes with the curriculum package has all of the answers needed for grading.

For more information, visit notgrass.com or call 1-800-211-8793.

The Citizen's Handbook

Civics in Action

The Citizen's Handbook: Civics in Action
Edited by Bethany Poore

ISBN 978-1-60999-048-0

Cover design by Mary Evelyn McCurdy
Interior design by John Notgrass

Printed in the United States of America

Notgrass Company
975 Roaring River Road
Gainesboro, TN 38562

1-800-211-8793
www.notgrass.com
books@notgrass.com

Table of CONTENTS

U.S. Capitol

Supreme Court

Flags at the Washington Monument

The Citizen's Handbook INTRODUCTION

These readings represent civics in action.

The ideas, laws, procedures, and systems of government that are discussed in these pages are not just theories—they live every day in every American town. Laws are passed which give people more freedom or less. People write to their Senators and Congressmen and influence real issues. Citizens vote, most of whom would not have had that freedom at previous times in our history. The procedures for becoming an American citizen are a framework for changed lives and new hopes. Government leaders are real people with ideas, failings, friends, families, and dreams for our country. The people they lead look to them as examples and depend on them to perform their duties with integrity. Government makes a difference in your life. It is an essential way we all interact with each other as Americans.

All the action, give-and-take, opinions, plans, and memories in these pages represent our government at work in everyday life. American government is not something trapped in marble statues, penned on fading documents, stuck in black-and-white photographs, or hidden in dusty books. The American government has a pulse. We see and feel that pulse when Congress votes on an important bill, when the President holds an emergency meeting with his Cabinet, when Supreme Court justices read late into the night to understand a case, when judges administer the oath of office, when government employees listen to people explaining their problems at length over the telephone, when a custodian at the Smithsonian unlocks the front doors in the morning, when a Glacier National Park ranger drives through the wilderness in a jeep, when citizens line up on a cold Tuesday morning in November to cast their votes, when a mayor opens a new school building, when jurors give up their daily responsibilities for the sake of justice, when men in orange vests repair the Interstate, when firemen jump off their cots to respond to a bell in the middle of the night, when policemen cruise downtown to keep an eye on things, and when far out in a distant ocean U.S. sailors raise the Stars and Stripes on a cruiser. Our government is living, breathing, changing, and always moving.

I hope the varied readings in this volume give you a greater respect and appreciation for the people that make our system of government work and for the key role you play in the life of the United States of America.

Bethany Poore

The Citizen's Handbook

Includes these types of original sources:

Journals, Memoirs, & Biographies

Poems

Documents

Songs

Newspaper & Magazine Articles

Letters

Virtue Stories

Speeches

My Country 'Tis of Thee
Samuel F. Smith

Samuel F. Smith wrote the following reply to an inquiry about the origins of his song, "America," commonly known as "My Country 'Tis of Thee."

Newton Centre, Massachusetts, June 5, 1887

Mr. J. H. Johnson:

Dear Sir: The hymn "America" was not written with reference to any special occasion. A friend (Mr. Lowell Mason) put into my hands a quantity of music books in the German language early in the year 1832—because, as he said, I could read them and he couldn't—with the request that I would translate any of the hymns and songs which struck my fancy, or, neglecting the German words, with hymns or songs of my own, adapted to the tunes, so that he could use the music. On a dismal day in February, turning over the leaves of one of these music books, I fell in with the tune, which pleased me—and observing at a glance that the words were patriotic, without attempting to imitate them, or even read them throughout, I was moved at once to write a song adapted to the music—and "America" is the result. I had no thought of writing a national hymn, and was surprised when it came to be widely used. I gave it to Mr. Mason soon after it was written, and have since learned that he greatly admired it. It was first publicly used at a Sabbath school celebration of Independence in Park Street Church, Boston, on the 4th of July, 1832.

Respectfully,
S. F. Smith.

My country, 'tis of thee,
Sweet land of liberty,
Of thee I sing.
Land where my fathers died,
Land of the pilgrims' pride,
From every mountain side
Let freedom ring!

My native country! Thee—
Land of the noble free,—
Thy name I love;
I love thy rocks and rills,
Thy woods and templed hills;
My heart with rapture thrills
Like that above.

Let music swell the breeze,
And ring from all the trees
Sweet freedom's song.
Let mortal tongues awake;
Let all that breathe partake;
Let rocks their silence break,—
The sound prolong.

Our fathers' God, to Thee,
Author of liberty,
To Thee we sing;
Long may our land be bright
With freedom's holy light;
Protect us by Thy might,
Great God, our King!

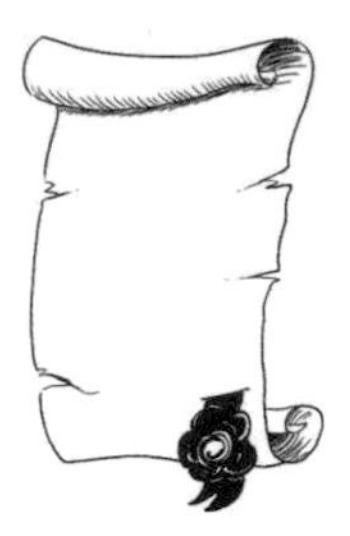

We, the People of . . .

Below are five examples of preambles (or introductions) to state constitutions. The preamble explains the purpose of the constitution and the perspective of the people who created it.

Preamble to the Constitution of the State of Ohio

We, the people of the State of Ohio, grateful to Almighty God for our freedom, to secure its blessings and promote our common welfare, do establish this Constitution.

Preamble to the Constitution of the State of Louisiana

We, the people of Louisiana, grateful to Almighty God for the civil, political, economic, and religious liberties we enjoy, and desiring to protect individual rights to life, liberty, and property; afford opportunity for the fullest development of the individual; assure equality of rights; promote the health, safety, education, and welfare of the people; maintain a representative and orderly government; ensure domestic tranquility; provide for the common defense; and secure the blessings of freedom and justice to ourselves and our posterity, do ordain and establish this constitution.

Preamble to the Constitution of the State of Maine

We the people of Maine, in order to establish justice, insure tranquility, provide for our mutual defense, promote our common welfare, and secure to ourselves and our posterity the blessings of liberty, acknowledging with grateful hearts the goodness of the Sovereign Ruler of the Universe in affording us an opportunity, so favorable to the design; and, imploring God's aid and direction in its accomplishment, do agree to form ourselves into a free and independent State, by the style and title of the State of Maine and do ordain and establish the following Constitution for the government of the same.

Preamble to the Constitution of the State of California

We, the People of the State of California, grateful to Almighty God for our freedom, in order to secure and perpetuate its blessings, do establish this Constitution.

Preamble to the Constitution of the State of Montana

We the people of Montana grateful to God for the quiet beauty of our state, the grandeur of our mountains, the vastness of our rolling plains, and desiring to improve the quality of life, equality of opportunity and to secure the blessings of liberty for this and future generations do ordain and establish this constitution.

You Dreamed Dreams of What America Was to Be
Woodrow Wilson

President Woodrow Wilson spoke to a group of brand-new American citizens at Convention Hall in Philadelphia on May 10, 1915. Following are excerpts of his address.

Mr. Mayor, Fellow Citizens: It warms my heart that you should give me such a reception; but it is not of myself that I wish to think tonight, but of those who have just become citizens of the United States.

. . . You have taken an oath of allegiance to a great ideal, to a great body of principles, to a great hope of the human race. You have said, "We are going to America, not only to earn a living, not only to seek the things which it was more difficult to obtain where we were born, but to help forward the great enterprises of the human spirit—to let men know that everywhere in the world there are men who will cross strange oceans and go where a speech is spoken which is alien to them if they can but satisfy their quest for what their spirits crave; knowing that whatever the speech there is but one longing and utterance of the human heart, and that is for liberty and justice.

Woodrow Wilson

. . . It is a very interesting circumstance to me, in thinking of those of you who have just sworn allegiance to this great Government, that you were drawn across the ocean by some beckoning finger of hope, by some belief, by some vision of a new kind of justice, by some expectation of a better kind of life. No doubt you have been disappointed in some of us. Some of us are very disappointing. No doubt you have found that justice in the United States goes only with a pure heart and a right purpose as it does everywhere else in the world. No doubt what you found here did not seem touched for you, after all, with the complete beauty of the ideal which you had conceived beforehand. But remember this: If we had grown at all poor in the ideal, you brought some of it with you. A man does not go out to seek the thing that is not in him. A man does not hope for the thing that he does not believe in, and if some of us have forgotten what America believed in, you, at any rate, imported in your own hearts a renewal of the belief. That is the reason that I, for one, make you welcome. If I have in any degree forgotten what America was intended for, I will thank God if you will remind me. I was born in America. You dreamed dreams of what America was to be, and I hope you brought the dreams with you. No man that does not see visions will ever realize any high hope or undertake any high enterprise. Just because you brought dreams with you, America is more likely to realize dreams such as you brought. You are enriching us if you came expecting us to be better than we are.

. . . You have come into this great nation voluntarily seeking something that we have to give, and all that we have to give is this: We cannot exempt you from work. No man is exempt from work anywhere in the world. We cannot exempt you from the strife and heartbreaking burden of the struggle of the day—that is common to mankind everywhere; we cannot exempt you from the loads that you must carry. We can only make them light by the spirit in which they are carried. That is the spirit of hope, it is the spirit of liberty, it is the spirit of justice.

When I was asked, therefore, by the Mayor and the committee that accompanied him to come up from Washington to meet this great company of newly admitted citizens, I could not decline the invitation. I ought not to be away from Washington, and yet I feel that it has renewed my spirit as an American to be here. In Washington men tell you so many things every day that are not so, and I like to come and stand in the presence of a great body of my fellow-citizens, whether they have been my fellow-citizens a long time or a short time, and drink, as it were, out of the common fountains with them and go back feeling what you have so generously given me—the sense of your support and of the living vitality in your hearts of the great ideals which have made America the hope of the world.

Newly Arrived Immigrants

The Archivist's Code
Wayne C. Grover

Wayne C. Grover began working at the National Archives in 1935, when it was a new organization. He previously worked as a journalist and a Senate aide. He rose quickly in the National Archives organization and became a skilled, trusted archivist. He was appointed by Harry S. Truman as the third Archivist of the United States in 1948. He served for 17 years, longer than any archivist before or since. He developed The Archivist's Code in 1955 to help archivists make decisions as they execute their responsibilities.

The archivist has a moral obligation to society to preserve evidence on how things actually happened and to take every measure for the physical preservation of valuable records. On the other hand, he has an obligation not to commit funds to the housing and care of records that have no significance or lasting value.

Wayne C. Grover

The archivist must realize that in selecting records for retention or disposal he acts as the agent of the future in determining its heritage from the past. Therefore, insofar as his intellectual attainments, experience, and judgment permit, he must be ever conscious of the future's needs, making his decisions impartially without taint of ideological, political, or personal bias.

The archivist must be watchful in protecting the integrity of records in his custody. He must guard them against defacement, alteration, or theft; he must protect them against physical damage by fire or excessive exposure to light, damp, and dryness; and he must take care to see that their evidentiary value is not impaired in the normal course of rehabilitation, arrangement, and use.

The archivist should endeavor to promote access to records to the fullest extent consistent with the public interest, but he should carefully observe any established policies restricting the use of records. Within the bounds of his budget and opportunities, he should work unremittingly for the increase and diffusion of knowledge, making his documentary holdings freely known to prospective users through published finding aids and personal consultation.

The archivist should respond courteously and with a spirit of service to all proper requests, but he should not waste time responding in detail to frivolous or unreasonable inquiries. He should not place unnecessary obstacles in the way of those who would use the records, but rather should do whatever he can to spare their time and ease their work. Obviously, he should not idly discuss the work and findings of one searcher with another; but where duplication of research effort is apparent, he may properly inform one searcher of the work of another.

The archivist should not profit from any commercial exploitation of the records in his custody, nor should he withhold from others any information he has gained as a result of his archival work in order to carry out private professional research. He should, however, take every legitimate advantage of his favored situation to develop his professional interests in historical and other research.

The archivist should freely pass on to his professional colleagues the results of his own or his organization's research that add to the body of archival knowledge. Likewise, he should leave to his successors a true account of the records in his custody and of their proper organization and arrangement.

Wayne C. Grover
Archivist of the United States

Work at the National Archives

Response to an Invitation from the Citizens of Washington
Thomas Jefferson

Thomas Jefferson received an invitation from Roger Weightman, mayor of Washington, D.C., to participate in the city's celebration of the 50th anniversary of the Declaration of Independence. Jefferson's response was the last letter he wrote. He died ten days later on July 4, 1826, the date of the 50th anniversary.

Monticello June 24. [18]26

Respected Sir

The kind invitation I receive from you on the part of the citizens of the city of Washington, to be present with them at their celebration of the 50th anniversary of American independence; as one of the surviving signers of an instrument pregnant with our own, and the fate of the world, is most flattering to myself, and heightened by the honorable accompaniment proposed for the comfort of such a journey. It adds sensibly to the sufferings of sickness, to be deprived by it of a personal participation in the rejoicings of that day. But acquiescence is a duty, under circumstances not placed among those we are permitted to control. I should, indeed, with peculiar delight, have met and exchanged there congratulations personally with the small band, the remnant of that host of worthies, who joined with us on that day, in the bold and doubtful election we were to make for our country, between submission or the sword; and to have enjoyed with them the consolatory fact, that our fellow citizens, after half a century of experience and prosperity, continue to approve the choice we made. May it be to the world, what I believe it will be, (to some parts sooner, to others later, but finally to all,) the Signal of arousing men to burst the chains, under which monkish ignorance and superstition had persuaded them to bind themselves, and to assume the blessings & security of self-government. That form which we have substituted, restores the free right to the unbounded exercise of reason and freedom of opinion. All eyes are opened, or opening, to the rights of man. The general spread of the light of science has already laid open to every view the palpable truth, that the mass of mankind has not been born with saddles on their backs, nor a favored few booted and spurred, ready to ride them legitimately, by the grace of God. These are grounds of hope for others. For ourselves, let the annual return of this day forever refresh our recollections of these rights, and an undiminished devotion to them.

I will ask permission here to express the pleasure with which I should have met my ancient neighbors of the City of Washington and of its vicinities, with whom I passed so many years of a pleasing social intercourse; an intercourse which so much relieved the anxieties of the public cares, and left impressions so deeply engraved in my affections, as never to be forgotten. With my regret that ill health forbids me the gratification of an acceptance, be pleased to receive for yourself, and those for whom you write, the assurance of my highest respect and friendly attachments.

Th. Jefferson

Thomas Jefferson

The First Prayer of the Continental Congress
Jacob Duché

Jacob Duché, Rector of Christ Church of Philadelphia, Pennsylvania, offered the first prayer before the Continental Congress on September 7, 1774, at 9:00 a.m.

O Lord our Heavenly Father, high and mighty King of kings, and Lord of lords, who dost from thy throne behold all the dwellers on earth and reignest with power supreme and uncontrolled over all the Kingdoms, Empires and Governments; look down in mercy, we beseech Thee, on these our American States, who have fled to Thee from the rod of the oppressor and thrown themselves on Thy gracious protection, desiring to be henceforth dependent only on Thee. To Thee have they appealed for the righteousness of their cause; to Thee do they now look up for that countenance and support, which Thou alone canst give. Take them, therefore, Heavenly Father, under Thy nurturing care; give them wisdom in Council and valor in the field; defeat the malicious designs of our cruel adversaries; convince them of the unrighteousness of their Cause and if they persist in their sanguinary purposes, of own unerring justice, sounding in their hearts, constrain them to drop the weapons of war from their unnerved hands in the day of battle!

Be Thou present, O God of wisdom, and direct the councils of this honorable assembly; enable them to settle things on the best and surest foundation. That the scene of blood may be speedily closed; that order, harmony and peace may be effectually restored, and truth and justice, religion and piety, prevail and flourish amongst the people. Preserve the health of their bodies and vigor of their minds; shower down on them and the millions they here represent, such temporal blessings as Thou seest expedient for them in this world and crown them with everlasting glory in the world to come. All this we ask in the name and through the merits of Jesus Christ, Thy Son and our Savior.

Amen.

Jacob Duché

Painting of the First Prayer in Congress

Three Branches—Excerpts from the Constitution

The United States Constitution outlines the division of power among three branches of government. The first three articles of the Constitution detail the organization and responsibilities of these three branches.

Article I.
Section 1.
All legislative Powers herein granted shall be vested in a Congress of the United States, which shall consist of a Senate and House of Representatives.

Article II.
Section 1.
The executive Power shall be vested in a President of the United States of America. He shall hold his Office during the Term of four Years, and, together with the Vice President, chosen for the same Term, be elected, as follows . . . .

Article III.
Section 1.
The judicial Power of the United States shall be vested in one supreme Court, and in such inferior Courts as the Congress may from time to time ordain and establish. The Judges, both of the supreme and inferior Courts, shall hold their Offices during good Behaviour, and shall, at stated Times, receive for their Services a Compensation, which shall not be diminished during their Continuance in Office.

Legislative

Executive

Judicial

Letter to the Governor of Connecticut

Roger Sherman and Oliver Ellsworth

Roger Sherman (1721-1793) and Oliver Ellsworth (1745-1807), delegates from Connecticut to the Constitutional Convention, sent a copy of the newly-created Constitution to the governor of their home state. They explained some of the ways the Constitution differed from the Articles of Confederation.

LETTER FROM THE HON. ROGER SHERMAN,
AND THE HON. OLIVER ELLSWORTH, ESQUIRES,
DELEGATES FROM THE STATE OF CONNECTICUT,
IN THE LATE FEDERAL CONVENTION,
TO HIS EXCELLENCY, THE GOVERNOR OF SAID STATE.

New London, September 26, 1787.

Sir: We have the honor to transmit to your excellency a printed copy of the Constitution formed by the Federal Convention, to be laid before the legislature of the state.

The general principles which governed the Convention in their deliberations on the subject, are stated in their address to Congress.

We think it may be of use to make some further observations on particular parts of the Constitution.

The Congress is differently organized; yet the whole number of members, and this state's proportion of suffrage, remain the same as before.

The equal representation of the states in the Senate, and the voice of that branch in the appointment to offices, will secure the rights of the lesser, as well as of the greater states.

Some additional powers are vested in Congress, which was a principal object that the states had in view in appointing the Convention. Those powers extend only to matters respecting the common interests of the Union, and are specially defined, so that the particular states retain their sovereignty in all other matters.

Oliver Ellsworth

The objects for which Congress may apply moneys are the same mentioned in the eighth article of the Confederation, viz., for the common defense and general welfare, and for payment of the debts incurred for those purposes. It is probable that the principal branch of revenue will be duties on imports. What may be necessary to be raised by direct taxation is to be apportioned on the several states, according to the number of their inhabitants; and although Congress may raise the money by their own authority, if necessary, yet that authority need not be exercised, if each state will furnish its quota.

The restraint on the legislatures of the several states respecting emitting bills of credit, making any thing but money a tender in payment of debts, or impairing the obligation of contracts by ex post facto laws, was thought necessary as a security to commerce, in which the interest of foreigners, as well as of the citizens of different states, may be affected.

The Convention endeavored to provide for the energy of government on the one hand, and suitable checks on the other hand, to secure the rights of the particular states, and the liberties and properties of the citizens. We wish it may meet the approbation of the several states, and be a means of securing their rights, and lengthening out their tranquility.

Roger Sherman

With great respect, we are, sir, your excellency's obedient, humble servants,

Roger Sherman,
Oliver Ellsworth

[To] His Excellency, Governor Huntington.

Mascot of the Marines

L. J. Weil and W. E. Burke

This letter arrived at the White House in November of 1943, in the midst of World War II. It was referred to the Marine Corps, a representative of which wrote the reply that follows. L. J. Weil is an example of the spirit of service and dedication to his country.

Dear Mr. President,

I really don't know how to write a letter to the President of the United States, but I'll try to do my best. The point is I'd like to be <u>mascot of the Marines</u>. I'm <u>12 years old</u> and a little young to get into anything right now, but when I'm a little older well just you wait and see. A lot of people are going to kid me about this letter but I don't care. And if sometimes you get tired up there in Washington you can come down South and stay with us a little while, "of course that's if you bring your ration book."

Your friend and also a Democrat,
L. J. Weil

Headquarters, U.S. Marine Corps
Washington, D.C.

12 November 1943

Dear Weil,

You letter of recent date, addressed to the President, relative to becoming a mascot in the Marine Corps, has been referred to this office for reply.

While instances are known where recruiting officers have appointed mascots informally and unofficially, no authority of law exists which permits the Marine Corps to name official mascots for our recruiting service.

The patriotic motive which prompted your offer of service, however, is appreciated, and hope that when you reach the required age for enlistment in the Marine Corps, you will avail yourself of the opportunity of becoming a real Marine.

Very truly yours,
W. E. Burke
Lt. Col. U.S. Marine Corps,
Enlisted Procurement Division

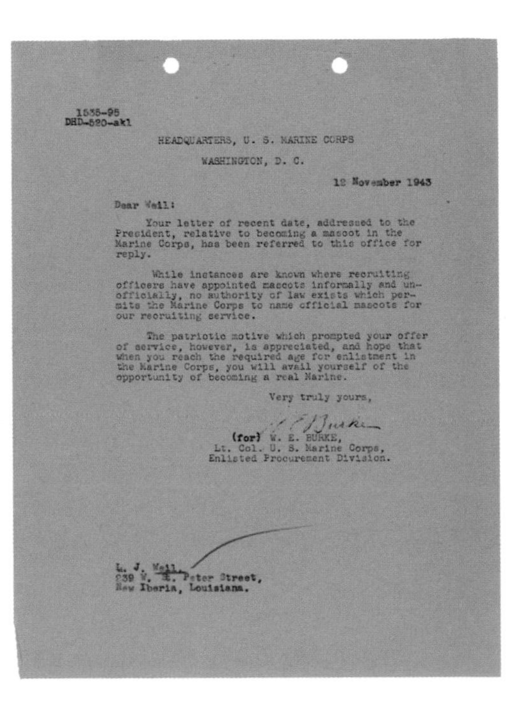

1535-95
DHD-520-akl

HEADQUARTERS, U. S. MARINE CORPS

WASHINGTON, D. C.

12 November 1943

Dear Weil:

Your letter of recent date, addressed to the President, relative to becoming a mascot in the Marine Corps, has been referred to this office for reply.

While instances are known where recruiting officers have appointed mascots informally and unofficially, no authority of law exists which permits the Marine Corps to name official mascots for our recruiting service.

The patriotic motive which prompted your offer of service, however, is appreciated, and hope that when you reach the required age for enlistment in the Marine Corps, you will avail yourself of the opportunity of becoming a real Marine.

Very truly yours,

(for) W. E. BURKE,
Lt. Col. U. S. Marine Corps,
Enlisted Procurement Division.

L. J. Weil,
239 W. St. Peter Street,
New Iberia, Louisiana.

The Flag Goes By

Henry Holcomb Bennett

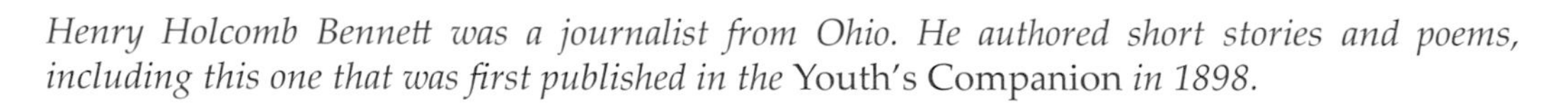

Henry Holcomb Bennett was a journalist from Ohio. He authored short stories and poems, including this one that was first published in the Youth's Companion *in 1898.*

Hats off!
Along the street there comes
A blare of bugles, a ruffle of drums,
A flash of color beneath the sky:
Hats off!
The flag is passing by!

Blue and crimson and white it shines,
Over the steel-tipped, ordered lines,
Hats off!
The colors before us fly;
But more than the flag is passing by.

Sea fights and land fights, grim and great,
Fought to make and save the State:
Weary marches and sinking ships;
Cheers of victory on dying lips;

Days of plenty and years of peace;
March of a strong land's swift increase;
Equal justice, right, and law,
Stately honor and reverend awe;

Sign of a nation, great and strong
To ward her people from foreign wrong:
Pride and glory and honor—all
Live in the colors to stand or fall.
Hats off!

Along the street there comes
A blare of bugles, a ruffle of drums;
And loyal hearts are beating high:
Hats off!
The flag is passing by!

Tim Oller

Newspaper Timeline of the Statue of Liberty

Newspapers across the country eagerly followed the progress of the arrival and erection of "Liberty Enlightening the World" in New York harbor. Below are excerpts from articles that appeared in newspapers during the lengthy process.

***The Morning Star and Catholic Messenger*, New Orleans, Louisiana, June 4, 1876**

The French people are signalizing our Centennial in sundry ways calculated to increase the friendship of the two countries. . . . Bartholdi's immense statue of Liberty, a gift from Frenchmen in honor of American Independence, is to be erected in New York harbor after its completion.

***New York Tribune*, New York City, New York, April 20, 1877**

Bedloe's Island to Be Evacuated.

Congress passed a law at the last session accepting the statue to be presented by the French Government, entitled "Liberty Enlightening the World," and directed the President to select a site either on Governor's Island or Bedloe's Island, in New York harbor, for its location. The President today selected Bedloe's Island, and the small garrison which has occupied the island for many years is ordered to be withdrawn. The lighthouse service has made arrangements to make the lighted torch of the statue one of the stations of the lighthouse service.

The Head of the Statue on Display in a Park in Paris

***Daily Globe*, St. Paul, Minnesota, May 10, 1883**

The Bartholdi Statue

New York, May 9.—The work of repairing the foundation for the Bartholdi monument at Bedloe's Island, was begun today, but was postponed until the families of the officers of the Marine hospital remove. Richard Butler, secretary of the committee, says: the chief Western powers are beginning to evince an interest in the work, and there is now no doubt as to the possibility of carrying the project through in time to erect the statue in the autumn of next year.

***New York World*, New York City, New York, March 16, 1885**

An appeal from the newspaper's publisher, Joseph Pulitzer, for the struggling pedestal fund

We must raise the money! The *World* is the people's paper, and now it appeals to the people to come forward and raise the money. The $250,000 that the making of the Statue cost was

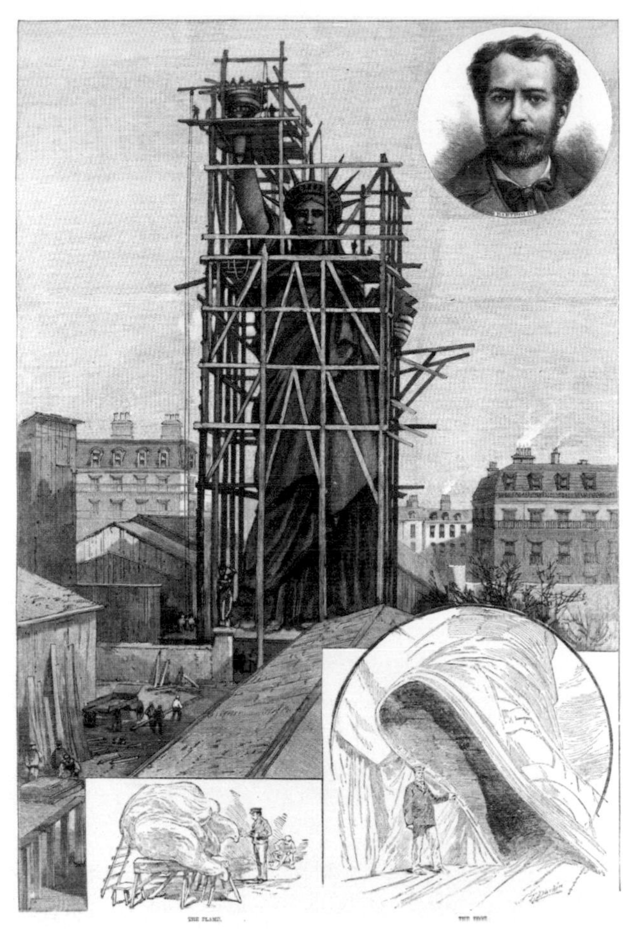

The Statue Under Construction in France

paid in by the masses of the French people—by the working men, the tradesmen, the shop girls, the artisans—by all, irrespective of class or condition. Let us respond in like manner. Let us not wait for the millionaires to give us this money. It is not a gift from the millionaires of France to the millionaires of America, but a gift of the whole people of France to the whole people of America.

***The National Tribune*, Washington, D.C., May 28, 1885**

This new Wonder of the World, which is now being loaded on the French transport *Isere* for shipment to this country, is the largest statue in the world. Some idea of its magnitude may be obtained from the fact that 40 persons found standing room within the head. A six-foot man standing on the level of the lips only just reached the eyebrow. . . . It is expected to arrive in New York about the 25th of May, where it will be erected on Bedloe's Island, this being the location selected for it by Gen. W. T. Sherman, who was appointed by the President to make the selection. . . . The committee in charge of the construction of the base and pedestal for the reception of this great work are in want of funds for its completion, and have prepared a miniature statuet, an exact counterpart of the original, six inches in height, the figure being made of bronze, the pedestal of nickel silver, which they are now delivering to subscribers throughout the United States for the small sum of $1 each. Aside from its being a lasting souvenir of this colossal statue, it will ornament our homes and bear testimony that we have contributed to the completion of one of the grandest works of modern times.

***Daily Globe*, St. Paul, Minnesota, June 18, 1885**

The steamer bearing the Bartholdi statue has arrived in New York harbor.

***Daily Evening Bulletin*, Maysville, Kentucky, October 22, 1885**

Gen. Stone is now laying the twenty-ninth course of stone on the pedestal, and is laying at the rate of five courses every two weeks. The rate can be maintained no matter how bad the weather. There are forty-six courses in the entire pedestal, consequently there are sixteen yet to be laid. Unless there is some unforeseen accident there will be no further delay. There are seventy stone cutters at work at the quarries in Connecticut, and a number of courses are ready to be shipped down. The money on hand is probably enough to complete the pedestal proper, but arrangements will yet have to be made for the raising of funds to pay for the steel fastenings, for the erection of the statue and for the clearing up of the island.

***New York Tribune*, New York City, New York, April 25, 1886**

The great Statue of Liberty is ready for the pedestal and the capstone of the pedestal has been laid. But it is necessary to raise $15,000 to meet the expenses of setting the mighty figure on the lofty base. An appeal which should meet with a prompt and generous response is published in our columns this morning. The American Committee asks for contributions to pay this $15,000. One agreeable and attractive way of contributing will be to attend the entertainment which will be given in Madison Square Garden tomorrow evening. The 22nd Regiment offer the entertainment and will be assisted by Gilmore's Band. There will be dancing.

***Omaha Daily Bee*, Omaha, Nebraska, October 26, 1886**

New York, October 25— . . . Three years and seven months ago work was begun on the foundation of the pedestal for Bartholdi's statue of Liberty. Today the last rivets in the copper sheathing are being hammered into place. On Thursday the unveiling will take place, and from thenceforth it will be "Liberty Enlightening the World," as the designer of the statue intended.

***The St. Johns Herald*, St. Johns, Apache County, Arizona Territory, November 4, 1886**

The great Franco-American statue of liberty was unveiled with imposing ceremonies in New York. William M. Evarts and President Cleveland were present and made short appropriate addresses.

The Unveiling of the Statue

The Statue of Liberty Today

Proclamation Number 5574

Ronald Reagan

At the request of Congress, Ronald Reagan issued this proclamation in 1986 declaring the rose the official flower of the United States.

PROC. NO. 5574. THE ROSE PROCLAIMED THE NATIONAL FLORAL EMBLEM OF THE UNITED STATES OF AMERICA

Proc. No. 5574, Nov. 20, 1986, 51 F.R. 42197, provided:

Americans have always loved the flowers with which God decorates our land. More often than any other flower, we hold the rose dear as the symbol of life and love and devotion, of beauty and eternity. For the love of man and woman, for the love of mankind and God, for the love of country, Americans who would speak the language of the heart do so with a rose. We see proofs of this everywhere. The study of fossils reveals that the rose has existed in America for age upon age. We have always cultivated roses in our gardens. Our first President, George Washington, bred roses, and a variety he named after his mother is still grown today. The White House itself boasts a beautiful Rose Garden. We grow roses in all our fifty States. We find roses throughout our art, music, and literature. We decorate our celebrations and parades with roses. Most of all, we present roses to those we love, and we lavish them on our altars, our civil shrines, and the final resting places of our honored dead. The American people have long held a special place in their hearts for roses. Let us continue to cherish them, to honor the love and devotion they represent, and to bestow them on all we love just as God has bestowed them on us. The Congress, by Senate Joint Resolution 159 [Pub. L. 99-449, now this section], has designated the rose as the National Floral Emblem of the United States and authorized and requested the President to issue a proclamation declaring this fact. NOW, THEREFORE, I, RONALD REAGAN, President of the United States of America, do hereby proclaim the rose as the National Floral Emblem of the United States of America. IN WITNESS WHEREOF, I have hereunto set my hand this twentieth day of November, in the year of our Lord nineteen hundred and eighty-six, and of the Independence of the United States of America the two hundred and eleventh.

Ronald Reagan.

The White House Rose Garden

Civility, Courage, Compassion, and Character
George W. Bush

George W. Bush took the oath of office in the first inauguration of the new millennium on January 20, 2001. In his inaugural address, he spoke of the timeless ideals that made our nation great and that must be observed if our country is to continue its greatness and its influence for good in the world.

. . . We have a place, all of us, in a long story, a story we continue but whose end we will not see. It is a story of a new world that became a friend and liberator of the old, the story of a slaveholding society that became a servant of freedom, the story of a power that went into the world to protect but not possess, to defend but not to conquer.

It is the American story, a story of flawed and fallible people united across the generations by grand and enduring ideals. The grandest of these ideals is an unfolding American promise that everyone belongs, that everyone deserves a chance, that no insignificant person was ever born. . . .

America has never been united by blood or birth or soil. We are bound by ideals that move us beyond our backgrounds, lift us above our interests, and teach us what it means to be citizens. Every child must be taught these principles. Every citizen must uphold them. And every immigrant, by embracing these ideals, makes our country more, not less, American.

Today we affirm a new commitment to live out our Nation's promise through civility, courage, compassion, and character.

America at its best matches a commitment to principle with a concern for civility. A civil society demands from each of us goodwill and respect, fair dealing and forgiveness.

Some seem to believe that our politics can afford to be petty because in a time of peace the stakes of our debates appear small. But the stakes for America are never small. If our country does not lead the cause of freedom, it will not be led. If we do not turn the hearts of children toward knowledge and character, we will lose their gifts and undermine their idealism. If we permit our economy to drift and decline, the vulnerable will suffer most.

We must live up to the calling we share. Civility is not a tactic or a sentiment; it is the determined choice of trust over cynicism, of community over chaos. And this commitment, if we keep it, is a way to shared accomplishment.

America at its best is also courageous. Our national courage has been clear in times of depression and war, when defeating common dangers defined our common good. Now we must choose if the example of our fathers and mothers will inspire us or condemn us. We must show courage in a time of blessing by confronting problems instead of passing them on to future generations. . . .

America at its best is a place where personal responsibility is valued and expected. Encouraging responsibility is not a search for scapegoats; it is a

George W. Bush

call to conscience. And though it requires sacrifice, it brings a deeper fulfillment. We find the fullness of life not only in options but in commitments. And we find that children and community are the commitments that set us free.

Our public interest depends on private character, on civic duty and family bonds and basic fairness, on uncounted, unhonored acts of decency, which give direction to our freedom. . . . The most important tasks of a democracy are done by everyone. . . .

What you do is as important as anything Government does. I ask you to seek a common good beyond your comfort, to defend needed reforms against easy attacks, to serve your Nation, beginning with your neighbor. I ask you to be citizens: citizens, not spectators; citizens, not subjects; responsible citizens building communities of service and a nation of character.

Americans are generous and strong and decent, not because we believe in ourselves but because we hold beliefs beyond ourselves. When this spirit of citizenship is missing, no Government program can replace it. When this spirit is present, no wrong can stand against it. . . .

We are not this story's Author, who fills time and eternity with His purpose. Yet, His purpose is achieved in our duty. And our duty is fulfilled in service to one another. Never tiring, never yielding, never finishing, we renew that purpose today, to make our country more just and generous, to affirm the dignity of our lives and every life. . . .

God bless you all, and God bless America.

Letter from Elizabeth E. Hutter

Elizabeth E. Hutter

Elizabeth E. Hutter wrote this letter to the newly-inaugurated President Benjamin Harrison. She shares a memory of the inauguration of his grandfather William Henry Harrison nearly 50 years before.

614 Race Street
Philadelphia

To His Excellency
General Benjamin Harrison
President, United States

My dear friend,

Allow me to congratulate you upon your inaugural address, it is a magnificent production.

When your grandfather was inaugurated, in 1840, Mr. Hutter, my husband, was present and stood by his side on the platform. They were warm friends and when death came and took him [William Henry Harrison] away so soon, Mr. Hutter predicted that some day our Heavenly Father would so ordain it that one of his grandsons would be elected president.

That God's choicest blessings will be showered upon you and sustain you, in your noble and trying position is the heartfelt prayer of your ever sincere friend,

Elizabeth E. Hutter
March 6th, 1889

The Inauguration of President Harrison and a Portrait of the President

Vermont Is a State I Love
Calvin Coolidge

Vermont, the home state of President Calvin Coolidge, was devastated by floods in 1927. The next year, President Coolidge toured areas that had been stricken by the floods to see Federal and state recovery efforts. He delivered this speech from the back of a train in Bennington, Vermont, on September 21, 1928.

My fellow Vermonters:

For two days we have been traveling through this state. We have been up the East side, across and down the West side. We have seen Brattleboro, Bellows Falls, Windsor, White River Junction and Bethel. We have looked toward Montpelier. We have visited Burlington and Middlebury. Returning we have seen Rutland.

I have had an opportunity of visiting again the scenes of my childhood. I want to express to you, and through the press to the other cities of Vermont, my sincere appreciation for the general hospitality bestowed upon me and my associates on the occasion of this journey.

It is gratifying to note the splendid recovery from the great catastrophe which overtook the state nearly a year ago. Transportation has been restored. The railroads are in a better condition than before. The highways are open to traffic for those who wish to travel by automobile.

Calvin Coolidge (right) With His Wife and Son

Vermont is a state I love. I could not look upon the peaks of Ascutney, Killington, Mansfield, and Equinox, without being moved in a way that no other scene could move me. It was here that I first saw the light of day; here I received my bride, here my dead lie pillowed on the loving breast of our eternal hills.

I love Vermont because of her hills and valleys, her scenery and invigorating climate, but most of all because of her indomitable people. They are a race of pioneers who have almost beggared themselves to serve others. If the spirit of liberty should vanish in other parts of the Union, and support of our institutions should languish, it could all be replenished from the generous store held by the people of this brave little state of Vermont.

Our Presidents
Isabel Ambler Gilman

The poem appeared in the book Poems Teachers Ask For, Volume 2. *It was published in 1925, which is why the poem includes the Presidents only through Calvin Coolidge.*

First on the list is Washington, Virginia's proudest name;
John Adams next, the Federalist, from Massachusetts came;
Three sons of old Virginia into the White House go—
'Twas Jefferson, and Madison, and then came James Monroe.

Massachusetts for one term sent Adams called John Q.,
And Tennessee a Democrat, brave Jackson staunch and true.
Martin Van Buren of New York, and Harrison we see,
And Tyler of Virginia, and Polk of Tennessee.

Louisiana Taylor sent; New York Millard Fillmore;
New Hampshire gave us Franklin Pierce; when his term was o'er
The keystone state Buchanan sent. War thunders shook the realm.
Abe Lincoln wore a martyr's crown, and Johnson took the helm.

Then U.S. Grant of Illinois who ruled with sword and pen;
And Hayes, and Garfield who was shot, two noble Buckeye men.
Chester Arthur from New York, and Grover Cleveland came;
Ben Harrison served just four years, then Cleveland ruled again.

McKinley—shot at Buffalo—the nation plunged in grief,
And "Teddy" Roosevelt of New York served seven years as chief.
Taft of Ohio followed him. Then Woodrow Wilson came—
New Jersey's learned Democrat; war set the world aflame;

And when the tide of strife and hate its baneful course had run,
The country went Republican and Warren Harding won.
No duty would he shirk,—he died while on a western trip;
Coolidge of Massachusetts then assumed the leadership.

The Constitution Is Yours
Grover Cleveland

President Grover Cleveland tried to follow the Constitution closely in his work as President. He vetoed many bills that Congress passed but that he thought would allow for wasteful spending. In this portion of his first inaugural address, delivered March 4, 1885, Cleveland explained how his oath to preserve, protect, and defend the Constitution should really be the oath of every citizen of the country.

. . . But he who takes the oath today to preserve, protect, and defend the Constitution of the United States only assumes the solemn obligation which every patriotic citizen—on the farm, in the workshop, in the busy marts of trade, and everywhere—should share with him. The Constitution which prescribes his oath, my countrymen, is yours; the Government you have chosen him to administer for a time is yours; the suffrage [vote] which executes [carries out] the will of freemen is yours; the laws and the entire scheme of our civil rule, from the town meeting to the state capitals and the national capital, is yours. Your every voter, as surely as your Chief Magistrate, under the same high sanction, though in a different sphere, exercises a public trust. Nor is this all. Every citizen owes to the country a vigilant watch and close scrutiny of its public servants and a fair and reasonable estimate of their fidelity and usefulness. Thus is the people's will impressed upon the whole framework of our civil polity—municipal, state, and Federal; and this is the price of our liberty and the inspiration of our faith in the Republic. . . .

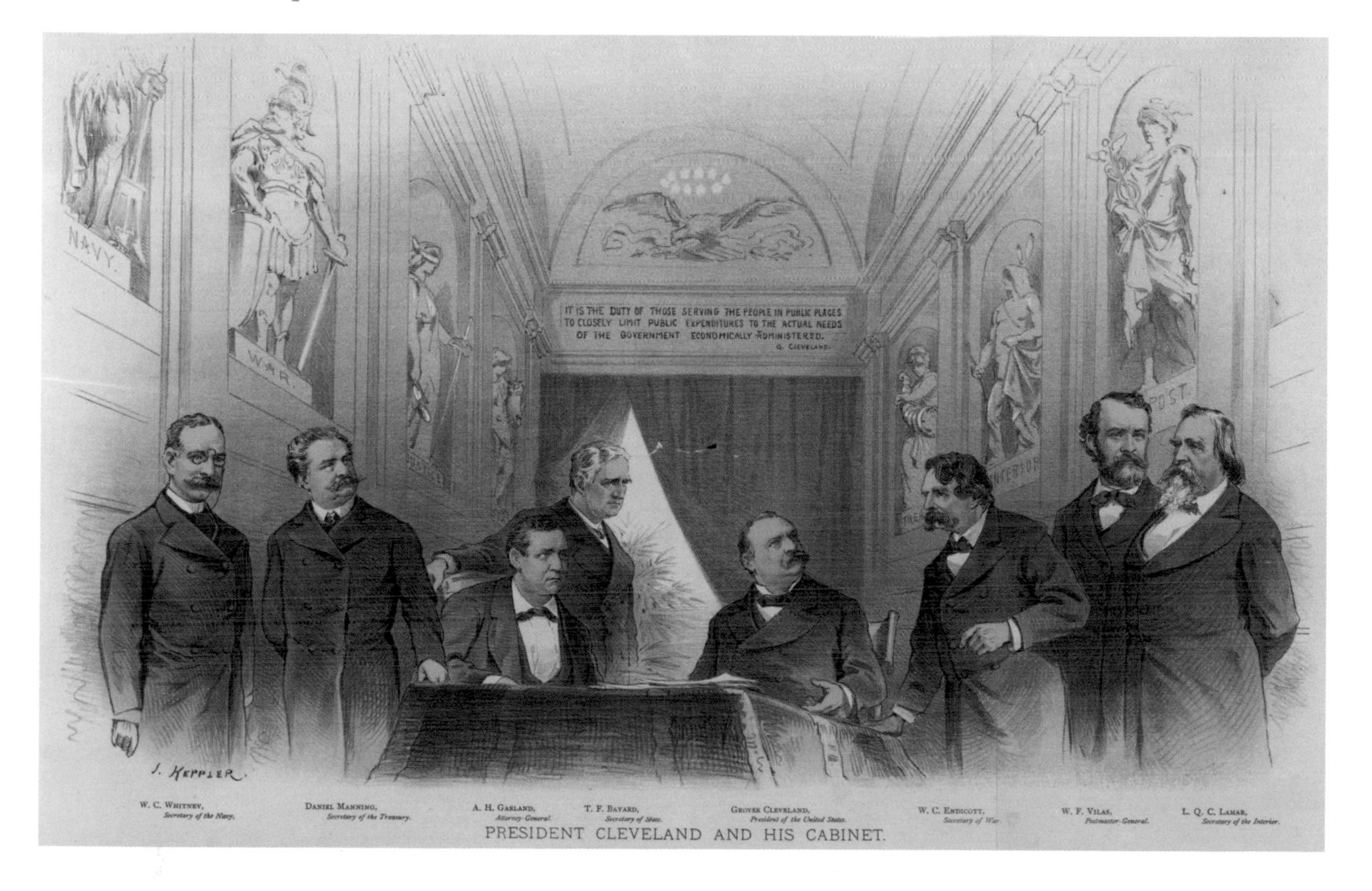

PRESIDENT CLEVELAND AND HIS CABINET.

Women Here Rejoice Over Right to Vote

This article appeared on the front page of The Evening Missourian *newspaper of Columbia, Missouri, on August 23, 1920.*

Women Here Rejoice Over Right to Vote

Sincerity and Spirit Mark Celebration at Methodist Church

Points Out Danger

Recognition as Equals Means Equal Responsibilities Says W. L. Nelson

"Well, well, women are people now! What do you think of that! Women can vote!"—what an old man said as he stumbled down the steps after the suffrage "celebration."

Seventy-five Columbia men and women, gathered in the auditorium of the Broadway Methodist Church last Saturday night, celebrated the passage of the Nineteenth Amendment by which the voting strength of Columbia and Boone County is doubled. The little group of people scattering among the pews took part in the program of speaking and singing with a sincerity and spirit which made their faces wet with tears and their voices husky.

William L. Nelson, congressman for the Eighth District, who made a short talk, said that the country expected women to effect many reforms. "Equal suffrage is fraught with danger," he said. "The danger is that women will not take advantage of the right to vote; that, having won recognition as equals with men, they will not shoulder the responsibilities of equals."

Mrs. Rosa Ingels, known as one of the most determined fighters for equal suffrage in the county, was in charge of the meeting. The tone of her remarks in opening the program set the pitch for the three speakers that followed. She said: "The passage of the Susan B. Anthony Amendment is the harbinger of a new era in American life: a cleaner, higher, better life wherein the men and women of America will work together to make this country the land of freedom and democracy, the land of new hope that the founders of the Nation prayed it might be."

"We will vote in politics but we will keep our souls above politics," said Mrs. Walter McNab Miller. "With the granting of the franchise to women there comes a hope that the words "political mire" may be erased and forgotten. As long as women are concerned with the welfare of the human race, as long as there are conditions which threaten their children, they will not be content to watch the clouds of war, child labor and rotten politics surround and blur the vision of the children of America."

"There is reason indeed," said Mrs. L. W. St. Clair-Moss, "for thanksgiving that the womanhood of America has at last been recognized as the equal of the [certain minorities] who have long had the right to make the laws by which American boys and girls have been reared to be American citizens. The mothers of these boys and girls, with the wisdom and loving insight concerning the needs of their children, can really help in making the laws which they must obey, and which their children must learn to revere and respect.

"Men are saying that women do not feel the weight of their new responsibilities. I think that men may come to realize their own responsibilities in the matter, if they keep on talking about it."

Women In Line to Vote

We Are Not Ready for That in Mississippi: The Story of Fannie Lou Hamer

Bethany Poore

An African American woman, wearing a knee-length print dress and carrying a white purse, made her way through the room crowded with white men in suits and ties. She sat down, faced the room, and introduced herself.

"Mr. Chairman, and to the Credentials Committee, my name is Mrs. Fannie Lou Hamer, and I live at 626 East Lafayette Street, Ruleville, Mississippi, Sunflower County, the home of Senator James O. Eastland, and Senator Stennis." She looked into the eye of the television camera that was broadcasting her words to the nation on the NBC television network. She immediately began telling the story that she felt the credentials committee and the people of the United States needed to hear.

Back in the summer of 1962, a group of strangers arrived in Fannie Lou's small Mississippi town. They organized a meeting at Williams Chapel Church. Curious, Fannie Lou attended. The strangers were young civil rights workers who had come to Mississippi to help black people register to vote. At the meeting that night, at age 44, Fannie Lou learned something she had never heard before: she, a black person, had the right to vote. Fannie Lou was interested. She determined to claim her right as a citizen of the United States.

Fannie Lou Hamer

As Fannie Lou told the credentials committee, "It was the 31st of August in 1962 that eighteen of us traveled twenty-six miles to the county courthouse in Indianola to try to register to become first-class citizens."

Powerful white people in the Mississippi of 1962 did not want to see black people voting. They believed that black people should "stay in their place" and let the white people make the decisions. They feared any changes in the segregated Mississippi way of life.

When Fannie Lou Hamer and the rest of the group entered the office for voter registration in the county courthouse, the clerk ordered all but two people to get out of his office. Only Fannie Lou and a young man would be allowed to register that day. They were subjected to a literacy test. The official showed Fannie Lou the 16th section of Mississippi's complex state constitution. He ordered her to copy it exactly, including every comma and period. Then the official told her to write her own interpretation of the meaning of the section. As the county officials had counted on, the task of interpretation was impossible for her. Fannie Lou failed the literacy test that day and was not allowed to register to vote.

Fannie Lou continued her story, "After we had taken this test and started back to Ruleville, we was held up by the City Police and the State Highway Patrolmen and carried back to Indianola where the bus driver was charged that day with driving a bus the wrong color." Too much yellow paint on the bus, the policeman said. He invented this excuse because it was against the law to arrest the driver for the real reason he had stopped the bus: too much black. The group pooled the money for the fine and Fannie Lou made it home.

Fannie Lou's home was a small house on the plantation owned by a white man where she was employed along with her husband and children. When she got back that day, her boss was furious. Fannie Lou had done something that black people weren't supposed to do. She had exercised her constitutional rights. Her boss said, "We are not ready for that in Mississippi." He ordered her to leave.

As Fannie Lou told the credentials committee, "I had to leave that same night."

Maybe Mississippi wasn't ready for black people to step into the full privileges of citizenship of the United States of America, but Fannie Lou Hamer was ready. After studying the Mississippi state constitution, she took the literacy test a second time and passed. She became a registered voter in the state of Mississippi. But gaining her own rights wasn't enough for Fannie Lou. Registering to vote was just the first step in her work for equality. She immediately began working to bring equality to all. This cause was the mission for the rest of her life.

In the presidential election of 1964, Mississippi sent a delegation to the Democratic National Convention as usual. The problem was that the Democratic party in Mississippi was controlled by white people who kept black people out of the process. The delegation to the convention was all white. Fannie Lou Hamer and other civil rights workers, black and white, organized an alternative delegation. They called themselves the Mississippi Freedom Democratic Party. They insisted that they truly represented Democrats in Mississippi and should be seated at the convention instead of the official Mississippi delegation. It was the job of the credentials committee to decide which representatives from Mississippi would get the seats.

That's why Fannie Lou Hamer, a poor African American woman who had lived her life on the plantations of the Mississippi delta, who had about six years of schooling off and on between working in the fields, a woman "sick and tired of being sick and tired," as she liked to say, pushed and pressed and fought through prejudice, hate, danger, persecution, and adversity to take a seat in front of the credentials committee and the people of the United States and tell her story. And finally, in 1964, people were starting to listen.

Fannie Lou Hamer and her fellow delegates were denied the seats they came for at the Democratic National Convention of 1964. They had tried their hardest. They had made history. But the answer was no. Still, the Mississippi Freedom Democratic Party did not give up. They were given a promise by the Democratic Party: things would be different at the convention of 1968.

Fannie Lou Hamer traveled around America telling her story, fighting the battle for civil rights. As a woman of vibrant faith in God, she believed in the principles of non-violent resistance. She worked passionately for equality, but she was not willing to hurt others in that fight, even though she was hurt herself. Her passion and commitment inspired others to keep moving ahead in the struggle. When times were hard, she encouraged her fellow workers by singing black spirituals in her strong and beautiful voice.

When the 1968 Democratic National Convention rolled around, the delegates stood and applauded thunderously for Fannie Lou Hamer as she took her seat as part of the integrated official delegation from her home state of Mississippi. Mississippi was a little bit more ready for that because of the work of Fannie Lou Hamer.

In 2006, President George W. Bush signed a bill that reaffirmed and made improvements to the Voting Rights Act of 1965. The Voting Rights Act Reauthorization And Amendments Act Of 2006 was named for three women who dedicated their lives to equality: Rosa Parks, Coretta Scott King, and Fannie Lou Hamer.

Fannie Lou Hamer Memorial Garden in Ruleville, Mississippi

To Do Well and Wisely with the Ballot
Theodore Roosevelt

Theodore Roosevelt wrote the following thoughts on voting in his autobiography, which was published in 1913, before women were given the right to vote in 1920. "Suffrage" means the right to vote. He addresses not only women's suffrage, but the responsibility carried by all voters.

Personally I feel that it is exactly as much a "right" of women as of men to vote. But the important point with both men and women is to treat the exercise of the suffrage as a duty, which, in the long run, must be well performed to be of the slightest value. I always favored woman's suffrage, but only tepidly, until my association with women like Jane Addams and Frances Kellor, who desired it as one means of enabling them to render better and more efficient service, changed me into a zealous instead of a lukewarm adherent of the cause—in spite of the fact that a few of the best women of the same type, women like Mary Antin, did not favor the movement. A vote is like a rifle: its usefulness depends upon the character of the user. . . . I believe in suffrage for women in America, because I think they are fit for it. I believe for women, as for men, more in the duty of fitting one's self to do well and wisely with the ballot than in the naked right to cast the ballot.

Theodore Roosevelt

"I Was Born Feb. 12, 1809 . . ."
Abraham Lincoln

Abraham Lincoln wrote this sketch of his life on December 20, 1859, at the request of a journalist with the Chester County Times *of West Chester, Pennsylvania, while Lincoln was pursuing the Republican nomination for President.*

I was born Feb. 12, 1809, in Hardin County, Kentucky. My parents were both born in Virginia, of undistinguished families—second families, perhaps I should say. My mother, who died in my tenth year, was of a family of the name of Hanks, some of whom now reside in Adams, and others in Macon counties, Illinois. My paternal grandfather, Abraham Lincoln, emigrated from Rockingham County, Virginia, to Kentucky, about 1781 or 2, where, a year or two later, he was killed by Indians, not in battle, but by stealth, when he was laboring to open a farm in the forest. His ancestors, who were Quakers, went to Virginia from Berks County, Pennsylvania. An effort to identify them with the New-England family of the same name ended in nothing more definite, than a similarity of Christian names in both families, such as Enoch, Levi, Mordecai, Solomon, Abraham, and the like.

My father, at the death of his father, was but six years of age; and he grew up, litterally without education. He removed from Kentucky to what is now Spencer county, Indiana, in my eighth year. We reached our new home about the time the State came in the Union. It was a wild region, with many bears and other wild animals still in the woods. There I grew up. There were some schools, so called; but no qualification was ever required of a teacher, beyond "readin, writin, and cipherin," to the Rule of Three. If a straggler supposed to understand Latin, happened to sojourn in the neighborhood, he was looked upon as a wizzard. There was absolutely nothing to excite ambition for education. Of course when I came of age I did not know much. Still somehow, I could read, write, and cipher to the Rule of Three; but that was all. I have not been to school since. The little advance I now have upon this store of education, I have picked up from time to time under the pressure of necessity.

Abraham Lincoln with Scenes from His Life

I was raised to farm work, which I continued till I was twenty two. At twenty one I came to Illinois, and passed the first year in Illinois—Macon county. Then I got to New-Salem, (at that time in Sangamon, now in Menard county), where I remained a year as a sort of Clerk in a store. Then came the Black-Hawk war; and I was elected a Captain of Volunteers - a success which gave me more pleasure than any I have had since. I went the campaign, was elated, ran for the Legislature the same year (1832) and was beaten - the only time I have been beaten by the people. The next, and three succeeding biennial elections, I was elected to the Legislature. I was not a candidate afterwards. During this Legislative period I had studied law, and removed to Springfield to practice it. In 1846 I was once elected to the lower House of Congress. Was not a candidate for re-election. From 1849 to 1854, both inclusive, practiced law more assiduously than ever before. Always a whig in politics, and generally on the whig electoral tickets, making active canvasses. I was losing interest in politics, when the repeal of the Missouri Compromise aroused me again. What I have done since then is pretty well known.

If any personal description of me is thought desirable, it may be said, I am, in height, six feet, four inches, nearly; lean in flesh, weighing, on an average, one hundred and eighty pounds; dark complexion, with coarse black hair, and grey eyes - no other marks or brands recollected.

Yours very truly,
A. Lincoln

Abraham Lincoln in May 1860

Candidate Cards

In local elections, candidates often announce their candidacy and introduce themselves to the public in the local newspaper. These announcements were called "Candidate Cards" in an August 13, 1910, edition of The Times and Democrat *newspaper of Orangeburg, South Carolina.*

I hereby announce myself a candidate for Cotton Weigher at Elloree and pledge myself to abide by the rules and regulations of the Democratic primary. Tilley D. Livingston

As I have been asked by several of my friends to run for cotton weigher, I hereby announce myself for cotton weigher at Springfield, subject to the rules of the Democratic Primary.
C. S. Gleaton

I beg to announce to my friends that I am a candidate for cotton weigher at Elloree. If elected I will use my best efforts to make myself worthy of the trust imposed upon me. I pledge to abide the result of the primary. Very truly, John W. Wactor

To my friends of the Elloree section: I beg to announce my candidacy for the position of Cotton Weigher, at Elloree, S.C. Having assisted in weighing cotton at Elloree during the last season, I feel that all are acquainted with my qualifications, and if elected will pledge you my best efforts to give each man a square deal and entire satisfaction. D. Wyman McEachern

THE TIMES AND DEMOCRAT SATURDAY, AUGUST 13, 1910

CANDIDATE CARDS

FIRE, LIFE, BURGLARY, TORNADO
INSURANCE!!!
ALSO
SURETY BONDS
Written by
H. C. Wannamaker

"Theodore Kohn Store"
We Are Going to Earn Your Trade With Good Goods
THEODORE KOHN,
"The Quality Store of Orangeburg"

You Should Buy The Best Paint
Lowe Brothers High Standard Liquid Paint
John McNamara

Peruvian Guano
Top-Dresser
A mixture of Peruvian Guano, Nitrate of Soda and Potash.
Wonderfully Quick!
Cheaper than Nitrate of Soda—and we are informed by our customers that last year it gave better results. The supply is limited—order now.
Peruvian Guano Corp.,
CHARLESTON, S. C.

LUZIANNE COFFEE

The Collar for all Farm Work

The Southern Marble & Granite Co.
Monuments, Coping and Headstones

Second-Hand School Books Wanted!!!
Sims Book Store

Every Farmer Needs This BOOK
It Is Free!
It tells how you can have telephone service in your home at very low cost.
Southern Bell Telephone & Telegraph Co.

L. E. Riley

Feeling that I have done my duty for my people I ask their endorsement for another term as a member of the Legislature subject to the Democratic Primary.
Respectfully, Bascom A. Shuler

The many friends of Mr. J. J. Fairey hereby announce him as a candidate for the position of Township Commissioner of Orange Township.

I hereby announce my candidacy for the office of Township Commissioner for Goodland Township in the coming primary. Pledging myself to abide by the results of the same.
Respectfully, Joseph A. Fanning

I hereby announce myself as a candidate for the Democratic nomination for Congress from the Seventh Congressional District of South Carolina and pledge myself to abide the rules and regulations of the Democratic primary. A. F. Lever

Prepare for the Coming Battle of the Ballots

The Omaha Daily Bee, *a Republican-supporting newspaper of Omaha, Nebraska, ran this full page advertisement in 1900 to encourage subscriptions to their newspaper. They reminded readers that the newspaper was an important resource to prepare for the upcoming presidential campaign.*

THE OMAHA DAILY BEE: FRIDAY, MARCH 9, 1900. 9

The Year 1900 is a Presidential Campaign Year

The battle royal for the control of the national government will be started by the great political parties with their nominating conventions in June, but the political forces are already being marshaled in opposing lines.

Prepare for the Coming Battle of the Ballots

Every patriotic citizen owes it as a duty to his country to keep himself fully abreast of all the movements in this great contest and to inform himself on the vital questions of public importance at issue between the contending parties.

The Bee as the foremost exponent of its party principles in this section of the country will furnish the most accurate, comprehensive, prompt and complete news of skirmishes, forays and battles of the political campaign of 1900. It will cover the political conventions, great and small, with uncolored reports of all that happens at them. It will give side lights on the men and measures before the people that will enable them to do their duty as citizens intelligently instead of in ignorance.

The Omaha Bee

Daily by mail $8.00 a year or $4.00 for six months.
Sunday $2.00 a year.
Weekly 65 cents a year—ten weeks' trial for 10 cents.

Populists

are threatened with a compulsory choice between the republican and democratic presidential tickets. The Bee will show them why it is to their advantage to prove their loyalty to their country by supporting republican rather than democratic candidates.

Republicans

will find in The Bee an enlightened organ of the republican party. Its editorial page will discuss fearlessly and logically the issues presented in the republican national platform and uphold the banner of the republican standard bearers chosen by the republican national convention. In the field of state politics The Bee will be an exponent of honesty and economy in state government and expose and oppose sham reform no matter where or by whom it is practiced.

The Omaha Bee

Subscribe for it now for the impending campaign.
Send it to your friends and neighbors.
The most effective republican campaign orator.

Democrats

who want to have both sides of the question can get no better exposition of republican doctrines than contained in The Bee from day to day and week to week. Always treating its opponents fairly, The Bee will in its news columns give the news of all parties.

Republicans can serve their party no better than to secure subscribers to The Bee. A copy of The Weekly Bee is a weekly argument at the fireside in favor of republicanism.

Remember the Presidential Campaign of 1900 is Upon Us

Subscribe for The Bee Now.

Subscriptions and Remittances to The Bee Publishing Co., Omaha, Neb.

Campaign Songs

Throughout American history, songs have held an important place in presidential campaigns. They are catchy, memorable, and fun. Some songs have been very effective in helping a candidate gain notoriety and votes. Read three examples of American campaign songs below.

Hurrah for Hayes and Honest Ways, 1876

Respectfully Dedicated to the Republican Centennial Presidential Candidate
Honorable Rutherford B. Hayes of Ohio
by E. W. Foster

Come on, ye jolly boys in gray,
And you my boys in blue;
We'll clasp the hand all o'er the land,
For gallant Hayes and Wheeler true.
For North and South, for East and West,
Long float the flag that's o'er us.
Hurrah! for Hayes, and Honest Ways,
With millions in the chorus!

Chorus
Come on! ye jolly boys in gray,
And you, my boys, in blue;
We'll clasp the hand all o'er the land,
For gallant Hayes, and Wheeler true,
For North and South, for East and West,
Long float the flag that's o'er us!
Hurrah for Hayes, and Honest Ways,
With millions in the chorus.

Ho! every one, both old and young,
That's past his one and twenty;
To vote for Hayes, and honest ways,
Means Freedom, Peace, and Plenty.
The names that from our banners flash,
Light up the way before us;
While all along, a mighty throng,
Roll up a rousing chorus! *(Chorus)*

Now let the blue deep vault resound,
While Fortune smiling o'er us,
Repeats to Fame, the magic name,
That fires the mighty chorus.
The Bird of Freedom soaring high,
Sees growing every minute,
The vote for Hayes, and Honest Ways,
And says, "there's millions in it!" *(Chorus)*

We've had enough of Sham in high,
And Sham in lowplace hiding;
The Men we want are on the flag,
Steel-true, and trust confiding.
There's naught but Truth and Honor pays;
Corruption's doom has met it;
Hurrah! for Hayes, and Honest Ways,
They'll win! don't you forget it! *(Chorus)*

Hurrah! for Hayes, and Honest Ways,
Hip! Hip! Hurrah! Hurrah!

President Taft, He's All Right, 1912
W. J. Applegate

Hurrah, Hurrah, Hurrah, Boys,
Hurrah for President Taft.
He's the man to fill the chair,
He has acted on the square,
So rally 'round his banners boys,
He'll right our wrongs and make our joys.
With Taft, with Taft to fight,
With him we're always right.

Chorus
Hurrah, Hurrah, Hurrah, Boys,
Hurrah for President Taft.
William Taft is always right,
He's the man to make the fight,
Who's allright? Why William Taft,
He's allright!

Hurrah, Hurrah, Hurrah, Boys,
Hurrah for President Taft.
He's the man to fill the bill,
He has smashed the grafter's mill,
The combinations they are sore,
That their machine can live no more.
With Taft, with Taft to fight,
With him we're always right. (*Chorus*)

Hurrah, Hurrah, Hurrah, Boys,
Hurrah for President Taft.
He's the man our country needs,
He's the man of radiant deeds,
In office he is on the square,
His methods with the best compare.
With Taft, with Taft to fight,
With him we're always right. (*Chorus*)

Stonewall Wilson, 1916
Robert Mortimer

Wilson by all tests has proven
He's the man to take command,
His no heedless, hasty action,
His the strong restraining hand.
No white feather in his make up,
He can bite as well as bark,
But he wastes no ammunition,
And he always hits the mark.

Chorus
Danger lurks upon the seas,
Foes are on the border,
But with Wilson at the front,
We'll keep our house in order.
Stonewall Wilson, Woodrow Wilson,
Our advance is steady,
And to keep you in the White House
You will find us ready,
You will find us ready,
You will find us ready!

Wilson by all tests has proven
He's the man to take the wheel,
He's the man we always look to,
When we want a good square deal.
Under Wilson peace and plenty,
Reign supreme from shore to shore,
Under Wilson we have prospered,
Could another give us more? (*Chorus*)

"And, Folks, Here's My Mamie!" The Story of Mamie Eisenhower

Bethany Poore

The train marked "Eisenhower Special" announced its arrival with a shrill whistle at the Keyser, West Virginia, station on the morning of September 25, 1952. An excited crowd 3,000 strong met the train. Schoolchildren dismissed from classes to attend the big event made the crowd all the more lively. Dwight D. Eisenhower, or "Ike," was the much-loved general who had served his country in World War II as Supreme Commander of the Allied Forces. He was campaigning to be America's next President. West Virginia's Republican candidate for governor introduced the general and the crowd erupted in cheers. Eisenhower gave his standard 10-minute campaign speech about the current administration, the war in Korea, the need for change, and promises for his own administration. After he finished his speech, he grinningly said to the crowd, "And, folks, here's my Mamie!" Eisenhower's wife Mamie stepped out onto the platform to stand beside her husband. She smiled warmly and waved to the crowd. The crowd burst into shouts and applause. The Eisenhowers received two special locally-produced gifts from the people of Keyser: a box of apples from Cheat Mountain Orchard and, especially for Mamie, a pair of soft deerskin gloves. With thanks and quick farewells, the Eisenhower Special chugged away from the waving crowd.

Mamie Doud and her future husband met at Fort Sam Houston near San Antonio, Texas, in 1915. He was a soldier stationed there and she was staying in San Antonio with her family. They were married in 1916 when Mamie was 19 and Ike was 25. They had been married for almost 53 years when Ike died in 1969. Even though Ike had a distinguished and busy military career spanning nearly 37 years, for most of their marriage Ike and Mamie were together. But for Mamie that meant packing up the household and moving many, many times as her husband was assigned to one post and then another. Mamie estimated that during her life she lived in 37 different houses. She moved with Ike to army bases all over the United States and to Panama, the Philippines, and France. Their first son, Doud Dwight, was born in 1917 and died in 1921 of scarlet fever. Their second son, John, was born in 1922. He grew up to become a soldier like his father and also served as Ambassador to Belgium.

Mamie Eisenhower

In the early 1950s, Ike was urged by influential Republicans to run for President. They believed that the country needed his proven leadership. Eisenhower became convinced that it was his duty to serve his country in that way.

Dwight and Mamie Eisenhower

Mamie was a modest, retiring woman who happily stayed out of the limelight that surrounded her world-famous husband. She had never before had the least political involvement. When her husband decided to try for the White House, she walked into the political arena by his side. Mamie, no longer able to stay quietly in the background, became a staunch, active advocate for her husband's election, working 16 hours a day because she believed as much as anyone else that he was the right man to be President. Ike's opinion was, "She's a better campaigner than I am."

Mamie connected with people by being herself: genuine and unpretentious. During the election, her hairstyle became a big conversation topic. She received many letters urging her to change it, but her hair stayed the way she liked it. When she was interviewed, she was able to converse sincerely as a normal American woman that understood other normal Americans and their worries about high grocery prices, taxes, and sending their sons off to war. During the campaign, Ike and Mamie said goodbye to their son, John, as he left to fight in the Korean War. Americans were drawn to her sincerity and caring. They could tell by the way she looked at Ike that she deeply loved and admired her husband of 36 years. No matter how many times she heard him give the same speeches, Mamie always listened with full attention when her husband spoke on the campaign trail. Her respect for him deepened the respect that other people had for Ike.

As the campaign progressed, Mamie became the first candidate's wife to have campaign songs written about her, called "Mamie" and "I Want Mamie." "I Like Ike" was the most famous slogan of Ike's campaign (and one of the most famous of all time). Mamie's fans coined the slogan, "I Like Ike, But I LOVE Mamie!" Campaign buttons read: "Mamie for First Lady" and "I Like Mamie, Too." Reporters liked Mamie, too. On one 6:45 a.m. whistle-stop in Salisbury, North Carolina, Ike and Mamie peeked out from their railroad car wearing their bathrobes and waved to the crowds. Photographers who hadn't been up that early asked Ike and Mamie to put on their bathrobes and do it again so they could catch it on film. The Eisenhowers smilingly complied.

Mamie Eisenhower accompanied her husband as his campaign wound its way over 51,276 miles, stopping at 232 towns in 45 states, traveling by train and propeller plane. She stepped out to stand beside Ike, smile, and wave many times.

Ike won 39 states on Election Day that November. He was inaugurated as the 34th president of the United States on January 20, 1953. After he took the oath of office, Ike turned to his most loyal supporter and became the first President in U.S. history to kiss his wife on the inauguration platform for all the world to see.

Reach Out to Potential Poll Workers

The U.S. Election Assistance Commission (EAC) was created by the Help America Vote Act, passed by Congress in 2002. The commission's job is to help states manage the voting process to make voting easier. The EAC published this list of ideas in 2006 for recruiting poll workers, an essential part of the voting process and one way average America citizens can step up to serve their country.

★ Advertise the need for poll workers by posting a sign-up sheet at polling places and early voting locations.

★ Use your office Web site by posting an online, interactive poll worker job application and job description. Partner with area businesses/corporations, city/county governments, chambers of commerce, etc., to post a link to your online recruitment application on their Web site.

★ Use technology by developing an e-mail blast to reach employees at city/county government and area businesses/corporations.

★ Use existing staff and poll workers as an army of recruiters. Ask them to talk to friends and relatives to encourage them to become poll workers.

★ Create an informational brochure to distribute at speaking engagements, make available at front counters, insert in mailings, etc.

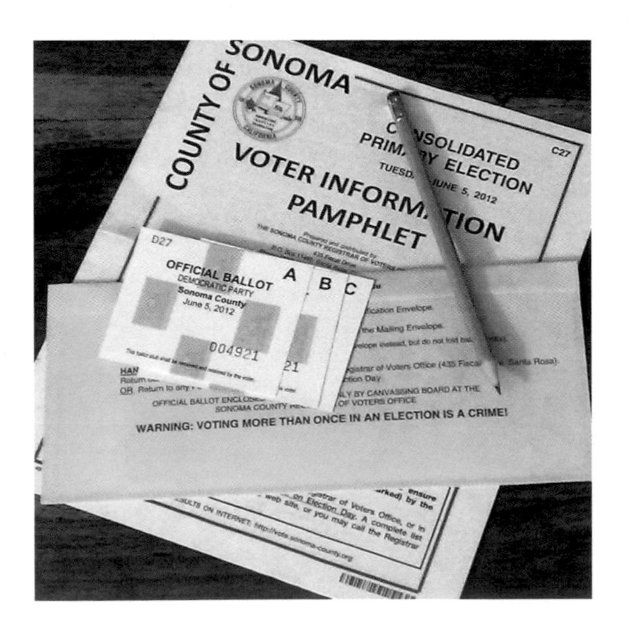

★ Advertise your need in area neighborhood association newsletters, city/chamber/school district newsletters, church publications, multilingual media publications, etc. Incorporate your need for poll workers with other election advertising needs. Example: Partner with your area cable public access channel to run public service announcements focusing on opportunities for poll workers.

★ Design and print recruitment posters. Display them at area grocery stores, in libraries, at movie theaters, at mass transportation systems, etc.

★ Reach out to the media with the specifics for the neighborhoods where you need poll workers—how many, etc.

★ Develop community recruiting partnerships:

  ★ City/County Government Employees—Work with local government management and elected officials to develop a program that encourages department heads to reassign some of their employees to the Election Office on Election Day.

  ★ High School Students—Establish a recruitment effort by contacting your local high school principals. If State law permits, assign at least one student to each polling place.

  ★ College Students—Contact college faculty at area universities and community colleges to develop a college poll worker program. College students could also be assigned to assist with pre-election operational needs and may also be available to assist as troubleshooters/rovers on Election Day.

  ★ Civic Organizations—Reach out to local civic groups and other membership organizations to recruit their membership to work at the polls. Promote this program by suggesting that members use working at the polls as a "fundraiser" with participating members voluntarily donating their stipends/earnings back to their organization or to the civic organization of their choice.

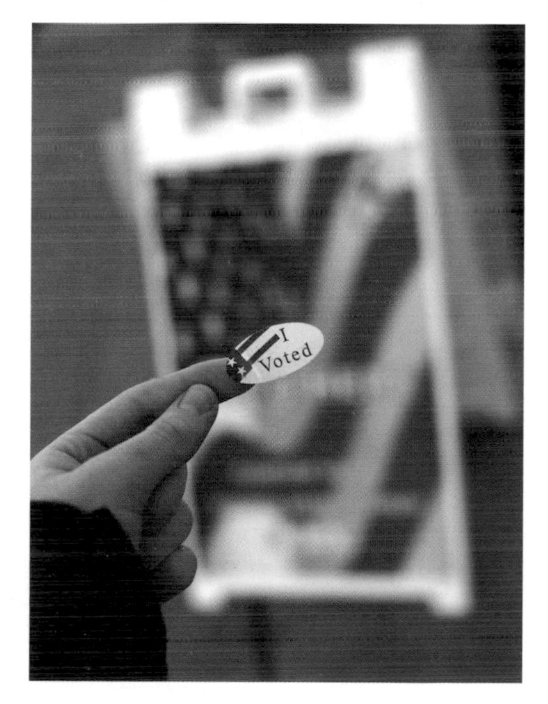

  ★ Corporations and Businesses—Reach out to companies and businesses to incorporate poll worker service as part of their ongoing community service program that encourages employees to serve as poll workers on Election Day. Promote this program by suggesting they use working at the polls as a "fundraiser" with participating employees voluntarily donating their stipends/earnings back to the civic organization of their choice.

The High School Tax Election

Mary Sloop

Eustace and Mary Sloop were a husband and wife doctor team in the Appalachian Mountains of Avery County, North Carolina, during the first part of the twentieth century. They did much to improve the lives of the people who lived there, physically, educationally, and spiritually. The selection below comes from Mrs. Sloop's 1953 autobiography, Miracle in the Hills. *In it she tells of the time when their community of Crossnore voted on whether or not they would establish their own high school. Hepsy was a young girl for whom Mrs. Sloop arranged a high school education in nearby Banner Elk. The "old-clothes money" refers to the revenue collected by selling second-hand clothes to residents of Crossnore and the surrounding countryside. The clothes were sent to the community by friends of the Sloops and other people who knew about their work in Crossnore.*

After Hepsy went off to school at Banner Elk and a little later four others had followed her, we began seriously to get into the business of sending children off to high school, for we had no adequate high-school course at Crossnore, and more and more boys and girls were wanting to go on with their education.

When that session at Banner Elk was over, those girls came home and were so enthusiastic about school that in the fall sixteen begged to go. I promised I'd see to it that somehow they got a chance to do it. Then it began to be told about the country that if a child wanted to go to a more advanced school than we had at Crossnore or elsewhere in that part of the country, they could just come to me and make arrangements.

Old-clothes money had to do the work. Contributions grew and grew, so that Uncle Gilmer had to drive his old mule Rhoda from the post office to his home, hitched to the little one-horse wagon, in order to haul the big boxes and packages sent by friends from various sections down in the lower country. The people came from miles around to buy, so that we began to obtain sizable funds from the sales. And we kept sending children off to school.

But we realized, in one sense, that it was the wrong thing to do. It would be far better to keep those children at home and provide them a high school at Crossnore. That would benefit the entire community. So we determined to have our own high school, and we set our caps to get it. I might add that before we were able to establish a high school at Crossnore, the old-clothes money had sent off that last year one hundred and four boys and girls to other schools. From one girl—Hepsy—to one hundred and four youngsters, and in just a few years, is not a bad record, even if I do mention it myself.

But, as I said, we were anxious to get plans under way for having our own high school. As the sale of old clothes grew and the interest of the children in going away for more advanced schooling increased, it seemed that you could see the community developing an enthusiasm for education. We began to hold meetings to discuss plans.

We had held meetings in the old schoolhouse to talk about plans for moving it and building the two-room structure, and we had held similar meetings in the two-room building to talk expansion again. We were great for holding meetings.

I recall one particularly.

Avery County, North Carolina

In those early days public meetings, even church meetings, often were the occasion for considerable disorder and sometimes actual bloodshed. Young men—and sometimes men not so young—would get themselves drunk on moonshine liquor and come to these meetings, oftentimes to wait for the meeting to end so they could walk their girls home. They would usually stay on the outside and frequently would get into altercations that sometimes ended in shooting.

We had had disorder at one of our school meetings and I was afraid that if such goings-on were not challenged, and challenged promptly, they would cause the more fearful and timid people to stay away, and that would very quickly end our movement for expanded school facilities.

So I made a plan, and I carried it out. I sent to Newland and got a deputy sheriff to agree to come over to Crossnore. Then I got three pistols and put them in my big handbag, and we went to the meeting, Doctor and I.

The deputy sheriff was there. And, of course, faithful Uncle Alex. I greeted the deputy sheriff and opened my big bag, so that everybody could see the pistols.

"Mr. Sheriff," I said, "we have been having disorder at our meetings, and this is against the law. I want you to deputize Uncle Alex and Doctor Sloop to help you maintain order here tonight."

The deputy sheriff had the two to raise their hands, and he swore them in. When he had done so I reached into my bag and brought out two pistols. I handed one to Doctor and the other to Uncle Alex.

"Now, gentlemen," I said, "in the name of the Lord and the State of North Carolina, I want you to shoot the first man who dares to interrupt our meeting. I'll handle this other pistol myself." I said it in a loud voice, too.

We called the meeting to order. And, brothers, it kept in order. Nobody offered to raise his voice, much less his shotgun or rifle. Those men very likely knew that the law wouldn't have allowed any of us to shoot just because someone had begun to talk loud or curse, but they didn't know that I knew it. And they weren't willing to risk Uncle Alex or Doctor or even the deputy sheriff. At any rate, the meeting proceeded in an orderly manner, even though, as I recall it now, a very heated argument developed between two fathers over the proposition of whether Crossnore School should teach that the world was round or flat.

A new North Carolina law greatly aided our efforts to get a high school. It decreed that any community could have a high school if it had a certain number of pupils in the high-school grades, provided the taxpayers of that community would vote on themselves a tax of thirty cents on the hundred dollars' property valuation to supplement the fund the state itself would provide toward the operation of a high school.

We had meetings, and we talked high school. We cornered little knots of people and talked high school. Before long the leaders in the community agreed that we should hold an election on the issue of voting the supplemental tax. They thought it would pass. So we called the election. And we began in earnest now to campaign in support of the tax. We chose two reliable and loyal politicians to go and visit all the homes in the school district. They went in different directions, and they covered the ground thoroughly. They came back with reports that many of the citizens were in favor of a high school and were willing to be taxed to support it, but they also had discovered quite a number who opposed the project. Then we knew that we really had a fight on our hands. Some days we'd get news that a convert had been made; on others we'd hear that folks just didn't want to be taxed that much. It would be a close vote.

So the morning came for the voting. They had put the two boxes out in front of the home of an old man who lived at the foot of a high hill directly west of the house. They grinned when I objected to the voting place—because that, I said, would make the sun set earlier and the voting was to stop, of course, at sunset. Several of those who favored the tax, I knew, lived at a considerable distance and I was afraid they might be late getting to the polls. But they wouldn't change the place, and I didn't know how to make them.

I was getting ready to go down to the voting place early that morning, when Dr. Sloop came back into the kitchen and told me that a neighbor had stopped by to say that he had been down at the voting place and that he didn't think that it would be safe for me to go. He said there were a great many men there from Buck Hill, that they were violently opposed to being taxed, and that every man had his gun. He was afraid there would be shooting before the day was over.

And Doctor said, "He advises you not to go."

I looked up at him and said, "And you know what I will do with his advice. Is the car ready?" For by that time we had a Model-T Ford.

He said, "Yes. You're going to risk it, are you?"

"It's not any risk," I replied. "Mountain men wouldn't shoot at me. You all don't respect them like I do. They won't hurt me one bit in the world."

We started off down the road. And though a Model-T was rather small then, and Doctor and I were never small, we passed two old people going down to vote, and question was, Shall we pick them up? Doctor said, "They'll vote against us."

I said, "I can't help it. I'm not going to let them walk down there." So the old man got in and took his wife in his lap and we went on down the road. We cast our vote for the special tax, and they cast their vote against it.

The election officials told us that the vote was still tied, that it had been tied for an hour. They couldn't get anybody to break it. When one person voted for it, there was always somebody who came up and voted against it.

And so the vote stayed tied for a long, long time. We argued with all the people standing around. Some of them had voted, some of them hadn't. But none of them seemed willing to vote for it. One man that I felt sure would be in favor of it said, "No, I don't mind the tax. I want my children to get an education, but there ain't no sense in children having to go to school nine months in the year. Four months is long aplenty for them to be kept indoors."

So we grew more and more anxious. Finally Doctor said, "I'm going up to Lee's. I don't believe Lee will refuse to do me the favor of coming down here and voting in favor of it, and we'll break the tie."

He got into his little car and drove off. Pretty soon somebody said, "Where's Doctor?" I told them where.

"It won't do a bit o' good," they said. "Lee left the county this morning before six o'clock. Said he couldn't never face Doctor and vote against it, and so he won't agoin' to be in the county this day."

Well, that made things look pretty serious. Then one man came up—and it was a man who had a little Ford too, a Model-T. It was in bad shape. I had always told him that he drove that Ford on will power—that it ran on will power, not on gasoline.

But he said to me, "Mrs. Sloop, I stopped at Uncle Abe's house last night and his sons were in there and they were all-fired mad about this tax being voted and were athreatenin' what they were agoin' to do if it was. Old Uncle Abe was alyin' in bed sick. But he said, 'If I could get up out o' this bed and get over there, I'd vote for it. I'd vote for anything that just woman said.'

"Now if I could go over there," he added, "I believe I could get Uncle Abe to come vote."

"Do you think he'd be able to come?" I asked him.

"Oh, yes," he said, "it wouldn't hurt him none. But he can't walk it, and they wouldn't bring him any other way."

He started to get in his car, turned around to me again. "I feel sure he'll come. You just pray that he will be awillin' to risk it."

I said, "I'll pray that your tires will last over that road, for there's never been an automobile over it."

"That's what they tell me," he said, "but we'll be acomin' back."

And he got in, and with its usual will power that little car started off, and I certainly prayed for those tires.

In just a little while before the sun was to set behind that high hill, he came back. The tires had held, the little car was still chugging, and Uncle Abe stepped out.

"Where's your box?" he said.

I didn't dare speak to him, because they'd say I had influenced him to vote. And I stepped back.

The registrar who was holding the election showed him where the box was. So he went over there, and they fixed his vote for him, and he put it in the box marked FOR. Then he turned slowly and walked back to the car. I stepped up to thank him.

"Uncle Abe," I said, "we appreciate your aid ever so much."

He looked right straight at me and said, "Hunn-n-h-h!" And he got in the car.

I never saw Uncle Abe again.

In a few moments a bearded man came up. I held my breath. Was he going to tie the vote again? "Waal-l-l," he said, "I ain't voted yet, but since Abe has give 'em the vote, I guess I'll add another one to it and make it two in majority."

We had voted our high school.

Sloop Chapel on the Campus of Crossnore School

Business of the Greatest Moment
Samuel Adams

Samuel Adams (1722-1803) was a key patriot, playing an important role in the founding of the United States as an independent republic. He signed the Declaration of Independence alongside his cousin John Adams. On April 2, 1781, Samuel Adams published a letter in the Boston Gazette *newspaper exhorting his fellow Americans to exercise their privilege of voting and to take the responsibility seriously. The following excerpts are from his letter, with his capitalizations.*

As we have a Constitution which is admired for its genuine Principles, I have been solicitous [anxious] to know, whether our Countrymen at large partook of the Spirit of those who formed it. I have conceived strong Hopes, that in organizing their Government and electing Persons to fill the important Places of Trust, no Consideration would avail, to govern their Suffrages [voting] in Favour of any Candidate, unless he was possessed of those Qualities which are necessary, to enable him to perform the Duties of the Office to be filled, to the Advantage of the Publick. I have flattered my self, that both the Governors and the Governed would have lain aside the gawdy Trappings of Monarchy, and put on that Simplicity which is the Ornament and Strength of a free Republick. How far it has been done, I am not able to judge at this Distance. It is a great Satisfaction to me to be informed, that some of the best Men in the Commonwealth have been elected into the Principal Departments of Government. . . .

I was sorry to hear, that the Number of Votes returned, the last Time, did not amount to a Quarter of the Number of qualified Electors in the Commonwealth. The Choice of Legislators, Magistrates and Governors, is surely a Business of the greatest Moment [importance], and claims the Attention of every Citizen. . . . Hence every Citizen will see, and I hope will be deeply impressed with a Sense of it, how exceedingly important it is to himself, and how intimately the welfare of his Children is connected with it, that those who are to have a Share in making as well as in judging and executing the Laws should be Men of singular Wisdom and Integrity. Such as are conscious that they are deficient in either of these Qualities, should even Tremble at being named as Candidates! I hope the great Business of Elections will never be left by the Many, to be done by the Few . . . Let each Citizen remember, at the Moment he is offering his Vote, that he is not making a Present or a Compliment to please an Individual, or at least that he ought not so to do; but that he is executing one of the most solemn Trusts in human Society, for which he is accountable to GOD and his Country.

Statue of Samuel Adams at Faneuil Hall in Boston

Lincoln's Farewell to the Citizens of Springfield
Abraham Lincoln

Soon to be inaugurated President, Abraham Lincoln left Springfield, Illinois, for Washington, D.C., on February 11, 1861. From the train platform, in a trembling voice, he bid farewell to his neighbors with these words.

Lincoln had this portrait taken shortly before he left Springfield.

My friends—No one, not in my situation, can appreciate my feeling of sadness at this parting. To this place, and the kindness of these people, I owe every thing. Here I have lived a quarter of a century and have passed from a young to an old man. Here my children have been born and one is buried. I now leave, not knowing when, or whether ever, I may return, with a task before me greater than that which rested upon Washington. Without the assistance of that Divine Being who ever attended him I cannot succeed. With that assistance I cannot fail. Trusting in Him, who can go with me, and remain with you and be every where for good, let us confidently hope that all will yet be well. To His care commending you, as I hope in your prayers you will commend me, I bid you an affectionate farewell.

The Lincoln Home in Springfield

Sample Letter from the Archivist to the Governors

Allen Weinstein

The National Archives and Records Administration provides an example of the type of letter the Archivist of the United States sends to the governor of each state to help them get organized and obey the law regarding the state's responsibility in the Electoral College process. Allen Weinstein was Archivist of the United States from 2005 to 2009.

The Honorable Madison Jefferson Monroe
Governor of Anystate
State Capitol, US 00000-0001

Dear Governor Monroe:

I am writing to inform you of your responsibilities in the upcoming Electoral College process and to offer the assistance of the National Archives and Records Administration (NARA). This year the Presidential election and selection of electors will occur on November 4, 2008 and the State meetings of the Electoral College will be held on December 15, 2008.

The Governor of each State performs certain duties to carry out the functions of the Electoral College. Each State is responsible for documenting the selection of electors and the electors' votes for President and Vice President, and for ensuring that properly executed certificates reach the appropriate Federal and State officials.

NARA administers the electoral process by receiving Certificates of Ascertainment of electors and Certificates of Vote from the States and the District of Columbia, reviewing them for legal sufficiency, making them available to the Congress for the official accounting of electors and votes, and providing the public with access to electoral documents and information about the Electoral College.

To assist you in carrying out your Electoral College duties, I am enclosing a set of procedural instructions and pamphlets containing the provisions of the U.S. Constitution and the United States Code that relate to the election of the President and Vice President. Please make these materials available to the officials who will administer the electoral process in your State.

I would greatly appreciate your assistance in ensuring the smooth operation of the Electoral College process this year. It is essential that the electoral certificates be prepared accurately and submitted as promptly as possible within the time periods allotted by law. If you have any questions regarding Electoral College procedures, please have your office or the appropriate State election officials contact the Legal Affairs Staff of NARA's Office of the Federal Register at (202) 741-6030.

Sincerely,
ALLEN WEINSTEIN
Archivist of the United States

Montana State Capitol

Washington in 1845
Marian Gouverneur

Marian Gouverneur (1821-1914) was the wife of Samuel L. Gouverneur Jr., grandson of James Monroe. Originally from Long Island, New York, she was a longtime resident of Washington, D.C., in adulthood, where she mingled with famous statesmen and everyday citizens. Her long and interesting life included accompanying her husband to China when he was appointed U.S. consul by President James Buchanan. This excerpt is from her 1911 autobiography.

My first visit to Washington was in 1845. I started from New York at eight o'clock in the morning and reached Philadelphia late the same afternoon. I broke the journey by spending the night at Jones's Hotel in the lower part of the city, which was the usual stopping place of travelers who made this trip. A few years later when the journey from New York to Washington was made in twelve hours, it was thought that almost a miracle had been performed.

Mrs. Winfield Scott in 1855 characterized the National Capital as "an ill-contrived, ill-arranged, rambling, scrambling village;" and it was certainly all of that when I first saw it. It is not improbable that the cause of this condition of affairs was a general feeling of uncertainty as to whether Washington would remain the permanent seat of government, especially as the West was naturally clamoring for a more centrally located capital. When I first visited the city the ubiquitous real-estate agent had not yet materialized, and corner lots, now so much in demand, could be purchased at a small price. Taxation was moderate and Congress, then as now, held itself responsible for one-half of the taxes. As land was cheap there was no necessity for economy in its use, and spacious fronts were built regardless of back-buildings. In other cases, when one's funds were limited, the rear of the house was first built and later a more imposing front was added. The contrast between the houses of New York, built closely together in blocks, and those in Washington, with the abundant space around them, was a great surprise to me. Unlike many other cities, land in Washington, then, as now, was sold and taxed by the square foot. . . .

Views of Washington, D.C., in the 1840s

My sister, Mrs. Eames, lived in a house on G Street near Twenty-first Street in what was then known as the First Ward. This general section, together with a part of Indiana Avenue, some portions of Capitol Hill, Sixth and Seventh Streets, and all of that part of the city bounded on the north by K Street, on the south by Pennsylvania Avenue, and westward of Fourteenth Street to Georgetown, was at this time the fashionable section of the city. Like many other places in its formative period, Washington then presented the picture of fine dwelling houses and shanties standing side by side. I remember, for example, that as late as 1870 a fine residence on the corner of I and Fifteenth Streets was located next to a small frame house occupied by a[n] . . . undertaker. The latter's business was prosperous, but his wealthy neighbor objected to the constant reminder of death caused by seeing from his fine bay window the numerous coffins carried in and out. He asked the undertaker to name his price for his property, but he declined, and all of his subsequent offers were ignored. Finally, after several years' patient waiting, during which offer after offer had been politely but positively rejected, the last one being an almost princely sum, the owner sold his home and moved away, leaving his humble neighbor in triumphant possession. This is simply a fair example of the conditions existing in Washington when I first knew it.

Two rows of houses on Pennsylvania Avenue, known as the "Six and Seven Buildings," were fashionable dwellings. Admiral David D. Porter, then a Lieutenant in the Navy, occupied one of them. Miss Catharine L. Brooke kept a girls' school in another, while still another was the residence of William Lee of Massachusetts. I have been informed that while serving in a consular office abroad, under the appointment of President Monroe, Mr. Lee was commissioned by him to select a dinner set for the White House.

Architects, if I remember correctly, were almost unknown in Washington at this time. When a person was sufficiently venturesome to build a house for himself, he selected a residence suited to his tastes and directed a builder to erect one like it. Speculative building was entirely unknown, and if any resident of the District had embarked upon such a venture he would have been regarded as the victim of a vivid but disordered fancy.

Mrs. C. R. Latimer kept a fashionable boarding house in a large brick dwelling facing Lafayette Square where the Belasco Theater now stands. Mr. and Mrs. Hamilton Fish boarded with her while the former was a Representative in Congress, and Mr. and Mrs. Sanders Irving, so well and favorably known to all old Washingtonians, also made this house their home. Many years later it was the residence of William H. Seward, and he was living there when the memorable attempt was made in 1865 to assassinate him. As is well known, it subsequently became the home of James G. Blaine. When Hamilton Fish was elected to the Senate, he purchased a house on H Street, between Seventeenth and Eighteenth Streets, which was afterwards known as the "Porter house." Previously it had been owned and occupied by General "Phil" Kearny.

The shops of Washington in 1845 were not numerous, and were located chiefly upon Pennsylvania Avenue, Seventh Street then being a residential section. The most prominent dry-goods store was kept by Darius Clagett at the corner of Ninth Street and Pennsylvania Avenue. Mr. Clagett, invariably cordial and courteous, always stood behind his counter, and I have had many pleasant chats with him while making my purchases. Although he kept an excellent selection of goods, it was usually the custom for prominent Washington folk to make their larger purchases in Baltimore. A little later Walter Harper kept a dry-goods store on

Pennsylvania Avenue, near Eighth Street, and some years later two others appeared, one kept by William M. Shuster on Pennsylvania Avenue, first between Seventh and Eighth Streets, and later between Ninth and Tenth; and the other by Augustus and Thomas Perry on the corner of Ninth Street and Pennsylvania Avenue. Charles Demonet, the confectioner, made his appearance a little later on Pennsylvania Avenue, between Seventeenth and Eighteenth Streets; but Charles Gautier, on Pennsylvania Avenue, between Twelfth and Thirteenth Streets, was his successful rival and was regarded more favorably in aristocratic circles. Madame Marguerite M. Delarue kept a shop on the north side of the same avenue, also between Twelfth and Thirteenth Streets, where small articles of dress dear to the feminine heart could be bought. There were several large grocery stores on the south side of Pennsylvania Avenue, between Sixth and Seventh Streets. Benjamin L. Jackson and Brother were the proprietors of one and James L. Barbour and John A. Hamilton of another, although the two latter had their business house at an earlier day on Louisiana Avenue. Louis Vavans was the accomplished cook and caterer, and sent to their rooms the meals of many persons temporarily residing in Washington. Joseph Redfern, his son-in-law, kept a grocery store in the First Ward. Franck Taylor, the father of the late Rear Admiral Henry C. Taylor, U.S.N., was the proprietor of a book store on Pennsylvania Avenue, near Four-and-a-Half Street, where many of the scholarly men of the day congregated to discuss literary and current topics. His store had a bust of Sir Walter Scott over its door, and he usually kept his front show-windows closed to prevent the light from fading the bindings of his books. The Center Market was located upon the same site as at present, but of course it has since been greatly enlarged and improved. All the stores on Louisiana Avenue sold at retail. I remember the grocery store of J. Harrison Semmes on Ninth Street and Louisiana Avenue, opposite the Center Market; and the hardware store kept by Joseph Savage on Pennsylvania Avenue, between Sixth and Seventh Streets, and at another time between Third and Fourth Streets.

On Fifteenth Street opposite the Treasury was another well-known boarding house, conducted by Mrs. Ulrich and much patronized by members of the Diplomatic Corps. Willard's Hotel was just around the corner on the site of the New Willard, and its proprietor was Caleb Willard. Brown's Hotel, farther down town, on Pennsylvania Avenue and Sixth Street, was a popular rendezvous for Congressional people. It was first called the Indian Queen, and was kept by that prince of hosts, Jesse Brown. After his death the name was changed to the Metropolitan.

The National Hotel

The National Hotel on the opposite corner was the largest hostelry in Washington. It boasted of a large Southern cliéntèle, and until President Buchanan's administration enjoyed a very prosperous career. . . . John Gadsby was its proprietor at one time, from whom it usually went by the name of "Gadsby's." President Buchanan was one of its guests on the eve of his inauguration.

Brackets, Stairs, Roofs &c.: The Story of James Hoban

Bethany Poore

The workday over, James Hoban walked home from the building site. The usual frustrations of supervising workmen, dealing with unexpected supply shortages, and keeping everything going on schedule had not bothered him today. He carried with him the expectation of the greatest honor of his life. His mind full of wonder and excitement, he had struggled throughout the day to focus on the work at hand.

Hoban entered the back door of 43 Trott Street, the combination house and workshop he shared with his friend Pierce Purcell. His home was a hive of activity, just as busy as the building site he had left. Apprentice boarders, pencils in hand, leaned over architectural drawings spread on tables or sawed and hammered to finish their day's projects. Slave craftsmen made final touches to interior pieces to be taken to building sites. Delicious smells stole from the kitchen where house slaves bustled through dinner preparations for the household. Hoban slipped past the busy hum and walked quietly to his bedroom. He had a little time to rest before dinner. Right afterward, his evening school students would arrive, and he would be immersed in teaching architectural drawing to a class of bright young men, hanging on his words, bending diligently over their desks, gripping a pencil in one hand and straight edge in the other. In their faces he recognized the young James Hoban, when he first started learning architecture himself.

A Cottage in County Kilkenny

James Hoban's life began in a small thatched cottage on the estate of the Cuffe family in County Kilkenny, Ireland, where his father, Edward, was a laborer. Young James attended the school offered for children on the estate. He was trained as a carpenter and wheelwright. He was good at what he did, but knew he could do more. In Dublin, there was a school where he could learn architecture from Ireland's best teachers. Was it an impossible dream for the poor laborer's boy?

James remembered the overwhelming jubilation that rushed through him the day he learned he had the support of Lord Otway Cuffee, lord of the estate where the Hoban family lived and worked, to attend the Dublin Society's Drawing School. To think that he, James Hoban, was going to Dublin to become a real architect!

Jubilation was smothered by fear, shyness, and a few tears the day he said goodbye to his family in the little thatched cottage and headed for Dublin. Trundling along the road in the wagon, he was headed for what seemed worlds away from home. The country boy had much to learn about life in the city, but at the Drawing School, James was in his element. He remembered fondly the wonder of working with the best tools, the relish of immersing himself in the abundant supply of books and models, and the generous dedication of his masters.

Behind the closed door of his quiet bedroom, James unlocked a drawer in his desk. For the first time in a long while, his hand closed around the medal that had rewarded him for the long nights of studying, the cramps in his hand and arm, and the many times he had carefully erased and started again. "Presented by the Dublin Society to James Hoban for Drawings of Brackets, Stairs, Roofs, & c. Nov. 23rd 1780." Every student at the Drawing School coveted the honor of receiving the Duke of Leinster's medal. He committed himself to becoming an excellent architect. Through the learning, striving, and working, James learned that the medal itself was not something to work for. He set his sights on working for the excellence that the medal recognized. And on that shining November day, the medal had followed.

Medal in hand, James earned an apprenticeship with architect Thomas Ivory, headmaster of the school. After working in Dublin and making his own mark on the city's architecture, James boldly decided to emigrate to the brand-new United States of America.

James remembered the early years in America, again tackling the task of building a reputation and proving what he was worth. His American clientele grew, first in Philadelphia, and then in Charleston. He prospered and gained the attention of some of the city's most prominent people. Excellent work earned the young Irish immigrant respect and a thriving business.

And now, who could have imagined? He was preparing for an honor beyond anything of his experience. All the years of work and dedication seemed to culminate in the news he had just received. George Washington wanted to meet with him. George Washington! James Hoban's adopted country's hero General and now its President. Charleston was honored by the great man's visit, and soon James Hoban would be himself.

George Washington was gathering information for one of his many tasks as President of the new country. The capital city rising out of the wilderness near the Potomac River needed a President's home. This was not a job for just any architect with just any design. While the fledgling government had to remember costs and practicality, the President's house must be a fine building that would proclaim to the nation and to its visitors from around the world that this United States of America was a real country. Though newly born, the United States was ready to take its place among the old nations with their revered palaces, courthouses, and parliamentary buildings. At just the right time, James Hoban's reputation for excellent work reached the ears of President George Washington, who consulted with the young Irish architect. Washington was quite impressed.

The next year, 1792, James Hoban saw this advertisement which was placed in newspapers by Washington's Secretary of State, Thomas Jefferson:

> *WASHINGTON, in the Territory of COLUMBIA.*
> *A PREMIUM OF FIVE HUNDRED DOLLARS, or a MEDAL of that value, at the option of the party, will be given by the Commissioners of the Federal Buildings, to the person who, before the fifteenth day of July next, shall produce to them the most approved PLAN, if adopted by them, for a PRESIDENT's HOUSE, to be erected in this City. The size of the building, if the artist will attend to it, will of course influence the aspect and outline of his plan; and its destination will point out to him the number, size, and distribution of the apartments. It will be a recommendation of any plan, if the central part*

of it may be detached and erected for the present, with appearance of a complete whole, and be capable of admitting the additional parts, in future, if they shall be wanting. Drawings will be expected of the ground plats, elevations of each front, and sections through the building, in such directions as may be necessary to explain the internal structure; and an estimate of the cubic feet of brick-work composing the whole mass of the walls.

March 14, 1792 *THE COMMISSIONERS*

James Hoban gathered up all the skill and creativity he had acquired through years of work and practice and drew a President's house—a view of the front, a bird's-eye view of the rooms, drawings of a house that was grand, but not ornate; gracious but not ostentatious: a perfect home for the leader of a proud and independent young republic. He submitted his design to the Commissioners as instructed in the advertisement. Because Washington had already become acquainted with Hoban's excellent work, he quickly chose Hoban's design from among the several entries. Before long, word arrived in Charleston—James Hoban was the winner!

Hoban's Design for the White House

Hoban proudly received the medal from the United States promised as payment for the winning design. He earned the medal not as an Irish immigrant, but as an American citizen. In 1791, James Hoban had become a naturalized citizen of the United States of America. American James Hoban was soon summoned to the Federal City to supervise the construction of the President's house.

James Hoban saw the White House to completion and went on to oversee construction of several other buildings for the new government. When the White House was damaged by fire by the British in 1814, James Hoban was commissioned to restore the house to its original state. He also superintended additions made during the presidencies of James Monroe and Andrew Jackson.

James Hoban spent the rest of his life as a valued member of the Washington community. Pierce Purcell, Hoban's business partner from Charleston, joined him in Washington and

A Sketch of Hoban's House in Washington, D.C.

the two established another successful business. Hoban served as captain of a local militia company, was a founding pillar of Washington's Roman Catholic community, and for many years served Washington as a city councilman. Always true to his Irish heritage, James Hoban used his influence in city politics to give a voice to Washington's many Irish laborers, and was a founding member of a society established to help Irish workers in need. Hoban also financially supported schoolteachers and a fire brigade. James Hoban married Susana Sewall in 1799 and the two had a family of ten children. James Hoban's sons Edward and Francis served in the United States Navy, Henry became a Jesuit priest, and James Jr. became district attorney of the District of Columbia.

The day after James Hoban's death on December 8, 1831, this was said about him in the obituary that appeared in Washington D.C.'s *National Intelligencer* newspaper:

> *In private life, Capt. Hoban possessed, in a very high degree, the esteem and confidence of his fellow citizens. He was hospitable, generous, and charitable. In his regard for the just claims and feelings of others, he was scrupulously nice and particular. Such men are blessings to society whilst they live, and, even after death, instruct by example.*

His excellence earned him an outstanding reputation. His reputation made him a sought-after architect with a successful practice. His success brought him financial plenty. He used his financial plenty to serve his community. James Hoban is remembered as the architect of the White House. The Irish architect built more than one of the world's most famous buildings: he built a life of excellence and service.

These United States Mint images show the 1992 commemorative coin that honored James Hoban and the 200th anniversary of laying the cornerstone of the White House.

The Crows at Washington
John Hay

At age 22, John Hay (1838-1905) was selected to be Abraham Lincoln's secretary. They became close friends. Hay went on to have a career in public service, serving as Ambassador to Great Britain and as Secretary of State under William McKinley and Theodore Roosevelt. He acquired an estate of over 1,000 acres in New Hampshire, part of which is now the John Hay Wildlife Refuge, administered by the U.S. Fish and Wildlife Service. Hay co-authored a biography of Lincoln and wrote many poems. This poem, published in 1890, mentions several famous Washington, D.C., landmarks.

Slow flapping to the setting sun
By twos and threes, in wavering rows.
As twilight shadows dimly close,
The crows fly over Washington.

Under the crimson sunset sky
Virginian woodlands leafless lie,
In wintry torpor bleak and dun.
Through the rich vault of heaven, which shines
Like a warmed opal in the sun,
With wide advance in broken lines
The crows fly over Washington.

Over the Capitol's white dome,
Across the obelisk soaring bare
To prick the clouds, they travel home,
Content and weary, winnowing
With dusky vans the golden air,
Which hints the coming of the spring,
Though winter whitens Washington.

The dim, deep air, the level ray
Of dying sunlight on their plumes,
Give them a beauty not their own;
Their hoarse notes fail and faint away;
A rustling murmur floating down
Blends sweetly with the thickening glooms;
They touch with grace the fading day,
Slow flying over Washington.

I stand and watch with clouded eyes
These dim battalions move along;
Out of the distance memory cries
Of days when life and hope were strong,
When love was prompt and wit was gay;
Even then, at evening, as to-day,
I watched, while twilight hovered dim
Over Potomac's curving rim,
This selfsame flight of homing crows
Blotting the sunset's fading rose,
Above the roofs of Washington.

John Hay (right) with Abraham Lincoln (center) and Lincoln's other private secretary John G. Nicolay (left)

Proclamation of Pardon
Gerald Ford

Richard Nixon resigned the presidency in 1974 because he had been accused of illegal actions. Vice President Gerald Ford became President. On September 8, 1974, Gerald Ford used his power of presidential pardon to clear Richard Nixon of all allegations. He made this speech to the citizens of the United States from the Oval Office when he signed Proclamation 4311 granting the pardon.

Ladies and gentlemen:

I have come to a decision which I felt I should tell you and all of my fellow American citizens, as soon as I was certain in my own mind and in my own conscience that it is the right thing to do.

I have learned already in this office that the difficult decisions always come to this desk. I must admit that many of them do not look at all the same as the hypothetical questions that I have answered freely and perhaps too fast on previous occasions.

My customary policy is to try and get all the facts and to consider the opinions of my countrymen and to take counsel with my most valued friends. But these seldom agree, and in the end, the decision is mine. To procrastinate, to agonize, and to wait for a more favorable turn of events that may never come or more compelling external pressures that may as well be wrong as right, is itself a decision of sorts and a weak and potentially dangerous course for a President to follow.

I have promised to uphold the Constitution, to do what is right as God gives me to see the right, and to do the very best that I can for America.

I have asked your help and your prayers, not only when I became President but many times since. The Constitution is the supreme law of our land and it governs our actions as citizens. Only the laws of God, which govern our consciences, are superior to it.

As we are a nation under God, so I am sworn to uphold our laws with the help of God. And I have sought such guidance and searched my own conscience with special diligence to determine the right thing for me to do with respect to my predecessor in this place, Richard Nixon, and his loyal wife and family.

Theirs is an American tragedy in which we all have played a part. It could go on and on and on, or someone must write the end to it. I have concluded that only I can do that, and if I can, I must.

There are no historic or legal precedents to which I can turn in this matter, none that precisely fit the circumstances of a private citizen who has resigned the Presidency of the United States. But it is common knowledge that serious allegations and accusations hang like a sword over our former President's head, threatening his health as he tries to reshape his life, a great part of which was spent in the service of this country and by the mandate of its people.

Gerald Ford Issuing the Proclamation of Pardon

After years of bitter controversy and divisive national debate, I have been advised, and I am compelled to conclude that many months and perhaps more years will have to pass before Richard Nixon could obtain a fair trial by jury in any jurisdiction of the United States under governing decisions of the Supreme Court.

I deeply believe in equal justice for all Americans, whatever their station or former station. The law, whether human or divine, is no respecter of persons; but the law is a respecter of reality.

The facts, as I see them, are that a former President of the United States, instead of enjoying equal treatment with any other citizen accused of violating the law, would be cruelly and excessively penalized either in preserving the presumption of his innocence or in obtaining a speedy determination of his guilt in order to repay a legal debt to society.

During this long period of delay and potential litigation, ugly passions would again be aroused. And our people would again be polarized in their opinions. And the credibility of our free institutions of government would again be challenged at home and abroad.

In the end, the courts might well hold that Richard Nixon had been denied due process, and the verdict of history would even more be inconclusive with respect to those charges arising out of the period of his Presidency, of which I am presently aware.

But it is not the ultimate fate of Richard Nixon that most concerns me, though surely it deeply troubles every decent and every compassionate person. My concern is the immediate future of this great country.

In this, I dare not depend upon my personal sympathy as a long-time friend of the former President, nor my professional judgment as a lawyer, and I do not.

As President, my primary concern must always be the greatest good of all the people of the United States whose servant I am. As a man, my first consideration is to be true to my own convictions and my own conscience.

My conscience tells me clearly and certainly that I cannot prolong the bad dreams that continue to reopen a chapter that is closed. My conscience tells me that only I, as President, have the constitutional power to firmly shut and seal this book. My conscience tells me it is my duty, not merely to proclaim domestic tranquillity but to use every means that I have to insure it.

I do believe that the buck stops here, that I cannot rely upon public opinion polls to tell me what is right.

I do believe that right makes might and that if I am wrong, 10 angels swearing I was right would make no difference.

I do believe, with all my heart and mind and spirit, that I, not as President but as a humble servant of God, will receive justice without mercy if I fail to show mercy.

Finally, I feel that Richard Nixon and his loved ones have suffered enough and will continue to suffer, no matter what I do, no matter what we, as a great and good nation, can do together to make his goal of peace come true.

[*The President began reading from the proclamation granting the pardon.*] "Now, therefore, I, Gerald R. Ford, President of the United States, pursuant to the pardon power conferred upon me by Article II, Section 2, of the Constitution, have granted and by these presents do grant a full, free, and absolute pardon unto Richard Nixon for all offenses against the United States which he, Richard Nixon, has committed or may have committed or taken part in during the period from [January] 20, 1969 through August 9, 1974." [*The President signed the proclamation and then resumed reading.*]

"In witness whereof, I have hereunto set my hand this eighth day of September, in the year of our Lord nineteen hundred and seventy-four, and of the Independence of the United States of America the one hundred and ninety-ninth."

General Instructions for the Western Trip
Charles S. Murphy

One of President Harry S. Truman's campaign efforts for re-election was a whirlwind train trip, leaving Washington, D.C., on June 3, 1948, and arriving in Los Angeles, California, on June 14. On this trip, Truman traveled through Maryland, Pennsylvania, Ohio, Indiana, Illinois, Iowa, Nebraska, Colorado, Wyoming, Idaho, Montana, Washington, and Oregon. Truman's aide Charles S. Murphy made a detailed plan and to-the-minute schedule, listing every member of the group, including the dozens of people working for the President and a host of representatives from newspapers, radio and television networks, newsreel services, and photographers. In his typed plan, he included these "General Instructions" for the traveling party.

Truman on the Train

General Instructions

Numerous "operating" and "platform" stops will be made during the Western trip. During these stops, if the President appears on the rear platform, correspondents, newsreel and still photographers will leave their cars and walk back to cover the proceedings. For the purpose of smooth and orderly train operating procedure an alert signal will be sounded over the train public address system immediately after the President concludes his remarks. This signal will be in the form of a RISING and FALLING sound. This sound will signal the end of the proceedings, the President's participation will have ended and NO MORE PICTURES WILL BE PERMITTED. The PRESS will get aboard at the opening provided at head end of NUMBER THREE car. The President's car, as well as NUMBER TWO car will be closed at all times to members of the press party getting aboard the train.

Do not go back to the rear of the train during "platform" or "operating" stops unless your duties require you to be there. To do so will interfere with the citizens seeing and hearing the President, obstruct the press and picture people, and handicap the police and secret service unnecessarily.

It is never advisable to leave the immediate platform adjacent to the car to which you are assigned or working in. If it is necessary for you to leave the train be sure to find a local police or railroad police officer, show him your identification and be sure he understands you are to come back the same way. Otherwise you may be cut off in the crowd and left behind.

The work of icing, watering, and servicing the train begins immediately upon arriving at an operating stop. These crews work at top speed and on a time limit. Please keep out of their way.

Be sure that every piece of your luggage is tagged with your name and the Pullman space assigned to you. It is advisable to take an overnight bag to be used for one-night off-the-train stops and leave your heavier baggage on the train. A laundry bag should also be included.

When you leave the train for overnight stops be sure to carry with you and hold on to important papers, envelopes, brief cases, etc., that you may need during the next few hours. Your overnight baggage and working equipment will follow you as soon as possible. However, the train is frequently switched to a distant yard for the necessary servicing and supply and may be inaccessible for some time except for emergency communications. Therefore, try to anticipate and carry with you anything you may need at off-train headquarters.

You will be advised on the trip west where and when you may obtain laundry service. Thus, the reason for a laundry bag so that you will be ready when "laundry day" arrives.

All meals and refreshments are to be paid for at time of service. Gratuities for Pullman porters will be collected at the end of the trip, but the personnel in the dining cars will change as we change from one railroad to another and these waiters should be taken care of at time of service.

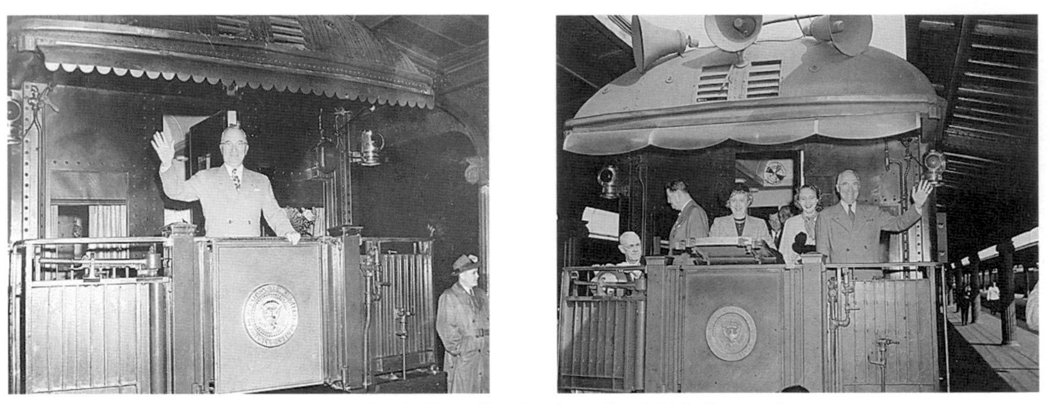

Truman and His Family During the 1948 Campaign

Debt of Gratitude
Theodore Roosevelt

This is an excerpt from Theodore Roosevelt's autobiography, published in 1913.

As for the men under me in executive office, I could not overstate the debt of gratitude I owe them. From the heads of the departments, the Cabinet officers, down, the most striking feature of the Administration was the devoted, zealous, and efficient work that was done as soon as it became understood that the one bond of interest among all of us was the desire to make the Government the most effective instrument in advancing the interests of the people as a whole, the interests of the average men and women of the United States and of their children. I do not think I overstate the case when I say that most of the men who did the best work under me felt that ours was a partnership, that we all stood on the same level of purpose and service, and that it mattered not what position any one of us held so long as in that position he gave the very best that was in him. We worked very hard; but I made a point of getting a couple of hours off each day for equally vigorous play. The men with whom I then played . . . we laughingly grew to call the "Tennis Cabinet . . ." There were many others in the public service under me with whom I happened not to play, but who did their share of our common work just as effectively as it was done by us who did play. Of course nothing could have been done in my Administration if it had not been for the zeal, intelligence, masterful ability, and downright hard labor of these men in countless positions under me. I was helpless to do anything except as my thoughts and orders were translated into action by them; and, moreover, each of them, as he grew specially fit for his job, used to suggest to me the right thought to have, and the right order to give, concerning that job. It is of course hard for me to speak with cold and dispassionate partiality of these men, who were as close to me as were the men of my regiment. But the outside observers best fitted to pass judgment about them felt as I did. At the end of my Administration Mr. Bryce, the British Ambassador, told me that in a long life, during which he had studied intimately the government of many different countries, he had never in any country seen a more eager, high-minded, and efficient set of public servants, men more useful and more creditable to their country, than the men then doing the work of the American Government in Washington and in the field.

President Roosevelt (left) and His Cabinet

Letter to Mrs. Abraham Lincoln

Frederick Douglass

Frederick Douglass was born a slave and escaped to freedom. He became a well-known speaker and writer against slavery. Frederick Douglass and Abraham Lincoln became friends during the Civil War.

Rochester. N.Y. August 17, 1865

Mrs. Abraham Lincoln:

Dear Madam: Allow me to thank you as I certainly do thank you most sincerely for your thoughtful kindness in making me the owner of a cane which was formerly the property and the favorite walking staff of your late lamented husband—the honored and venerated President of the United States. I assure you, that this inestimable memento of his presidency will be retained in my possession while I live—an object of sacred interest—a token not merely of the kind consideration in which I have reason to know that the President was pleased to hold me personally, but as an indication of his humane interest [in the] welfare of my whole race.

With every proper sentiment of Respect and Esteem,

I am, Dear Madam, your obedient,

Frederick Douglass

Frederick Douglass

Mary Lincoln

Remembering Mr. and Mrs. Madison
Paul Jennings

Paul Jennings was born a slave on James Madison's estate in 1799. He worked as Madison's personal attendant and went to Washington, D.C., with the Madisons during their presidential years. After James Madison's death, Senator Daniel Webster purchased Paul Jennings' freedom, which Jennings paid back in work. Later, Paul Jennings worked in the Pension Office of the Department of the Interior. There he met a fellow employee named John Brooks Russell who was fascinated by Jennings' recollections of the Madisons. He published Jennings' stories in a magazine in 1863, and they were later published as a book titled A Colored Man's Reminiscences of James Madison. *(At the time, "colored" was a polite way to refer to African Americans, though it is no longer.) These excerpts are from Jennings' book.*

James Madison

About ten years before Mr. Madison was President, he and Colonel Monroe were rival candidates for the Legislature. Mr. Madison was anxious to be elected, and sent his chariot to bring up a Scotchman to the polls, who lived in the neighborhood. But when brought up, he cried out: "Put me down for Colonel Monroe, for he was the first man that took me by the hand in this country." Colonel Monroe was elected, and his friends joked Mr. Madison pretty hard about his Scotch friend, and I have heard Mr. Madison and Colonel Monroe have many a hearty laugh over the subject, for years after.

When Mr. Madison was chosen President, we came on and moved into the White House; the east room was not finished, and Pennsylvania Avenue was not paved, but was always in an awful condition from either mud or dust. The city was a dreary place.

Mr. Robert Smith was then Secretary of State, but as he and Mr. Madison could not agree, he was removed, and Colonel Monroe appointed to his place. Dr. Eustis was Secretary of War rather a rough, blustering man; Mr. Gallatin, a tip-top man, was Secretary of the Treasury; and Mr. Hamilton, of South Carolina, a pleasant gentleman, who thought Mr. Madison could do nothing wrong, and who always concurred in every thing he said, was Secretary of the Navy.

. . . Mrs. Madison was a remarkably fine woman. She was beloved by everybody in Washington, white and colored. . . . In the last days of her life, before Congress purchased her husband's papers, she was in a state of absolute poverty, and I think sometimes suffered for the necessaries of life. While I was a servant to Mr. Webster, he often sent me to her with a market-basket full of provisions, and told me whenever I saw anything in the house that I thought she was in need of, to take it to her. I often did this, and occasionally gave her small sums from my own pocket, though I had years before bought my freedom of her.

Dolley Madison

Mr. Madison, I think, was one of the best men that ever lived. I never saw him in a passion, and never knew him to strike a slave, although he had over one hundred; neither would he allow an overseer to do it. Whenever any slaves were reported to him as stealing or "cutting up" badly, he would send for them and admonish them privately, and never mortify them by doing it before others. They generally served him very faithfully.

. . . I have heard Mr. Madison say, that when he went to school, he cut his own wood for exercise. He often did it also when at his farm in Virginia. He was very neat, but never extravagant, in his clothes. He always dressed wholly in black—coat, breeches, and silk stockings, with buckles in his shoes and breeches. He never had but one suit at a time. He had some poor relatives that he had to help, and wished to set them an example of economy in the matter of dress. He was very fond of horses, and an excellent judge of them, and no jockey ever cheated him. He never had less than seven horses in his Washington stables while President.

. . . After Mr. Madison retired from the presidency, in 1817, he invariably made a visit twice a year to Mr. Jefferson—sometimes stopping two or three weeks—till Mr. Jefferson's death, in 1826.

I was always with Mr. Madison till he died, and shaved him every other day for sixteen years. For six months before his death, he was unable to walk, and spent most of his time reclined on a couch; but his mind was bright, and with his numerous visitors he talked with as much animation and strength of voice as I ever heard him in his best days. I was present when he died. That morning Sukey brought him his breakfast, as usual. He could not swallow. His niece, Mrs. Willis, said, "What is the matter, Uncle James?" "Nothing more than a change of mind, my dear." His head instantly dropped, and he ceased breathing as quietly as the snuff of a candle goes out. He was about eighty-four years old, and was followed to the grave by an immense procession of white and colored people. The pall-bearers were Governor Barbour, Philip P. Barbour, Charles P. Howard, and Reuben Conway; the two last were neighboring farmers.

Montpelier, the Home of the Madisons

White House Menus

Here are examples of menus served at the White House.

Everyday menu served in the
Truman White House
Thursday, October 16, 1947

Luncheon

Hot Bouillon
Melon Ring Salad
(Filled with Bing Cherries)
Melba Toast
Half Grapefruit

Dinner

Minted Orange Cup
Broiled Lamp Chops
Buttered Peas
Buttered Carrots
Curled Celery
Assorted Olives
Baked Apples

Stag Dinner for
Prince Charles Regent of Belgium
Hosted by Harry S. Truman
Tuesday, April 6, 1948

Oysters on Half Shell Saltines

Clear Soup
Fairy Toast
Curled Celery Assorted Olives

Broiled Red Snapper
Sour Cream Cucumbers Dinner Rolls

Roast Stuffed Turkey
Giblet Gravy Cranberry Sauce
Casserole of Sweet Potatoes
Asparagus Glazed Carrots

Tomato Aspic Cheese Sticks

Ice Cream Molds Sponge Drops

Demitasse

State Dinner
for Chancellor
Helmut Schmidt
of West Germany
Hosted by Jimmy Carter
July 13, 1977

Chilled Crab Gumbo
Cheese Straws

Glazed Virginia Ham
with Brandied Peaches
Corn Pudding
Green Squash

Bibb Lettuce Salad
Sharp Cheddar Cheese

Lemon Chiffon Pie

Demitasse

State Dinner for David Cameron,
Prime Minister of the United Kingdom and
Northern Ireland and Samantha Cameron
Hosted by Barack Obama
March 14, 2012

Crisped Halibut with Potato Crust
Shaved Brussels Sprouts,
Applewood Smoked Bacon

Spring Garden Lettuces,
Shallot Dressing, Shaved Breakfast Radish,
Cucumbers and Avocados

Bison Wellington
Red Wine Reduction, French Beans,
Cipollini Onion

Warm Meyer Lemon Steamed Pudding
with Idaho Huckleberry Sauce
and Newton Pippin Apples

Field Trip to the Capitol

The United States Capitol Visitor Center provides this information for school groups planning to visit the United States Capitol.

Reservations

The Capitol is open to school groups for guided tours only. Tours are conducted from 8:50 a.m. to 3:20 p.m. Monday through Saturday. (The Capitol is not available for tours on Sundays.)

You may want to include additional time in your schedule to view the House and Senate Chamber galleries and to visit your Representative and Senators' offices. The gallery of the Senate Chamber is open to visitors when the Senate is in session and during scheduled recesses of one week or more from 9 a.m. to 4:30 p.m. The House of Representatives Chamber gallery is open to visitors when the House is in session and additionally 9 a.m. – 4:15 p.m., Monday through Friday when the House is not in session. Gallery passes may be obtained from the offices of your Senators or Representative. Visit their web sites at www.senate.gov or at www.house.gov for further information.

No passes or reservations are required to visit the Capitol Visitor Center itself, including the Exhibition Hall, the Gifts Shops and the Restaurant. (A pass is required to view the orientation film and to participate in a tour of the historic Capitol).

Painting of the Surrender of Lord Cornwallis in the U.S. Capitol

How much time should we allow for a U.S. Capitol visit?

Plan to spend at least two hours viewing the 13-minute orientation film, touring the Capitol, and exploring the Exhibition Hall.

Where can we eat?

The Capitol Visitor Center Restaurant is open 8:30 a.m. – 4 p.m., Monday through Saturday. Box lunches are available for school groups. For details and to reserve lunches, contact our restaurant facility through our main number, 202.226.8000.

What should we wear?

The Capitol is a working office building. Therefore, you are expected to dress appropriately for a business environment and behave in a respectful manner. We recommend that you wear comfortable shoes (you will climb many stairs as you move through the Capitol and tour the grounds). During the spring and summer months, you may want to bring a hat (it is very sunny and hot) as well as a foldable rain poncho for sudden rainstorms during warm weather.

Capitol Etiquette

When entering the Capitol Visitor Center:

★ Everyone will be asked to present all carried items for inspection upon entering the Capitol Visitor Center. We ask that students leave their backpacks or large bags and metal jewelry behind on the bus to help expedite the security check.

★ Food, beverages (including bottled water) are prohibited in the building.

★ The Capitol is a working office building. Therefore, you are expected to dress appropriately and behave in a respectful manner in this business environment.

While in the Capitol Visitor Center and the historic Capitol:

★ Turn off and do not use your cell phone or other electronic devices during the orientation film and while touring the Capitol.

★ Use your quiet voice when walking through the Capitol and exploring the Capitol Visitor Center's Exhibition Hall.

★ Please DO NOT TOUCH art objects including sculptures, statues, walls, and cases. The oils and acids even in clean hands can cause irreparable damage to works of art.

★ Refrain from leaning on the walls or using the walls, display cases, or pedestals for note-taking.

★ Do not sit on displays or sculptures for picture-taking.

★ Do not block doorways or aisles or sit on stairs or floors. Seating is provided throughout the buildings.

★ Stay together as a group. Be attentive to your guide's instructions at all times and especially when moving from one area to another in the Capitol. Watch your step, always use handrails when on the stairs, and use escalators with caution.

★ Respect any areas that are roped off.

★ Please don't run, push, shove, or take any other actions that may endanger other visitors or the works of art and the items in the Exhibition Hall.

Following these requests ensures that everyone will have a fun and memorable experience.

The Highest Good of the Country: The Story of Edmund G. Ross

Bethany Poore

Thousands of visitors flooded Washington, D.C., from all over the country. For the first time, the government of the United States was trying out the guidelines given in the Constitution for removing a President from office. Some visitors hoped to influence politicians, others just wanted to be part of the excitement, and many hoped to benefit from the upheaval by obtaining a position in the new government.

Opinions and emotions were intense as the bitter struggle neared its end. President Andrew Johnson had been on trial for several weeks. The Senate had to decide whether he would continue as President or walk away in disgrace. Johnson's many opponents had done everything they could, legal and illegal, to try to make sure he was found guilty.

As the controversy developed and the trial began, the United States was already a battered and weary nation. States had battled states, brother had slain brother in the tragedy of the Civil War. Cities, homes, farms, and lives were wrecked. Just as the war ended, Abraham Lincoln had been shot. This was the landscape that Lincoln's Vice President, Andrew Johnson, inherited when he took office.

The war was over, but the difficult work of peacemaking lay ahead for Johnson and the rest of the government. The Confederate States of America had lost, surrendered, and asked to be readmitted to the Union. Andrew Johnson wanted to make that process as quick and smooth as possible, but Radical Republicans in Congress thought the Southern states should be treated like conquered foes.

The Republicans in Congress had a large majority. They clashed with the President again and again. Not every member of Congress or the Senate was against the President, but his opponents controlled the power and their voices were loud. It was no longer North fighting South—the executive and legislative branches of the United States government were at war.

The war of laws, appointments, removals, vetoes, and overrides of vetoes between the U.S. Capitol and the White House climaxed in 1868. Johnson's opponents in Congress decided he should no longer be President. The Constitution gives instructions for how a President must be removed if necessary: first, he has to be impeached (officially accused of doing wrong) by the House of Representatives. The Senate must then hold a trial. The Chief Justice of the Supreme Court presides as judge, and the Senators are the jury. To remove the President, two-thirds of the Senators must vote for a guilty verdict.

In 1868, there were 54 Senators. 42 were Republicans and twelve were Democrats. Thirty-six votes were needed to remove the President. Most Senators made no pretense of waiting until the end of the trial to announce their verdict. They freely informed fellow Senators, others in government, newspapers, and the public.

Tickets were issued for admission to the impeachment trial.

Near the end of the trial, the Republicans held a meeting to make certain how many of their number they could count on. Fiery conversations burst forth in different parts of the room. Party leaders worked their way through the group, ready to intimidate as necessary. Clerks rushed in with urgent messages. Heads craned to see if anyone was missing. The atmosphere was charged with frenzied excitement. The Radical Republicans could smell victory.

"Surely, sir, we can count on you to see that justice is done and our nation is secure?"

"Guilty! Absolutely! I never heard such overwhelming evidence against a man in my life!"

"I came to Washington to represent my state, and every last man of them wants to see him gone."

"I will not fail in my loyalty to the Republican Party in the hour of its greatest need."

The goal seemed closer and closer as man after man promised to find Johnson guilty. Then suddenly the room gasped and every face turned toward a strong, steady voice. "In my opinion, the evidence brought forward is not enough to convict the President. In good conscience, I must vote not guilty."

The room erupted. Traitor! Weakling! He's one of our own party! Simply unbelievable!

When the last promise had been spoken, 35 had confidently promised a guilty vote, while six brave men had announced that they had not heard enough evidence of wrongdoing to find Johnson guilty. The Radical Republicans had exactly six Republican votes to spare to have enough for a two-thirds majority to declare Johnson guilty and boot him out of office. Despite these six renegade Republican senators who would not cooperate, was the guilty verdict secure? They still didn't know for sure.

One lone Republican senator, Edmund G. Ross of Kansas, simply would not say what his vote would be. When the House had impeached Johnson, Ross had remarked to another senator, "Well, Sprague, the thing is here; and so far as I am concerned, though a Republican and opposed to Mr. Johnson and his policy, he shall have as fair a trial as an accused man ever had on this earth."

So Ross could not be counted on. Republican leaders were furious and worried. This one man could jeopardize their entire plan! He and the six who had also stood up to Republican party leaders were hounded with demands, slander, and threats of violence and the ruin of their political careers.

Ross and his fellow Senator from Kansas received a telegram from home:

> *Kansas has heard the evidence and demands the conviction of the President.*
> *Signed: D.R. Anthony and 1000 others of our truest and best men.*

Ross replied to "D.R. Anthony and 1000 Others":

> *I do not recognize your right to demand that I shall vote either for or against conviction. I have taken an oath to do impartial justice according to the Constitution and laws, and trust that I shall have the courage and the honesty to vote according to the dictates of my judgment, and for the highest good of the country.*

May 16, 1868: the day the Senate would vote on President Johnson's fate. The House of Representatives adjourned and its members hurried to the Senate chamber. Every extra seat on the Senate floor and every square foot of standing room was filled. Some in the crammed visitors galleries had paid enormous prices for tickets. Even that morning, those on the side of the Radical Republicans targeted certain Senators who were against conviction, applying last-minute pressure for a guilty vote.

The Impeachment Trial of Andrew Johnson

Chief Justice Salmon Chase called the packed chamber to order. He sternly warned the visitors that "complete silence and perfect order are required," and threatened the immediate arrest of anyone who caused a disturbance. He ordered the Chief Clerk, "Call the roll."

The Chief Clerk called out the name of each Senator one by one, in alphabetical order. When his name was called, each Senator stood solemnly and was addressed by the Chief Justice,

"Mr. Senator Anthony, how say you? Is the respondent, Andrew Johnson, President of the United States, guilty or not guilty of a high misdemeanor, as charged in this article?"

"Guilty," said Mr. Anthony.

One by one each Senator called out his vote, some answering, "Not guilty," most answering "Guilty." Many spectators carefully marked down the votes on a list of the Senators that had been printed especially for the occasion. So far, twenty-four for guilty and ten for not guilty. Then the clerk called, "Mr. Ross."

Eleven more guilty votes were sure or almost sure from Senators who would vote after Ross, totaling 35 of the 36 needed votes for impeachment. Here was the agonizing moment of suspense on which the impeachment scheme hinged. If Senator Ross of Kansas voted guilty, Andrew Johnson would be removed and the Radical Republicans would win the day. One of their own, Benjamin Wade, was next in line to assume the presidency as president *pro tempore* of the Senate. With Wade in office, Radical Republican power would be boundless!

Visitors in the gallery leaned tensely forward, keeping absolutely silent. Senators leaned over their desks toward Ross, trying not to miss a syllable. No one but Ross himself knew how he had determined to vote. The face of the Chief Justice betrayed emotion as he asked "How say you, Senator Ross? Is the respondent, Andrew Johnson, guilty or not guilty under this article?" He joined those leaning forward toward Senator Ross, his forehead knit with anxiety. The nation held its breath. From the very center of the maelstrom, surrounded by silent, intense faces full of hope or fear, weighted with the knowledge that this one action would have a decisive impact on the future of his country and his own life, Ross spoke.

"Not guilty."

The strain snapped. All was now in the light. The intense observers fell back in their chairs. Gasps, shuffling feet, murmurs, fury, and relief grew quickly louder as everyone reacted and watched the reactions of those around them. With a forceful effort, the Chief Justice restored order and continued asking for votes. But everyone already knew the ending: impeachment had failed.

Senator Ross had made an unpopular choice, and the consequences were immediate and intense. Newspapers viciously maligned him. The people of Kansas cried out that he had betrayed them. He was called a liar, a wretch, and a traitor. When his one term in the Senate ended in 1871, he and his family returned home to Kansas.

Why would a Senator sacrifice so much to keep an opponent in office? Edmund G. Ross had admitted he was against Johnson and his policies. If he had voted guilty, Ross would have been on the winning side of a successful impeachment. He might have enjoyed more power in the new government and the jubilant approval of his friends and his home state.

Senator Ross voted "not guilty" because he had the wisdom to see beyond the bitter contest of the moment. He realized that the Senate was not simply voting on the guilt or innocence of a single man, but was setting the course for the future governance of the United States.

Was it acceptable for the Congress to remove a President just because the majority disagreed with his decisions and saw him as standing in their way? The evidence against Johnson brought forth at the trial failed to prove that he was guilty, but most of his Republican opponents didn't care. The point was not the evidence; the point was to get him out of office however they could. But was that acceptable?

If the first impeachment trial of a President had determined that the chief executive could be removed by Congress because of differences of opinion, then the legislative branch would ever after be in control. The President would be the puppet of Congress, easily removed if he caused problems. The framers of the U.S. Constitution knew the wisdom of checks and balances in our government, and Edmund G. Ross cast his vote for those wise choices to continue as the law of the land.

A Loyal Kansan
T. C. Hill

After Senator Edmund G. Ross rendered his unpopular verdict in the impeachment trial of Andrew Johnson, one of his fellow Kansans sent him this letter of loyal support.

Americus, Lyon County, Kansas
June 12, 1868

Hon E. G. Ross

Dear Sir,

From what I see in the papers I fear you must almost be afraid to open a letter for fear of reading some miserable slang.

So far as I am concerned I cannot see why you have not as much of a right to render a verdict according to law & evidence as any juror consequently I have no reason for abusing you as some do.

I am glad to see one man who feels as though he should do justice to all even [if] their politics or color may differ. I am sure you have more friends in Kansas as yet than many represent. A few of the fool Rads have spoken their piece and it might appear to one at a distance that all Kansas had come down on you. I notice such as L. D. Bailes, F. G. Hunt and other sore heads appear to think it a fine opportunity to pounce upon you. I do not know that I can say or do anything that would give you any pleasure more than to show you that I cannot feel like condemning you for doing what your judgment dictated to you was right.

Yours Respectfully,
T. C. Hill

Edmund G. Ross

Senate Firsts

First Senators Elected	First (Former) Senator to Become President	First Senator Who Had Been President

Robert Morris (pictured) and William Maclay of Pennsylvania were elected September 30, 1788.	*James Monroe represented Virginia in the Senate from 1790 to 1794. He became President in 1817.*	*Andrew Johnson became a Senator on March 4, 1875, representing Tennessee.*
First Hispanic Senator	**First Female Senator**	**First Elected Female Senator**

Octaviano Larrazolo became the first Hispanic Senator in 1928. He was a Republican from New Mexico.	*Rebecca Felton was appointed to the Senate. She took the oath of office on November 21, 1922, and served for one day.*	*Hattie Ophelia Wyatt Caraway was elected to the Senate in 1932. The Democrat from Arkansas served until 1945.*

★ **First Radio Broadcast from Senate Chamber**—The first radio broadcast from the chamber of the Senate was on March 4, 1929.

★ **First Television Broadcast from Senate Chamber**—The first television broadcast from the Senate chamber aired December 19, 1974, covering Nelson Rockefeller taking the oath of office to become Vice President.

First "First Lady" Senator	First Chinese American Senator	First African American Senator

Hillary Clinton took the oath of office on January 3, 2001. She was still serving as First Lady.	*In 1959, Hiram L. Fong became the first Senator of Chinese ancestry. He was a Republican from Hawaii.*	*Hiram R. Revels took the oath of office on February 25, 1870. He was a Republican from Mississippi.*
First Female African American Senator	**First Senator in Space**	**First Father and Son Senators Serving Together**

Carol Moseley-Braun of Illinois became the first African American female to be a U.S. Senator in 1993.	*In 1998 Senator John Glenn, a former astronaut, returned to space aboard the Space Shuttle.*	*Henry Dodge (top) represented Wisconsin from 1848 to 1857. His son Augustus represented Iowa from 1848 to 1855.*

★ **First Page**—The first Senate page was nine-year-old Grafton Hanson in 1929. The first female pages were 16-year-olds Paulette Desell and Ellen McConnel in 1971.

★ **First C-SPAN Coverage in the Senate**—In 1986 C-SPAN began to air regular television coverage of proceedings on the floor of the Senate.

★ **Senate Movie**— Forty-five senators attended the 1939 world premiere of "Mr. Smith Goes to Washington" at Constitution Hall in Washington, D.C.

Pages of the House

From its early days, the House of Representatives employed pages to assist in tasks such as carrying documents, messages, and letters between offices and Congressmen. Over time, the House began to employ teenage boys to perform these duties. The first records of teenage boys serving as employees of the house dates from the 20th Congress (1827-1829). As new states entered the Union, the number of pages increased, reaching about 70 pages serving modern Congresses. Until the passage of the Compulsory School Act in 1925, pages were not required to attend school. The House started a one-room school in the basement of the Capitol, which eventually grew to include pages from the Senate and the Supreme Court. The first class of the Page School graduated in 1932. Girls permanently joined the ranks in 1973. The most recent pages were high school juniors from around the country who served for a spring, summer, or fall session and lived in the Page Residence Hall. In 2011 Speaker of the House John Boehner and Democratic Leader Nancy Pelosi decided to close the House Page program. They issued the following press release on August 8, 2011.

Citing advances in technology that have reduced the need for services traditionally provided by congressional Pages, as well as the high cost of the program, House Speaker John Boehner (R-OH) and Democratic Leader Nancy Pelosi (D-CA) have directed the Clerk of the House and other House officials to take the steps necessary to conclude the House Page Program. Speaker Boehner and Leader Pelosi have advised the Page Board of their decision, which was based in part on an independent review of the program conducted jointly by Strategic Assets Consulting and Fieldstone Consulting, Inc. Specifically, the independent review found:

Pages, once stretched to the limit delivering large numbers of documents and other packages between the U.S. Capitol and House office buildings, are today rarely called upon for such services, since most documents are now transmitted electronically;

Dozens of Pages, once needed on the House floor to deliver a steady stream of phone messages to lawmakers, are no longer required for that purpose as most Members are contacted directly via electronic devices;

The annual cost to operate the program exceeds $5 million, not including capital costs associated with the Page dormitory and school; and the "per Page" cost per school year is between $69,000 and $80,000, more than the most expensive boarding schools, as well as most colleges and universities.

Speaker Boehner and Leader Pelosi issued the following statement: "We have great appreciation for the unique role that Pages have played in the history and traditions of the House of Representatives. This decision was not easy, but it is necessary due to the prohibitive cost of the program and advances in technology that have rendered most Page-provided services no longer essential to the smooth functioning of the House. Although the traditional mission of the Page Program has diminished, we will work with Members of the House to carry on the tradition of engaging young people in the work of the Congress."

Speaker Boehner and Leader Pelosi also directed the House Historian to prepare an official history of the House Page Program as a tribute to the many Pages, Members of Congress and congressional staff who have contributed to the program over the years.

House Pages

Moving the Books
Thomas Jefferson

The British burned the Capitol and Library of Congress in 1814 during the War of 1812. At that time, Thomas Jefferson had the largest personal library in the United States, which he offered to sell to Congress to begin their library again. After debate, Congress accepted the offer and paid Jefferson $23,950 for 6,487 volumes, more than twice the number that were in the library at the time of the fire. Jefferson wrote to Washington-area bookseller Joseph Milligan requesting him to come to Monticello, Jefferson's home, to supervise the packing and transportation of the books to Washington.

Monticello Feb 27, 1815

Dear Sir,

The library committee of Congress having concluded to take my library without further valuation, at the amount of your estimate, I shall on receipt of the catalogue proceed to review it, arrange and number all the books according as they stand in the catalogue. As on this review many will doubtless be found missing and irrecoverable, deductions proportioned to their size and number must of course be made from the amount of compensation. Besides this there should be some one skilled in packing to attend to that and see that the fine bindings should not be destroyed by the joltings of the wagons. You were so kind, in one of your letters, as to say you would come and see to this. I have therefore proposed to Mr. Smith to have you authorized by the committee as their agent, and I hope if it meets their approbation that yours will not be wanting. When I have finished the review I am to give him notice that all is ready. I have mentioned to him too that wagons can be had here at L.D. to take 2500 [pounds?] each, and an accurate estimate makes 11 such wagon loads. But I have suggested to him the necessity of sending a wagon load of book binders paper-parings and waste paper, the former to fill the [spaces] between the books and shelves, the latter to wrap the best bindings, and for slips between all the books. I should be very sorry to have them injured by the way. I suppose the review will employ me near a fortnight, and immediately after that and before the possibility of any new derangement I should be anxious to have the delivery made. If these propositions should be accepted I hope your concurrence will not be wanting, and that we shall have the pleasure of receiving you here in the course of the next month. Accept the assurance of my great esteem and respect.

Th. Jefferson

The Dimensions of a Kind Deed
Calvin Coolidge

In 1841 a fourteen-year-old Japanese boy named Manjiro and four shipmates were caught in a sudden violent storm while fishing near their village on the coast of Japan. They were driven to a rocky island 300 miles away. After more than five months, they were rescued by an American whaling vessel from Massachusetts. The captain of the ship, William Whitefield, took notice of the intelligent young Manjiro, and invited him to return with him to Massachusetts. His shipmates were left in Hawaii. Manjiro attended school in Fairhaven, Massachusetts, for three years. He became a successful whaler.

The law of Japan demanded isolation and dealt severe consequences to those who returned to the country after contact with foreigners. In 1851 Manjiro decided to risk his life and return to Japan. After interrogation and imprisonment, he was reunited with his mother and siblings. In 1853 American Admiral Matthew Perry came to Japan in hopes of establishing friendly relations between Japan and the United States. As an expert on the United States, Manjiro was summoned to advise and assist in the consideration of the treaty. His influence helped open his country to contact with the rest of the world. He became a teacher, preparing young Japanese to live in a far different Japan than the one Manjiro had known as a boy.

On July 4, 1918, in Fairhaven, Massachusetts, lieutenant governor Calvin Coolidge received the gift of a samurai sword from the 1300s to commemorate Manjiro's rescue and the kindness of the people of Fairhaven. The sword was given by Manjiro's eldest son, Dr. Toichiro Nakahama, and presented by Viscount Kikujiro Ishii, Japan's Ambassador to the United States. The following is the speech made by Coolidge on the occasion.

We have met on this anniversary of American independence to assess the dimensions of a kind deed. Nearly four score years ago the master of a whaling vessel sailing from this port rescued from a barren rock in the China Sea some Japanese fishermen. Among them was a young boy whom he brought home with him to Fairhaven, where he was given the advantages of New England life and sent to school with the boys and girls of the neighborhood, where he excelled in his studies. But as he grew up he was filled with a longing to see Japan and his aged mother. He knew that the duty of filial piety lay upon him according to the teachings of his race, and he was determined to meet that obligation. I think that is one of the lessons of this day. Here was a youth who determined to pursue the course which he had been taught was right. He braved the dangers of the voyage and the greater dangers that awaited an absentee from his country under the then existing laws, to perform his duty to his mother and to his native land. In making that return I think we are entitled to say that he was the first Ambassador of America to the Court of Japan, for his extraordinary experience soon brought him into the association of the highest officials of his country, and his presence there prepared the way for the friendly reception which was given to Commodore Perry when he was sent to Japan to open relations between that government and the government of America.

The Presentation Ceremony at Fairhaven High School

Calvin Coolidge

And so we see how out of the kind deed of Captain Whitefield, friendly relations which have existed for many years between the people of Japan and the people of America were encouraged and made possible. And it is in recognition of that event that we have here today this great concourse of people, this martial array, and the representative of the Japanese people—a people who have never failed to respond to an act of kindness.

Kikujiro Ishii

It was with special pleasure that I came here representing the Commonwealth of Massachusetts, to extend an official welcome to His Excellency Viscount Ishii, who comes here to present to the town of Fairhaven a Samurai sword on behalf of the son of that boy who was rescued long ago. This sword was once the emblem of place and caste and arbitrary rank. It has taken on a new significance because Captain Whitefield was true to the call of humanity, because a Japanese boy was true to his call of duty. This emblem will hereafter be a token not only of the friendship that exists between two nations but a token of liberty, of freedom, and of the recognition by the government of both these nations of the rights of the people. Let it remain here as a mutual pledge by the giver and the receiver of their determination that the motive which inspired the representatives of each race to do right is to be a motive which is to govern the people of the earth.

Manjiro

Whatever May Be Our Wishes: The Story of John Adams

Ray Notgrass and Bethany Poore

"Fire! Fire at the Treasury building!" The cries broke into the quiet evening. Citizens rushed from their homes to help. The new United States of America was struggling to establish a capital city in the wilderness along the Potomac River, and now their six-month-old Treasury building was in flames. "Bring buckets! Bucket brigade!" As fast as they could, the men of Washington passed buckets of water hand-to-hand toward the burning building, and passed empty buckets back to be re-filled. One man in line passing the buckets, getting sloshed with water and splashed with mud, had rushed from the Executive Mansion next door in answer to the urgent cries. He was President John Adams.

Doing the right thing regardless of the cost to himself was the way Adams had lived his entire professional life. His first call to render selfless public service had come thirty years earlier in 1770.

On a cold March evening, John Adams relaxed at the home of Mr. Henderson Inches with a group of friends. The urgent sound of ringing bells broke into their conversation. "It's a fire! Come along, we must lend a hand!" They snatched their hats and cloaks and hurried out. A throng of people formed a strong current flowing down the street.

"What has happened? What has caught fire?" Adams asked a man passing by.

"Nothing is afire, sir. The filthy redcoats have fired on our townsmen," he replied.

"Some are killed! Some wounded!" a woman yelled over her shoulder as she rushed along.

The group of friends turned to each other with alarm. "God have mercy on us," one murmured. They fell in with the crowd and walked to the Town House. Nervous, ears alert, they listened for the crack of guns. They heard nothing but the frenzied excitement of the crowd. By the time they arrived at the Town House, the violence was over and the soldiers had regained control. Apparently the killed and wounded had already been taken away. A few cannons and a tense guard stood before the Town House door. The crowd of Bostonians looked and pointed and whispered. John Adams walked slowly around the building and convinced himself that all was quiet.

Abigail and John Adams

John Adams knew that his wife must have heard the news at home. Mrs. Adams was expecting a baby, and her husband worried about the effect of such a shock. As he headed for home, he came upon one or two companies of redcoats lined up in front of a church with muskets shouldered and bayonets fixed. He had to pass right in front of the entire line through the tiny space they had left for foot travelers. The soldiers were like marble statues as John Adams walked by, looking straight ahead. Mrs. Adams was calm; she had heard of the violence, but then heard that all was under control. Apparently, all was quiet for the night, and the Adamses were left to wonder and worry about what this event foretold for the future.

The next morning, John Adams sat working in his law office. He looked up when a man entered. He recognized his visitor and greeted him, "Good morning, Mr. Forrest."

Mr. Forrest looked at Adams with tears streaming from his eyes. "I am come with a very solemn message from a very unfortunate man, Captain Preston, in prison." Captain Preston had played a part in the tragedy of the preceding day. He would be put on trial with eight other British soldiers who had been arrested for the deaths of five citizens in the incident now known as the Boston Massacre.

Depiction of the Boston Massacre by Paul Revere

How could he get a fair trial in this city seething with anger and hatred? What American lawyer would risk his reputation defending the hated British for the killing of five martyrs of American freedom? But Mr. Preston had heard of John Adams' integrity. He felt he could trust his life to him. Adams was committed to truth and the law. Despite the risk, Adams agreed to take the case. It was the right thing to do.

In the trial, Adams argued convincingly that the disturbance was actually caused by colonists attacking the soldiers, and that the soldiers were only acting in self-defense. This in fact was true. On the evening of the Massacre, a small crowd threatened a single soldier who was standing guard at the government custom house. Eight more soldiers came alongside their comrade as reinforcements. The crowd grew to several hundred people, many of whom began throwing snowballs, stones, and other objects at the soldiers. At some point, the soldiers opened fire. The people of Boston were understandably angry about the British treatment of the colonies, and especially about the policy of requiring colonists to house British soldiers; but this did not justify the crowd's actions toward the soldiers.

"Facts are stubborn things," said Adams during the trial, "and whatever may be our wishes, our inclinations, or the dictums [commands] of our passions, they cannot alter the state of facts and evidence."

Adams would later become a leader in the cause of American independence. He had no defense of the British policies toward the colonies. But on this occasion, to Adams the evidence was clear. He was not defending British policy. Instead, he was defending the truth and the right of any accused person to receive a fair trial by an impartial jury.

All of the soldiers were found not guilty except two, who were convicted of manslaughter. They were punished by being branded on their thumbs. Defending British soldiers charged with killing Americans in colonial, emotion-charged Boston was not easy. But the right to a fair trial, even for people who are not popular, was a fundamental part of British (and later American) justice. John Adams defended the soldiers because it was the right thing to do.

In 1785, after the American Revolution, the time came for the two former adversaries, Great Britain and the United States, to exchange ambassadors. Who could serve—who would want to serve—as American ambassador to Britain? Once again, the United States called upon John Adams; and Adams accepted the job. It was not easy, but it was the right thing to do.

During the time that Adams was President, France was at war with Great Britain. American relations with Great Britain had improved, and a significant amount of trade took place between the two countries. Although France was also friendly toward the United States, the French seized American trading ships bound for Britain in the name of their war effort. Many Americans were furious and demanded that the nation declare war against France. But President Adams knew that the United States military and its tiny navy were far too weak to win such a war. Adams sent a diplomat to Paris to negotiate an agreement to end the hostility between the two nations. The successful conclusion of these negotiations ended the threat of war, but it cost Adams dearly in the realm of public opinion. Still, Adams knew it was the right thing to do.

When Adams ran for re-election in 1800, two opposing political parties had formed. Adams was a member of the Federalist Party, while his Vice President, Thomas Jefferson, sided with the Democratic-Republicans. Jefferson agreed to run against Adams. Newspapers that supported Jefferson printed vicious lies about Adams, and Federalist papers printed scandalous stories about Jefferson. Even some Federalists published material that was sharply critical of Adams. Adams was deeply hurt by these attacks and by the opposition from his old friend Thomas Jefferson. But Adams did not stoop to reply to the slander, and he did not engage in any negative campaigning himself. Adams lost the election by eight electoral votes. If only one state with enough electoral votes had gone the other way, Adams would have won. But if Adams had sacrificed his integrity in order to win an election, he would have lost much more.

Everyone faces decisions in which they have to decide whether to do the right thing or the easy thing, the principled thing or the popular thing. Everyone who is involved in public service has to make decisions under pressure about whether to do what is right or to do what will win re-election and praise. During over thirty years of public service, from putting out the fire of political injustice after the Boston Massacre to helping put out a literal fire in the Treasury building in the District of Columbia, John Adams was a strong example of someone who had the integrity to do the right thing.

John Adams at Age 88

Diplomat's Wife
Lillie De Hegermann-Lindencrone

Lillie De Hegermann-Lindencrone (1844-1928), originally of Cambridge, Massachusetts, married Denmark's Ambassador to the United States. Her letters describing her experiences as a diplomat's wife were published as The Sunny Side of Diplomatic Life *in 1913.*

WASHINGTON, November, 1875.

Lillie De Hegermann-Lindencrone

Dear Mother,—After my hurriedly written letter of the 24th you will know that we have arrived here safely. My first introduction to my first post as diplomat's wife was made unwittingly by a gentleman walking with a friend just behind me. "Who is that gentleman?" said he, indicating Johan. "That? That is the Minister of Denmark." I, struggling with an arm-load of flowers culled from well-intentioned friends at different stations on the road, my maid and Johan's valet bringing up the rear with the overflow of small baggage, passed unnoticed. Now we are quite established here, and I have already commenced my diplomatic duties. There seems to be no end of card-leaving and card-receiving, and a list of rules on etiquette (the Ten Commandments of a Diplomat) as long as your arm. I never knew of anything so confusing. I try to remember the things that I must do and the things that I must not do. How many cold shower-baths of reproval have I already received; how many unruly things have I already done! We are invited to many dinners, luncheons, and entertainments of all kinds. I am knee-deep in engagements, actually wading in them. The engagement-book you gave me is already overfilled. . . .

It would take more than one letter of mine written on foolscap paper to tell you of our colleagues and friends. I can do it in sections when I have time. But, oh, when can I get the time!

I have had my "audience" (Johan calls it an "audience"; I call it a "call on Mrs. President Grant at the White House"). There was nothing formal or formidable about it. Mrs. Grant and I sat on the sofa together and talked generalities. Johan could not tell me what to expect. He said his audience with the President had been a surprise, unprecedented by anything he had ever seen. As it was his first post as Minister, he had pictured to himself that it would be somewhat like the ceremonies abroad—very solemn and impressive. Of course he was in his red gala uniform, with all his decorations. A hired landau brought him to the steps of the White House, which he mounted with conscious dignity. His written speech, nicely folded, he carried in his hand. In Europe there would have been a crowd of gorgeous chamberlains to receive him, but here he found a negro, who, on seeing him, hurriedly donned a coat and, with an encouraging wave of the hand, said: "Come right along in, sir. I'll let them know you're here, sir." Johan was shown into a room and waited with patience until the President and Mr. Hamilton Fish came in. Mr. Grant was dressed

Julia Grant

in a gray walking-suit and wore a colored tie; and Mr. Hamilton Fish (Secretary of State) had evidently just come in from a walk, as his turned-up trousers signified.

Johan read his speech, and the President answered by reading, with some difficulty, a paper which Mr. Fish handed to him at the last moment. After this exchange of formalities Johan shook hands with the President, and without further ceremony he left the room, the door this time being opened by a white servant in black clothes. Mr. Fish at parting casually observed that the weather was fine.

I was officially presented on their reception days to the wives of all the Ministers, and made my visits to the members of the Corps Diplomatique. We were invited to dinner at the White House—a dinner given to the Corps Diplomatique. I was taken in by M. de Schlözer, the German Minister, and sat between him and Sir Edward Thornton (the English Minister), who sat on the right of Mrs. Grant. We were opposite to the President. I noticed that he turned his wine-glasses upside down, to indicate, I suppose, that he did not drink wine during dinner. Afterward we amused ourselves by walking in the long Blue Room. The President disappeared with some of the gentlemen to smoke and was lost to view. The company also faded gradually away. Mrs. Grant did not seem inclined to gaze on us any longer, and appeared to be relieved when we shook her outstretched hand and said "Good night."

A dinner to which we went, given by the Schiskines (the Russian Minister) in honor of the Grand-Duke Constantine of Russia, was most delightful. The Grand Duke is very charming, natural, with a sly twinkle in his mild blue eye. He has a very handsome face, is extremely musical, and plays the piano with great finesse, having a most sympathetic touch.

After dinner we darned stockings. This sounds queer, but nevertheless it is true. The Schiskines had just bought a darning-machine. They paid eighty-six dollars for it; but to darn, one must have holes, and no holes could be found in a single decent stocking, so they had to cut holes, and then we darned. The Grand Duke was so enchanted with this darning that he is going to take a machine home to the Grand Duchess, his august mother.

The darning done, we had some music. M. de Schlözer improvised on the piano, and after the Grand Duke had played some Chopin I sang. M. de Schlözer went through his little antics as advance-courier of my singing: he screwed the piano-stool to the proper height (he thinks it must be just so high when I accompany myself); he removed all albums from sight for fear people might be tempted to glance in them; he almost snatched fans from the hands of unoffending ladies, fearing they might use them; no dogs were to be within patting distance, and no smoking; he turned all the chairs to face the piano so that no one should turn his back to it. These are all heinous crimes in his eyes. He would, if he could, have pulled down all the portières and curtains, as he does in his own house when I sing there. What must people think of him?

. . . The charity concert, of which I was dame patronesse, went off with success. We made a great deal of money. M. de Schlözer paid twenty dollars for his ticket. My chorus covered itself with glory and was encored. As the concert finished at ten, we adjourned to the Zamaconas' (Minister of Mexico) first ball, and I hope, for them, their only one. It was one of those soirées where people appropriate the forks and spoons. It cost, they say, ten thousand dollars. . . .

A Better Day for Humankind—Here and Everywhere
Franklin D. Roosevelt

On December 24, 1943, President Franklin D. Roosevelt delivered one of his famous Fireside Chats. These were a series of informal radio speeches he made to the American people during his presidency. World War II had separated families and taken millions of brave service personnel into danger. The message was broadcast to families in America and to Americans fighting all over the world. This excerpt of Roosevelt's hopeful message rings true for the dedicated men and women serving in our armed forces today.

President Franklin Roosevelt

. . . Less than a month ago I flew in a big Army transport plane over the little town of Bethlehem, in Palestine.

Tonight, on Christmas Eve, all men and women everywhere who love Christmas are thinking of that ancient town and of the star of faith that shone there more than nineteen centuries ago.

American boys are fighting today in snow-covered mountains, in malarial jungles, on blazing deserts; they are fighting on the far stretches of the sea and above the clouds, and fighting for the thing for which they struggle. I think it is best symbolized by the message that came out of Bethlehem.

On behalf of the American people—your own people—I send this Christmas message to you who are in our armed forces:

In our hearts are prayers for you and for all your comrades in arms who fight to rid the world of evil.

We ask God's blessing upon you—upon your fathers, mothers, wives and children—all your loved ones at home.

We ask that the comfort of God's grace shall be granted to those who are sick and wounded, and to those who are prisoners of war in the hands of the enemy, waiting for the day when they will again be free.

And we ask that God receive and cherish those who have given their lives, and that He keep them in honor and in the grateful memory of their countrymen forever.

God bless all of you who fight our battles on this Christmas Eve.

God bless us all. Keep us strong in our faith that we fight for a better day for humankind—here and everywhere.

American Bomber During World War II

1918 Resolution: The Story of Martin A. Treptow
by Bethany Poore

Company M of the 168th Infantry crossed the Ourcq river and continued toward their objective, Hill 212. The advance was costly, for the Germans had a good defensive position to fire on the American soldiers. In the noise and confusion of battles such as this one, commanders depended on brave runners to carry messages from regiment to battalion, battalion to company, company to platoon. The task was frequently deadly as messengers had to cross unprotected through large open areas. Several soldiers were frequently sent with the same message in hopes that at least one would make it through enemy fire.

American Soldiers in France, 1918

"Who will take this message?" The commander looked around at his company of young soldiers. He knew what he was asking. He was asking them to offer their very lives for their country.

"I'll take it," Private Martin Treptow volunteered.

Carrying this vital information for his comrades, Martin set out. He had trained for this. He was ready. He would do all in his power to get the message across for the welfare of his buddies and the success of their fight. Heart beating fast, mind focused on his goal, he rushed away from comparative safety and into danger. His ears rang with machine gun and artillery fire. Keep going! Any cover? Any better path to take? He looked around. He tried to be invisible. Almost there! In a few moments, the precious message would be safely delivered. But suddenly a German shell struck at his feet. He was killed instantly. He fell in France on July 28, 1918, in the midst of World War I, fighting with the Allies in what would prove to be the decisive Second Battle of the Marne. He was 24 years old.

German Soldiers and Tanks at the Second Battle of the Marne

When his body was recovered, his comrades found Private Treptow's diary safely preserved in his shirt pocket. Martin had used the diary to record upbeat notes on his day-to-day life in the army. On New Year's Eve of 1917, Martin wrote a "1918 Resolution:"

America shall win the War
Therefore I will work,
I will save,
I will sacrifice
I will endure
I will fight cheerfully and do my utmost,
as if the whole issue of the struggle
depended on me alone.

That July day on the fighting fields of France, Martin Treptow was asked to prove the worth of his resolution. Unshirking, Martin Treptow did his duty to his country, and made the greatest sacrifice he had to offer.

Martin Treptow had an American experience like many others. His parents were born in Germany and came to America as children with their families. Martin was born in 1894, the middle child of five siblings. He grew up on the family farm near Bloomer in western Wisconsin, hunting, fishing, swimming in the creek in the summer, skiing in the winter, and attending the country schoolhouse.

As a young man, he decided he wanted to be a barber, and he became a good one. His work took him to Cherokee, Iowa. After America entered World War I in 1917, President Woodrow Wilson called for volunteers to serve their country. Martin Treptow answered the summons and enlisted. He trained in Iowa and New York before shipping out to France in late 1917.

Martin had a sweetheart in Cherokee named Pearl Van de Steeg. She played the piano at the local vaudeville and movie theaters (films were silent in those days and had live music to accompany them) and was an accompanist and music teacher at Cherokee High School.

Before Martin left for the war, he and Pearl exchanged snapshots of each other. On the back of her photo, Pearl inscribed, "With all the Love in the World for 'Trep.'" Martin penciled under her message, "In Case of accident, please send this picture to My sweetheart. Box 222 Cherokee, Iowa."

U.S. newspapers in the United States printed an official War Casualty List provided by the War Department on September 27, 1918. Columns of names in tiny print listed those who were killed in action, missing, wounded, dead of disease or accident, or in enemy prisons. The list of Killed in Action included the line "Martin A. Treptow, Bloomer, Wis." The snapshot was returned to Pearl Van de Steeg. The Treptow family received Martin's diary.

Frank Slupecki, Toledo, O.
Wm. P. Taylor, Amazonia, Mo.
James F. Tennimon, Selma, Ala.
Carl Thompson, Columbus, Ga.
Wade Thompson, Sellars, S. C.
Henry W. Toepfer, Charles City, Ia.
Martin A. Treptow, Bloomer, Wis.
Alex Tyska, Detroit.
Peter Verde, Billings, Mont.
John J. Walsh, Utica, N. Y.
Clarence Wenlock, Phila., Pa.

Casualty lists with hundreds of names were printed in newspapers across the country. This clipping is from the September 29 issue of the Bisbee Daily Review *in Arizona.*

On January 20, 1981, over sixty years after Martin Treptow died carrying a message across the battlefield, his nephew Lyle, 65, and niece Doris, 59, were watching Ronald Reagan's inaugural speech on television. All of a sudden, they were shocked to hear something very familiar. The new President was talking about their uncle, and quoting his words that had been so important in their family life.

Reagan spoke of the price that has been paid for American freedom, and he used as an example, ". . . Martin Treptow, who left his job in a small town barbershop in 1917 to go to France with the famed Rainbow Division. There, on the western front, he was killed trying to carry a message between battalions under heavy artillery fire.

"We're told that on his body was found a diary. On the flyleaf under the heading, "My Pledge," he had written these words: "America must win this war. Therefore I will work, I will save, I will sacrifice, I will endure, I will fight cheerfully and do my utmost, as if the issue of the whole struggle depended on me alone."

Ronald Reagan Giving His First Inaugural Address

For a few moments, people all across the country were thinking about Martin Treptow. His solemn words of love for and devotion to his country settled into their minds. His tragic ending touched their hearts. His words no doubt inspired many of his fellow Americans, those serving in the military and those serving their country in other ways.

But on December 31, 1917, when Martin Treptow wrote those words, he wasn't famous. No one was making speeches about him. He was just a plain, simple, small-town American who loved his country. As he took up his diary and pen in a French village on the other side of the world from Bloomer, Wisconsin, and thought about the new year ahead, he pledged to do his duty. A few months later, Martin Treptow proved that he meant what he said.

Remembering West Point Years
Ulysses S. Grant

Grant included these memories of his West Point years in his autobiography, Personal Memoirs of U.S. Grant, *published in 1885. Despite his early lack of interest in military life, Grant went on from West Point to become one of the greatest soldiers in the history of the United States.*

In the winter of 1838-9 I was attending school at Ripley, only ten miles distant from Georgetown, but spent the Christmas holidays at home. During this vacation my father received a letter from the Honorable Thomas Morris, then United States Senator from Ohio. When he read it he said to me, "Ulysses, I believe you are going to receive the appointment."

"What appointment?" I inquired.

"To West Point; I have applied for it."

"But I won't go," I said.

He said he thought I would, and I thought so too, if he did. I really had no objection to going to West Point, except that I had a very exalted idea of the acquirements necessary to get through. I did not believe I possessed them, and could not bear the idea of failing. . . .

The Honorable Thomas L. Hamer, one of the ablest men Ohio ever produced, was our member of Congress at the time, and had the right of nomination. He and my father had been members of the same debating society (where they were generally pitted on opposite sides), and intimate personal friends from their early manhood up to a few years before. In politics they differed. Hamer was a life-long Democrat, while my father was a Whig. They had a warm discussion, which finally became angry—over some act of President Jackson, the removal of the deposit of public moneys, I think—after which they never spoke until after my appointment. I know both of them felt badly over this estrangement, and would have been glad at any time to come to a reconciliation; but neither would make the advance. Under these circumstances my father would not write to Hamer for the appointment, but he wrote to Thomas Morris, United States Senator from Ohio, informing him that there was a vacancy at West Point from our district, and that he would be glad if I could be appointed to fill it. This letter, I presume, was turned over to Mr. Hamer, and, as there was no other applicant, he cheerfully appointed me. This healed the breach between the two, never after reopened.

Besides the argument used by my father in favor of my going to West Point—that "he thought I would go"—there was another very strong inducement. I had always a great desire to travel. I was already the best travelled boy in Georgetown, except the sons of one man, John Walker, who had emigrated to Texas with his family, and immigrated back as soon as he could get the means to do so. In his short stay in Texas he acquired a very different opinion of the country from what one would form going there now.

I had been east to Wheeling, Virginia, and north to the Western Reserve, in Ohio, west to Louisville, and south to Bourbon County, Kentucky, besides having driven or ridden pretty much over the whole country within fifty miles of home. Going to West Point would give me the opportunity of visiting the two great cities of the continent, Philadelphia and New York. This was enough. When these places were visited I would have been glad to have had a steamboat or railroad collision, or any other accident happen, by which I might have received a temporary injury sufficient to make me ineligible, for a time, to enter the Academy. Nothing of the kind occurred, and I had to face the music. . . .

I took passage on a steamer at Ripley, Ohio, for Pittsburgh, about the middle of May, 1839. Western boats at that day did not make regular trips at stated times, but would stop anywhere, and for any length of time, for passengers or freight. I have myself been detained two or three days at a place after steam was up, the gang planks, all but one, drawn in, and after the time advertised for starting had expired. On this occasion we had no vexatious delays, and in about three days Pittsburgh was reached. From Pittsburgh I chose passage by the canal to Harrisburg, rather than by the more expeditious stage. This gave a better opportunity of enjoying the fine scenery of Western Pennsylvania, and I had rather a dread of reaching my destination at all. At that time the canal was much patronized by travelers, and, with the comfortable packets of the period, no mode of conveyance could be more pleasant, when time was not an object. From Harrisburg to Philadelphia there was a railroad, the first I had ever seen, except the one on which I had just crossed the summit of the Allegheny Mountains, and over which canal boats were transported. In traveling by the road from Harrisburg, I thought the perfection of rapid transit had been reached. We traveled at least eighteen miles an hour, when at full speed, and made the whole distance averaging probably as much as twelve miles an hour. This seemed like annihilating space. I stopped five days in Philadelphia, saw about every street in the city, attended the theatre, visited Girard College (which was then in course of construction), and got reprimanded from home afterwards, for dallying by the way so long. My sojourn in New York was shorter, but long enough to enable me to see the city very well. I reported at West Point on the 30th or 31st of May, and about two weeks later passed my examination for admission, without difficulty, very much to my surprise.

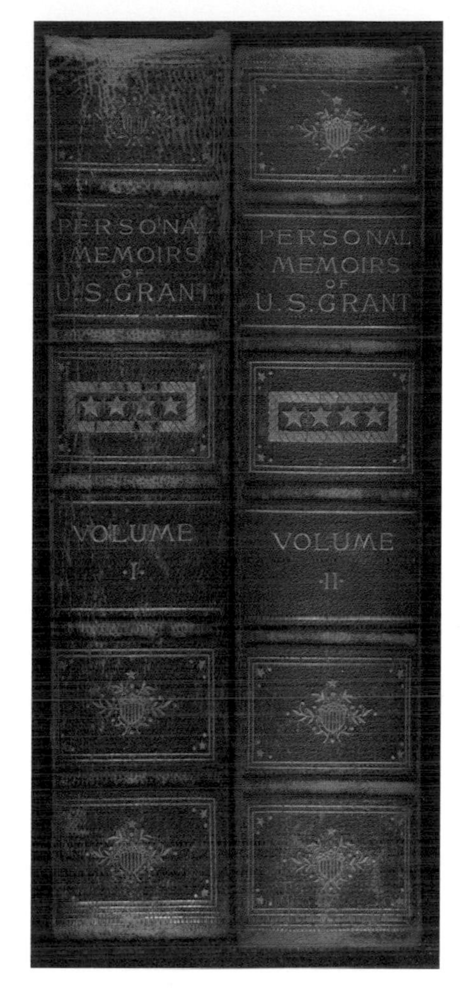

A military life had no charms for me, and I had not the faintest idea of staying in the army even if I should be graduated, which I did not expect. The encampment which preceded the commencement of academic studies was very wearisome and uninteresting. When the 28th of August came—the date for breaking up camp and going into barracks—I felt as though I had been at West Point always, and that if I staid to graduation, I would have to remain always. I did not take hold of my studies with avidity, in fact I rarely ever read over a lesson the second time during my entire cadetship. I could not sit in my room doing nothing. There is a fine library connected with the Academy from which cadets can get books to read in their quarters. I devoted more time to these, than to books relating to the course of studies. Much of the time, I am sorry to say, was devoted to novels, but not those of a trashy sort. I read all of Bulwer's then published, Cooper's, Marryat's, Scott's, Washington Irving's works, Lever's, and many others that I do not now remember. Mathematics was very easy to me, so that when January came, I passed the examination, taking a good standing in that branch. In French, the only other study at that time in the first year's course, my standing was very low. In fact, if the class had been turned the other end foremost I should have been near head. I never succeeded in getting squarely at either end of my class, in any one study, during the four years. I came near it in French, artillery, infantry and cavalry tactics, and conduct.

Early in the session of the Congress which met in December, 1839, a bill was discussed abolishing the Military Academy. I saw in this an honorable way to obtain a discharge, and read the debates with much interest, but with impatience at the delay in taking action, for I was selfish enough to favor the bill. It never passed, and a year later, although the time hung drearily with me, I would have been sorry to have seen it succeed. My idea then was to get through the course, secure a detail for a few years as assistant professor of mathematics at the Academy, and afterwards obtain a permanent position as professor in some respectable college; but circumstances always did shape my course different from my plans.

At the end of two years the class received the usual furlough, extending from the close of the June examination to the 28th of August. This I enjoyed beyond any other period of my life. My father had sold out his business in Georgetown—where my youth had been spent, and to which my day-dreams carried me back as my future home, if I should ever be able to retire on a competency. He had moved to Bethel, only twelve miles away, in the adjoining county of Clermont, and had bought a young horse that had never been in harness, for my special use under the saddle during my furlough. Most of my time was spent among my old school-mates—these ten weeks were shorter than one week at West Point. . . .

The last two years wore away more rapidly than the first two, but they still seemed about five times as long as Ohio years, to me. At last all the examinations were passed, and the members of the class were called upon to record their choice of arms of service and regiments. I was anxious to enter the cavalry, or dragoons as they were then called, but there was only one regiment of dragoons in the Army at that time, and attached to that, besides the full complement of officers, there were at least four brevet second lieutenants. I recorded therefore my first choice, dragoons; second, 4th infantry; and got the latter. Again there was a furlough—or, more properly speaking, leave of absence for the class were now commissioned officers—this time to the end of September. . . .

Lieutenant Grant at Age 21

Having made alternate choice of two different arms of service with different uniforms, I could not get a uniform suit until notified of my assignment. I left my measurement with a tailor, with directions not to make the uniform until I notified him whether it was to be for infantry or dragoons. Notice did not reach me for several weeks, and then it took at least a week to get the letter of instructions to the tailor and two more to make the clothes and have them sent to me. This was a time of great suspense. I was impatient to get on my uniform and see how it looked, and probably wanted my old school-mates, particularly the girls, to see me in it.

The Service Flag
William Herschell

The tradition of the service flag began during World War I when Army Captain Robert Queissner designed a small banner to honor his two sons who were serving in France. The symbol quickly became popular with other families of servicemen. The Department of Defense now regulates the design, manufacture, and display of service flags. Companies must have a certificate of authority to manufacture service flags. During a time of war or hostilities, service flags may be displayed in the homes of immediate family members of service personnel on active duty, and by their employers, churches, schools, and other organizations. When a member of the armed forces gives his or her life in the line of duty, the family or organization covers the blue star with a gold star. Two national organizations who serve the military and their families take their name from the service flag tradition: American Gold Star Mothers began in 1928 and Blue Star Mothers of America began in 1942. "The Service Flag" is a World War I poem first published in The Indianapolis News *of Indianapolis, Indiana.*

Dear little flag in the window there,
Hung with a tear and a woman's prayer,
Child of Old Glory, born with a star—
Oh, what a wonderful flag you are!

Blue is your star in its field of white,
Dipped in the red that was born of fight;
Born of the blood that our forebears shed
To raise your mother, The Flag, o'er-head.

And now you've come, in this frenzied day,
To speak from a window—to speak and say:
"I am the voice of a soldier son,
Gone, to be gone till the victory's won.

"I am the flag of The Service, sir:
The flag of his mother—I speak for her
Who stands by my window and waits and fears,
But hides from the others her unwept tears.

"I am the flag of the wives who wait
For the safe return of a martial mate—
A mate gone forth where the war god thrives,
To save from sacrifice other men's wives.

"I am the flag of the sweethearts true;
The often unthought of—the sisters, too.
I am the flag of a mother's son,
Who won't come home till the victory's won!"

Dear little flag in the window there,
Hung with a tear and a woman's prayer,
Child of Old Glory, born with a star—
Oh, what a wonderful flag you are!

World War II Service Flag

A Civil War Letter from Nashville
Ely Parker

Ely Parker (1828-1895) was a Native American of the Seneca tribe, born on the Tonawanda reservation in New York. Because he was proficient in English, he represented the Seneca tribe in treaty negotiations with the U.S. government while still in his teens. He worked for several years as an engineer for the U.S. government, working on Erie Canal improvements, Great Lakes lighthouses, and government buildings. He served as a soldier and as General Ulysses S. Grant's aide during the Civil War. He attended Lee's surrender at Appomattox Court House that ended the war. When Grant became President, he appointed Parker the first Native American to serve as Commissioner of the Bureau of Indian Affairs. Toward the end of his life, Ely Parker worked in the New York City police department. This letter was written while he was stationed in Nashville, the capital of Tennessee, during the Civil War. The Hermitage, which he describes in this letter, still stands and is a popular tourist attraction in the Nashville area.

Nashville
Feb. 2nd, 1864
Dear Brother,

A View of Nashville from the Capitol, 1864

The preceding letter was written in anticipation of my being ordered away on special service, which Staff Officers are sometimes obliged to make and are never heard from more. But as I closed I found I was not going, and therefore, laid aside the communication. Upon looking it over at this date I find that it contains nothing improper or contraband, and cannot consequently well avoid sending it, if not for your edification, at least for your information. Since I found the preceding letter I have made myself more acquainted with the City and its vicinity. The City is beautifully laid out in squares, that is to say that every street is at right angles to every street crossing it. The Cumberland River which passes through this city forms its base. This City you are aware, is the capitol [*sic*] of the state of Tennessee and therefore the State House is here, and a most elegant limestone fireproof building it is, and located upon the highest eminence or hill in the city. Very many beautiful residences or country villas are in the vicinity.

. . . The Hermitage (General Jackson's home and estate,) is about 12 miles from the city. I visited the same on the last day of last month. Our picket lines not extending out that distance, it is considered unsafe for Federal Soldiers to go out there. A Major and myself however, having set our minds on visiting this place, guerillas or no guerillas, armed ourselves capapie with 3 pistols each and trusty sabers, took an escort of 10 men and rode out there. We had a delightful ride and a pleasant visit with Andrew Jackson Donelson, the adopted son of the old general, the present owner and occupant of the estate. The house in which the General lived and died is about 40 years old. Very many interesting and valuable relics are in the house. Among them, Washington's official chair used by him when the seat of the government was in Philadelphia. The old General's tomb is in the garden. The Major and I met with no adventures and returned safely home without having seen a single guerilla. They are said to be about but luckily they did not choose to pay us their compliments. Ex-President Polk's residence was in this city. His monument was erected in his front door yard. A singular taste.

War news at this date is not amounting to much. Fighting at Knoxville continues. Several expeditions are starting upon our whole front and by which we anticipate and hope to gain great advantage over the rebels. We are having most delightful spring weather. The trees have commenced budding out and the blue birds pipe forth their jubilant notes.

When you write, tell me what news may now be stirring among the Indians. Do dissensions and bitter animosities still live and burn among them? Will they attempt the recovery of the Kansas interests and claims? I judge so from the fact that Sam George has been in Washington.

Major General Grant is now I suppose a Lt. General. If he accepts this rank I am afraid we will lose his service in the field, as he will of necessity be compelled to go to Washington. Whether his staff will go with him is yet to be determined.

From your Brother,
Ely S. Parker

Parker (second from right) with Other Officers

Ely Parker After the War

Kentucky's New State Capitol Building Dedicated at Frankfort

This article appeared in The Citizen *newspaper of Berea, Kentucky, on June 2, 1910, the day Kentucky's current state capitol was dedicated.*

New Building Formally Opened With Elaborate Program— Three Addresses Are Delivered At the Dedication Exercises

Frankfort—Every true Kentuckian viewed with heart full of pride the dedication of the new state Capitol, for the Capitol building of this grand old commonwealth is one of the finest in the United States and stands as a monument to the honesty and integrity of the people who made it possible.

The capitol commission, composed of Governor A. E. Willson, Treasurer E. Parley, Auditor Frank P. James, Secretary of State Bruner and Attorney General Breathitt, arranged the dedication exercises. United States Senator William O. Bradley delivered the principal address, and short talks were made by Gov. Willson, former Gov. J. C. W. Beckham and Mayor James H. Polagrove, mayor of Frankfort.

Kentucky's New State Capitol Building Dedicated at Frankfort

New Building Formally Opened With Elaborate Program-- Three Addresses Are Delivered At the Dedication Exercises--Some Historical Kentucky Facts.

KENTUCKY'S HANDSOME NEW STATE CAPITOL BUILDING AT FRANKFORT.

INSIDE VIEW NEW STATE CAPITOL LOOKING FROM HALL OF THE HOUSE TOWARD THE SENATE CHAMBER.

AUGUSTUS E. WILLSON

HER LAST WORD

Following the formal exercises the building was opened for inspection by the public. Gov. Willson and the other state officials received during the evening in the governor's reception room.

The members of the 1910 general assembly were all present and the majority of the members of the general assemblies of 1906 and 1908 who appropriated the money for the erection of the building were also present to rejoice with the citizens that so great a work has been accomplished and that no taint of corruption attaches.

. . .The grounds surrounding the Capitol were not entirely completed, but the visitors got a fairly good idea of the beauty of the approach to the building when completed.

. . .The new Capitol building, grounds, electric light plant, landscape gardening and other improvements will cost when completed two and a half million dollars, and there has never been the least suspicion of graft connected with the work.

The building of a new state house commensurate with the wealth and dignity of the Commonwealth had long been considered and discussed at many sessions of the General Assembly, but it was not until 1894, under the administration of Gov. Beckham, that an appropriation of one million dollars was made to begin the work.

The commission . . . together with Architect F. M. Andrews, decided that the grounds occupied by the old state house were not large enough, or that its location in the center of the city was not a suitable place for the new building.

Accordingly, in 1905, Gov. Beckham convened the legislature in extraordinary session to consider the matter of a new location. After some weeks' consideration it was decided to purchase a new site at the extreme south limit of South Frankfort, about a mile from the old, and an appropriation was made to buy the forty or more acres selected.

Ground was broken for the new building in 1906, and the magnificent building was completed and occupied in less than four years. It is one of the most complete and convenient Capitol buildings in the country, many persons who are familiar with public buildings throughout the United States pronounce it without a superior for the purpose for which it was erected.

. . . The various offices for the departments are commodious and convenient. Nothing that would conduce to the dispatch of business or the comfort of the officials seems to have been overlooked or neglected. After many years of wishing and waiting those who have felt a pride in Kentucky's wealth and greatness are rejoiced that she is no longer ashamed to invite a stranger to visit her Capitol.

Kentucky State Capitol

Circular Letter to the State Governors

George Washington

After America won the Revolutionary War, General George Washington thought he had accomplished his duty of service to his country. He looked forward to retiring to his beloved home at Mount Vernon near present-day Washington, D.C. He didn't know that he would soon be called upon to spend several more years away from home, serving the United States of America as its first President. As he made plans to resign and retire to his home after the war, he wrote a long letter to be sent to the Governor of each state. Washington was concerned about the infant country and knew that the cooperation of all the states was essential to its success. From his position of respect and influence, he addressed his concerns and advised leaders in each state on what was needed from them in the coming days. Cooperation of state Governors in what is best for the whole country is something we take for granted today, but the leadership and spirit of unity shown by state Governors and legislators is a key part of what keeps our country running smoothly. Excerpts of Washington's letter are below, with his own capitalizations.

Head Quarters, Newburgh, June 14, 1783

Sir:

The great object for which I had the honor to hold an appointment in the Service of my Country, being accomplished, I am now preparing to resign it into the hands of Congress, and to return to that domestic retirement, which, it is well known, I left with the greatest reluctance, a Retirement, for which I have never ceased to sigh through a long and painful absence, and in which (remote from the noise and trouble of the World) I meditate to pass the remainder of life in a state of undisturbed repose; But before I carry this resolution into effect, I think it a duty incumbent on me, to make this my last official communication, to congratulate you on the glorious events which Heaven has been pleased to produce in our favor, to offer my sentiments respecting some important subjects, which appear to me, to be intimately connected with the tranquility of the United States, to take my leave of your Excellency as a public Character, and to give my final blessing to that Country, in whose service I have spent the prime of my life, for whose sake I have consumed so many anxious days and watchful nights, and whose happiness being extremely dear to me, will always constitute no inconsiderable part of my own.

Impressed with the liveliest sensibility on this pleasing occasion, I will claim the indulgence of dilating the more copiously on the subjects of our mutual felicitation. When we consider the magnitude of the prize we contended for, the doubtful nature of the contest, and the favorable manner in which it has terminated, we shall find the greatest possible reason for gratitude and rejoicing; this is a theme that will afford infinite delight to every benevolent and liberal mind, whether the event in contemplation, be considered as the source of present enjoyment or the parent of future happiness; and we shall have equal occasion to felicitate ourselves on the lot

Washington Resigning His Commission in the Army

which Providence has assigned us, whether we view it in a natural, a political or moral point of light.

. . .There are four things, which I humbly conceive, are essential to the well being, I may even venture to say, to the existence of the United States as an Independent Power:

1st. An indissoluble Union of the States under one Federal Head.

2dly. A Sacred regard to Public Justice.

3dly. The adoption of a proper Peace Establishment, and

4thly. The prevalence of that pacific and friendly Disposition, among the People of the United States, which will induce them to forget their local prejudices and policies, to make those mutual concessions which are requisite to the general prosperity, and in some instances, to sacrifice their individual advantages to the interest of the Community.

. . . I have thus freely disclosed what I wished to make known, before I surrendered up my Public trust to those who committed it to me, the task is now accomplished, I now bid adieu to your Excellency as the Chief Magistrate of your State, at the same time I bid a last farewell to the cares of Office, and all the employments of public life.

It remains then to be my final and only request, that your Excellency will communicate these sentiments to your Legislature at their next meeting, and that they may be considered as the Legacy of One, who has ardently wished, on all occasions, to be useful to his Country, and who, even in the shade of Retirement, will not fail to implore the divine benediction upon it.

I now make it my earnest prayer, that God would have you, and the State over which you preside, in his holy protection, that he would incline the hearts of the Citizens to cultivate a spirit of subordination and obedience to Government, to entertain a brotherly affection and love for one another, for their fellow Citizens of the United States at large, and particularly for their brethren who have served in the Field, and finally, that he would most graciously be pleased to dispose us all, to do Justice, to love mercy, and to demean ourselves with that Charity, humility and pacific temper of mind, which were the Characteristics of the Divine Author of our blessed Religion, and without an humble imitation of whose example in these things, we can never hope to be a happy Nation.

Six of the State Governors in Office in 1783 (from left to right): Benjamin Harrison V of Virginia, John Dickinson of Pennsylvania, John Hancock of Massachusetts, William Paca of Maryland, Lyman Hall of Georgia, and George Clinton of New York.

Proclamations by the Governor
Brian Sandoval

State Governors issue proclamations to increase public awareness of an issue, honor a person or group in their state, and encourage citizens to do good things. These proclamations were issued in 2012 by Brian Sandoval, who became Governor of Nevada on January 3, 2011.

State of Nevada
Executive Department
A Proclamation by the Governor

Whereas, the first pioneers in Nevada were miners and farmers and ranchers, some of whom became Governors of Nevada, who provided food and fiber to those engaged in mining and other enterprises; and

Whereas, the descendants of those original pioneers and those influenced by their agricultural endeavors continue the customs and traditions established long ago; and

Whereas, in Nevada, cowboys and ranchers have created a unique style universally recognized as the Great Basin Buckaroo which continues these traditions through their daily work and in their celebrations such as rodeo; and

Whereas, through that cultural influence and the spirit of competition those hardworking ranchers, cowboys, and cowgirls established rodeo in Nevada beginning with competitions in Elko and Reno 100 years ago, and continuing today all over Nevada culminating with The National Finals Rodeo in Las Vegas each year in December; and

Whereas, through their hard work, honesty, and perseverance, cowboys and cowgirls have earned a reputation of integrity, patriotism, and a desire to preserve the uniquely American traditions of their trade; and

Whereas, the young people of this country have embraced the lifestyle of the cowboy through organized activities such as Future Farmers of America, 4-H, High School Rodeo and other educational endeavors to prepare them for their role in the western lifestyle and agricultural careers; and

Whereas, today's cowboys and cowgirls continue to strive to serve, preserve, and perpetuate this heritage through the efforts of working cowboys and cowgirls and through the efforts of the many statewide organizations that recognize and work to preserve the significance and value of the cowboy and western lifestyle; and

Governor Brian Sandoval

Whereas, the cowboy, buckaroo, and cowgirl continue to be vital to the nation and in particular to the economy of Nevada; and

Whereas, through determination and skill, commitment and sacrifice the rancher, cowboy, buckaroo and cowgirl continue and will continue to produce the products that feed and clothe this nation and continue the traditions, heritage and customs of the cowboy and the western lifestyle;

Now, therefore, I, Brian Sandoval, Governor of the State of Nevada, do hereby proclaim the 4th Saturday of July 2012 as

National Day of the Cowboy in Nevada

In Witness Whereof, I have hereunto set my hand and caused the Great Seal of the State of Nevada to be affixed at the State Capitol in Carson City, this 16th day of July, 2012.

B Sandoval, Governor
Ross Miller, Secretary of State

State of Nevada
Executive Department
A Proclamation by the Governor

Whereas, on September 11, 2012, we pay tribute to the selfless heroes and innocent victims of the September 11, 2001 tragedy that called forth in all of us a sense of unity, service, and patriotism; and

Whereas, Nevadans will join together with Americans across the country to participate in the "I Will" campaign to promote greater unity, compassion and peace in our world; and

Whereas, Americorps members through the state, who give a year of service to our local communities, will be focusing their service on this day to collect donations for our military service members and veterans; and

Whereas, each individual has unique talents, interests, and skills to share through service; and

Whereas, Nevada Volunteers, the state's commission on service and volunteering, encourages everyone to find a way to serve their community in observance of this day; and

Whereas, service above self is a cornerstone of this administration;

Now, therefore, I, Brian Sandoval, Governor of the State of Nevada, do hereby proclaim September 11, 2012 as

Day of Service and Remembrance in Nevada

In Witness Whereof, I have hereunto set my hand and caused the Great Seal of the State of Nevada to be affixed at the State Capitol in Carson City, this 20th day of August, 2012.

B Sandoval, Governor
Ross Miller, Secretary of State

State of Nevada
Executive Department
A Proclamation by the Governor

Whereas, as text messaging has grown in popularity, so has the incidence of texting while driving; and

Whereas, it is important that Nevadans recognize that texting while driving is irresponsible and that a driver who attempts to send or read text messages while driving is not just a hazard to himself or herself, but to passengers, other drivers and pedestrians; and

Whereas, information and education are the keys to dissuading drivers of all ages from texting while driving; and

Whereas, AT&T and others are dedicating a day to highlight the need to educate the public about the danger of texting while driving and Nevada applauds the companies and individuals who are supporting an ongoing education effort; and

Whereas, Nevadans are encouraged to always pay attention to the road and never text while driving;

Now, Therefore, I, Brian Sandoval, Governor of the State of Nevada, do hereby proclaim September 19, 2012 as

No Text On Board Pledge Day in Nevada

In Witness Whereof, I have hereunto set my hand and caused the Great Seal of the State of Nevada to be affixed at the State Capitol in Carson City, this 20th day of August, 2012.

B Sandoval, Governor
Ross Miller, Secretary of State

State Flag of Nevada

Changes and Improvements Made in Boston

Charles Bulfinch and Ellen Susan Bulfinch

Charles Bulfinch had a tremendous impact on public life at the city, county, state, and national levels. He is best known for his architectural career. He also served on the Board of Selectmen of his hometown of Boston for about 25 years, including 21 years as Chairman, a position similar to mayor. Charles Bulfinch was born in Boston in 1763. As a child, he spent time on the estate of his grandfather. Grandfather Bulfinch had designed the estate himself and had a fine collection of books about architecture. The younger Bulfinch was thirteen years old when the Declaration of Independence was signed. He watched the Battle of Bunker Hill from the roof of his family's home in Boston. Charles Bulfinch graduated from Harvard when he was eighteen. Four years later he went on an eighteen-month tour of Europe, visiting places suggested to him by Thomas Jefferson.

After returning to America, Bulfinch began his career in architecture and design. He designed a host of public and private buildings, including Massachusetts General Hospital, buildings at Harvard University, courthouses, schools, jails, banks, and homes. His body of work also includes the Massachusetts State House (capitol building), Connecticut's Old State House, and the Maine State House. When President James Monroe visited Boston in 1817, Bulfinch accompanied the President as he toured the city. Monroe was impressed with Bulfinch's work and soon hired him as Architect of the Capitol in Washington, D.C. The Architect of the Capitol oversees improvements in the Capitol and manages its maintenance. Bulfinch served in this role from 1818 to 1829. The following is an excerpt from The Life and Letters of Charles Bulfinch, Architect, *which was written and edited by his granddaughter, Ellen Susan Bulfinch. Most of the following excerpt is Charles Bulfinch's own notes on improvements that were made in the city of Boston during and after his tenure on the Board of Selectmen.*

Charles Bulfinch

The position which Charles Bulfinch now filled of chairman of the Board of Selectmen was similar in many respects to that occupied by the mayor of the city. He was charged with the first responsibility regarding the order, cleanliness, and economy of the town administration; with its health and safety; and also with the privilege of representing the town on occasions of state, and receiving its honored guests.

. . . Of this period of Mr. Bulfinch's life, covering, in all his relations to the administration of town affairs, between twenty and thirty years, his son Thomas wrote:

"It would require a long detail to enumerate the works of public improvement by which the crooked were made straight, and the rough places smooth, under his influence, during this long period of the history of our city. In the course of these improvements he necessarily was often brought into collision with individuals whose interests were to be made to yield to the public exigency [need]. In all instances these collisions were dealt with in such a mild and reasonable spirit as to allay to a great degree the irritation which arose, and in many cases to convert into warm friends those who at first met him in the most hostile spirit.

. . . I find the following statement in my grandfather's handwriting concerning the changes and improvements made in Boston during his administration of its affairs, and in the years immediately succeeding. It was probably written near 1840:

C. Bulfinch was a junior member of the Board of Selectmen from 1789 to 1793; he was Chairman from 1797 to 1818, 21 years, during which time he was Superintendent of Police, salary $600, till the last two years, when it was raised to $1,000.

By his exertions a law of the State was obtained, giving powers to the Selectmen to widen streets and regulate pavements, another to establish the Municipal Court. In consequence of these points:

- Congress Street was opened at entrance on State Street.
- The West end of Court Street widened, leading to Bowdoin Square.
- The lower part of State Street and Merchants Row and Back Street widened.
- Hanover Street and Beacon Street, by Governor Hancock's and High Street, ditto.
- Exchange Street widened throughout.
- New Cornhill opened, leading from Tremont Street to Dock Square.
- Part of Avon Street widened after a fire.
- Charles Street laid out and filled over the marsh.
- West Mall formed and planted.
- The Neck Lands laid out in streets and squares.
- The Mill Pond laid out in streets.
- South Boston laid into streets.
- All streets regulated with sidewalks, wherever new paved.
- Faneuil Hall building enlarged to four times it original size.
- Almshouse in Leverett Street built.
- Stone Court House, now City Hall, built.
- Derne Street and Belknap Street opened, and part of Batterymarch Street.

All these improvements were made by the Town and paid for, so that when C.B. was invited to Washington, to rebuild the Capitol, the debt of the Town was only fourteen thousand dollars. Population in 1818, 40,000.

Besides these public improvements, others were made during the same period by the State and companies of individuals:

- The State House built, from plans of C.B.
- West Boston Bridge
- Canal Bridge, so called, from Leverett Street
- Front Street and South Boston Bridge
- Boylston Market
- Board Street and India Wharf
- Central Wharf
- The General Hospital from plans by C.B.
- Franklin Place, Colonnade Row, Park Street

The increase of the population and the wealth of the citizens has enabled the City authorities to make improvements on a more extended scale, viz. [namely]:

- The Quincy Market and streets adjacent, new court house, jail in Leverett Street, almshouse and other buildings at South Boston.
- Tremont Street continued over the flats to Roxbury.
- Several streets widened.
- Portions of Washington, Portland, and Friend Streets, Elm Street and others.

These undertakings are important improvements and add to the convenience and beauty of the City, but they have occasioned a debt of one million, six hundred thousand dollars; the interest of which is more than the whole annual tax of 1818.

Since the incorporation of the City the following important improvements have been made by private companies:

- The Western Avenue to Brooklyne
- Commercial Street with the noble wharfs projecting from it.
- Tremont and several other large hotels.
- The South Cove land—3 railroad depots, Louisbourg and Pemberton Squares.

Architectural Drawing of New South Church in Boston, attributed to Charles Bulfinch

Dedication of Weston Town-House
Calvin Coolidge

As Governor of Massachusetts, Calvin Coolidge traveled to Weston, Massachusetts, to take part in the dedication ceremony for the new Weston Town-House on November 27, 1917. He makes reference to World War I, which America had entered on April 6 of that year.

I was interested to come out here and take part in the dedication of this beautiful building in part because my ancestors had lived in this locality in times gone past, but more especially because I am interested in the town governments of Massachusetts. . . .

The history of Weston has been long and interesting, beginning, as your town seal designates, back in 1630, when Watertown was recognized as one of the three or four towns in the Commonwealth; set off by boundaries into the Farmers' Precinct in 1698, and becoming incorporated as a town in 1713. There begins a long and honorable history. Of course, the first part of it gathered to a large degree around the church. The first church was started here, I think, in 1695, and I believe that the land on which it was to be erected was purchased of a man who bore my name. Your first clergyman seems to have been settled about 1702; and the long and even tenor of your ways here and your devotion to things which were established is perhaps shown and exemplified in the fact that during the next one hundred and seventy-four years, coming clear down to 1876, you had but six clergymen presiding over that church. You have an example here now, along the same line, in the long tenure of office that has come to your present town clerk, he having been first elected, I believe, in 1864 and having held office from that time to this, probably serving as long, if not longer, than any of the town clerks of Massachusetts, certainly, I believe, the longest of any present living town clerk.

There are many interesting things connected with the history of this town. It bore its part in the Indian Wars. Here was organized an Indian fighting expedition that went to the North, and, though some of the men in that expedition were lost and the expedition was not altogether successful, it showed the spirit, the resolution, the bravery, and the courage which animated the men of those days. . . .

Calvin Coolidge

Of course, there are many other interesting events in the history of this town. You had here many men who have seen military service. You furnished a large number for the Revolutionary War and a large amount of money. You furnished as your quota one hundred and twenty-six soldiers that went into the army from 1861 to 1865. But you were doing here what they were doing all over the Commonwealth of Massachusetts. . . .

So this town has had a long and interesting history, and has done its part in building up Massachusetts and giving her strength to take her part in the history of this great Nation. And it is pleasant to see how the work that the fathers have done before us is bearing fruit in these times of ours. It is interesting to see this beautiful building. It is interesting to know that you have a town planning committee who are placing this building in a situation where it will contribute to the physical beauty of this historic town. . . .

Weston is doing something along these lines and building her public buildings and laying out her public square or her common (as it was known in the old days) so they will be things of beauty as well as things of use. Let us dedicate this building to these new purposes. Let us dedicate it to the glorious history of the past. Let us dedicate it to the sacrifice that is required in these present days. Let us dedicate it to the hope of the future. Let us dedicate it to New England ideals—those ideals that have made Massachusetts one of the strong States of the Nation; strong enough so that in Revolutionary days we contributed far in excess of our portion of men and money to that great struggle; strong enough so that the whole Nation has looked to Massachusetts in days of stress for comfort and support.

We are very proud of our democracy. We are very proud of our form of government. We believe that there is no other nation on earth that gives to the individual the privileges and the rights that he has in America. The time has come now when we are going to defend those rights. The time has come when the world is looking to America, as the Nation has looked to Massachusetts in the past, to stand up and defend the rights of the individual. Sovereignty, it is our belief, is vested in the individual; and we are going to protect the rights of the individual. It is an auspicious moment to dedicate here in New England one of our town halls, an auspicious moment in which to dedicate it to the supremacy of those ideals for which the whole world is fighting at the present time; that the rights of the individual as they were established here in the past may be maintained by us now and carried to a yet greater development in the future.

Weston Town Hall (or Town-House)

Crow Tribe, United States and State of Montana Sign Historic Water Compact

U.S. Department of the Interior

The U.S. Department of the Interior Bureau of Indian Affairs issued this press release on April 27, 2012. It is an example of tribal, state, and Federal governments working together.

WASHINGTON, D.C. – The Crow Tribe Apsáalooke Nation, the United States of America and the State of Montana executed the Crow Tribe-Montana Water Rights Compact in an historic signing ceremony today at the U.S. Department of the Interior.

Secretary of the Interior Ken Salazar, Crow Chairman Cedric Black Eagle and Montana Governor Brian Schweitzer signed the compact—marking a major milestone in implementing the Crow Tribal Water Rights Settlement Act of 2010.

Today's event signifies the resolution of more than three decades of litigation and negotiations, clearing the way to address pressing needs on the Crow Reservation for safe drinking water and the rehabilitation of the dilapidated Crow Irrigation Project.

"The Obama Administration is proud to be a party to the Crow-Montana Compact. Signing the Compact today demonstrates the Administration's continued commitment to resolving Indian water rights and providing settlements that truly benefit Indian tribes," Secretary Salazar said. "The Compact not only ensures delivery of a much-needed safe supply of water for the Crow community, but will also bolster their economic security."

With signing of the Compact today, the Settlement Act authorizes $460 million, calling for the Bureau of Reclamation to plan, design and construct a Municipal, Rural and Industrial (MR&I) water system for the tribe and to rehabilitate and improve the Crow Irrigation Project.

"Today is a significant day for the Crow people," said Chairman Black Eagle. "We began negotiating the Crow-Montana Compact over a decade ago and with continued commitment by all of the parties, including the State and the United States, we were able to come together

Montana Governor Brian Schweitzer, Secretary of the Interior Ken Salazar and Crow Tribe Apsáalooke Nation Chairman Cedric Black Eagle signed the compact—marking a major milestone in implementing the Crow Tribal Water Rights Settlement Act of 2010

today and sign the Compact," said Chairman Black Eagle. "Water is life. This Compact ensures that Crow people will have water and the necessary infrastructure for generations to come. Now the hard work continues to implement the Compact and Settlement legislation to ensure that Crow people realize these benefits from the settlement."

"Today is an important day in Montana history," Governor Schweitzer said. "The signing of the Crow-Montana Compact evidences the State's dedication to successfully resolving both Indian and Federal reserved water rights claims through settlement negotiations."

The signatories also thanked both U.S. Senators from Montana—Senator Max Baucus and Senator Jon Tester—for their leadership. As Chairman of the Senate Finance Committee, Senator Baucus worked diligently to build a bipartisan compromise around the Crow-Montana Water Rights Compact to help successfully pass the legislation in 2010. Senator Tester has been a strong supporter of the Crow Water Settlement both during his time as a Montana State Senator and as a U.S. Senator.

The signing ceremony with tribal, state and federal representatives was livestreamed to the public, including participants at the reservation in Montana. . . .

On December 8, 2010, President Obama signed Public Law 111-291, the Claims Resolution Act of 2010. Title IV of the Act, the Crow Tribe Water Rights Settlement, authorizes and directs the Secretary of the Interior to execute the Compact.

Together, the Settlement Act and the Compact quantify the Tribe's water rights and authorize funding of $131.8 million for the rehabilitation and improvement of the Crow Irrigation Project and $246.4 million for the design and construction of the MR&I water system to serve numerous reservation communities, as well as funding totaling more than $81 million for tribal water administration and for a portion of costs for the irrigation and municipal water systems. The Settlement also provides funding to boost energy development projects such as hydropower generation at Yellowtail Afterbay Dam, clean coal conversion, and other renewable energy projects.

The existing drinking water system on the reservation has significant deficiencies in terms of both capacity and water quality, and many tribal members at times must haul water. The Crow Irrigation Project is in a state of significant disrepair and currently cannot support the Reservation's mainstay of farming and ranching.

Litigation concerning the Tribe's water rights has been ongoing since 1975. Negotiations with the State of Montana and the Crow Tribe on the Compact began nearly thirty years ago in the mid-1980's. In June 1999, after reaching agreement with the Tribe, the State legislature ratified the Compact.

In March 2011, the members of the Tribe voted to ratify the Compact and Settlement Act. On July 15, 2011, Secretary Salazar and Bureau of Reclamation Commissioner Mike Connor visited the Crow Indian Reservation to participate with Chairman Black Eagle and a crowd of 200 celebrating the Crow Tribe Water Rights Settlement.

The Crow Reservation is the largest reservation in Montana, encompassing about 2.3 million acres, and is home to approximately 8,000 of the 11,900 enrolled Crow tribal members.

Post Office in Crow Agency, Montana

To Fight for My Down-Trodden Race
Sarah Winnemucca Hopkins

Sarah Winnemucca Hopkins (c.1844-1891) was the daughter and granddaughter of Paiute (or Piute) chiefs and grew up to be a leader and advocate for her people. She published an autobiography in 1883 entitled Life Among the Piutes: Their Wrongs and Claims. *The following excerpt is the beginning of her autobiography.*

I was born somewhere near 1844, but am not sure of the precise time. I was a very small child when the first white people came into our country. They came like a lion, yes, like a roaring lion, and have continued so ever since, and I have never forgotten their first coming. My people were scattered at that time over nearly all the territory now known as Nevada. My grandfather was chief of the entire Piute nation, and was camped near Humboldt Lake, with a small portion of his tribe, when a party traveling eastward from California was seen coming. When the news was brought to my grandfather, he asked what they looked like. When told that they had hair on their faces, and were white, he jumped up and clasped his hands together, and cried aloud,

"My white brothers,—my long-looked for white brothers have come at last!"

He immediately gathered some of his leading men, and went to the place where the party had gone into camp. Arriving near them, he was commanded to halt in a manner that was readily understood without an interpreter. Grandpa at once made signs of friendship by throwing down his robe and throwing up his arms to show them he had no weapons; but in vain—they kept him at a distance. He knew not what to do. He had expected so much pleasure in welcoming his white brothers to the best in the land, that after looking at them sorrowfully for a little while, he came away quite unhappy. But he would not give them up so easily. He took some of his most trustworthy men and followed them day after day, camping near them at night, and traveling in sight of them by day, hoping in this way to gain their confidence. But he was disappointed, poor dear old soul!

I can imagine his feelings, for I have drank deeply from the same cup. When I think of my past life, and the bitter trials I have endured, I can scarcely believe I live, and yet I do; and, with the help of Him who notes the sparrow's fall, I mean to fight for my down-trodden race while life lasts.

Sarah Winnemucca Hopkins, c. 1883

The Horse Patrol: Running Neck and Neck with Technology

Linda Kane

This article appeared in the October/November 2003 issue of Customs and Border Protection Today, *a newsletter of U.S. Customs and Border Protection (CBP). The U.S. Border Patrol is a division of CBP.*

Who would have thought that in the 21st century Border Patrol agents on horseback patrolling our borders would still have an edge over all-terrain vehicles, 4x4s, helicopters, and planes?

No one could argue that a mounted agent in full dress uniform provides the utmost in pomp and circumstance for ceremonial settings, but in this age of cutting-edge technology, can horse patrols do more? Read on. The answer may surprise you.

A rich heritage. From the beginning, horses were an important part of the Border Patrol, and they remain so today. Mounted guards, the predecessors of today's Border Patrol, were a colorful group who, as they watched the border for illegals, embodied the independence and love of the land associated with the old West. In 1915, Congress authorized the Mounted Patrolmen, a more formal group of officers on horseback, until finally, in 1924, the Border Patrol was established.

Border Patrol Agent in Texas, 1942

The first Border Patrol agents provided their own transportation—they had to own a horse and tack (equestrian rigging-saddles, bridles, harness.) Uncle Sam paid their salary and provided animal feed.

Why ride? Horse patrol agents still ride through the night, stopping bad guys, and carrying on the tradition of those early line-watchers. However, don't fall into the romantic notion that these patrolmen are just modern day "cowboys." Sure, they have wranglers, fellows who take care of the horses back at the station, and just like the riders of old, they share a closeness with their animals.

Make no mistake, today's horse patrol agents are highly trained and sophisticated law enforcement officers. Some, like Senior Patrol Agent Arnoldo A. Martinez III, the El Centro sector's equine instructor and wrangler, hold degrees in agribusiness or range management. So why do they ride? D'Arcy Rivers, Supervisory Border Patrol agent in the El Centro sector says, "The whole idea of being around horses is so appealing to me. While horses are a tool, they are so much more than that—they represent a lifestyle."

A typical day. Mounted agents start their shifts by grooming their horses, brushing them, doing a sort of "pre-flight" inspection for bruises or injuries, then "tacking up"—putting on their saddles, bridles, reins. The horses are trailered and driven to an operating area. Agents, usually riding in groups of three or four but at least in pairs, decide where they will ride based on intelligence developed by agents during the previous shift. Once out in the field, the agents scour the landscape, looking for footprints, disturbances in the brush, or other indicators of alien traffic. If there are no tracks, they may respond instead to movement sensors hidden in the landscape along the border.

These agents put in four and sometimes up to eight hours of saddle time per day, depending upon the season and the situations they encounter. And riding as a job rather than as a hobby is hard work. Jeff Jeude, senior Border Patrol agent, former Navy helicopter pilot, and a member of the horse patrol says, "I love the job, but it is the most physically demanding work I have ever done. I've been out freezing on a mountain at midnight and then riding in the scorching midday sun."

At the end of the day, each horse is brought back to the stable and inspected, de-tacked, and hosed off until the next day when the cycle starts all over again.

Selection and training. Agents who seek the sense of freedom and camaraderie that comes with being a member of the horse patrol have to respond to announcements for volunteers in writing. Candidates go through a two-phase selection process that consists of a face-to-face interview with unit supervisors and a riding skills test conducted by current horse patrol agents. Although most applicants have had experience with horses, novices can also apply. Unit supervisors rate the greenhorns based upon their potential to complete the training. The length and type of training novices receive varies from sector to sector, and reflects differences in the terrain and in the type of riding skills required in each sector.

Horse patrol agents at the San Diego sector train for eight weeks studying horsemanship, equine anatomy, veterinary care, trailering, and related subjects. After graduating from CBP's training program, all sector agents attend the Royal Canadian Mounted Police School's Basic Course. Instructors and agents alike must complete advanced training which includes handcuffing techniques, arrest procedures, formation riding and riot control. The San Diego sector mounted patrol is a classically trained unit, which uses lightweight endurance saddles that are suited not only for range work but also for urban work, such as crowd control. Even experienced Western-style riders must receive training to adapt to the "classical seat" or dressage riding.

The El Centro sector rides Western style and uses Western-style saddles. Riders in this sector spend four weeks in training; initially they ride bareback to learn the "feel" of a horse, then they learn the intricacies of proper saddling. This training is followed by fieldwork—learning the trails and adjusting to being five feet above ground on horseback.

American Quarter horses are the preferred breed, and color is important: sorrels, chestnuts, bays, or horses whose colors provide camouflage by night top the list. CBP buys its horses through brokers or scouts them out at local ranches and feedlots.

And the horses get their share of training, too. Each rider is responsible for keeping up his or her horse's training unless a performance problem develops. Then a professional wrangler or certified horse trainer is called to help with retraining or fixing the problem.

Technology has its limits. Four-wheel drive and all-terrain vehicles allow the Border Patrol to cover rough terrain and patrol areas that might otherwise be off limits. Helicopters and airplanes provide a bird's-eye view expanding the patrol range and making it more difficult for illegal immigrants to cross border territory undetected—but the 171 Border Patrol agents who mount up daily are a reminder that technology has its limitations.

Horse patrols can travel places that ATVs and motorized vehicles cannot. And they can do it faster. "The area where we work has heavy mansanita brush that can be six feet high. A group of illegal immigrants will scatter and run away from a ground agent or helicopter that has stopped them. Add a couple of horses to the mix, and it changes the dynamic. Horses can get into the brush, and they have the advantage of being able to look down," explains Agent Jeude.

The roar of an ATV engine or headlights presents another advantage that horses have over motorized vehicles—stealth. Horses are quiet, and they can see at night, making it possible for a horse patrol agent to get close to camps or groups of illegals without being detected.

Horses also bring an air of authority to explosive situations. Their size and speed can be intimidating, but they also have a calming effect on a large group detained by authorities. An agent on horseback can prevent a group of illegals from "making a run for it," fleeing in different directions into the wild. Horse and rider can shepherd the immigrants so they can be safely "walked out" of rough or dangerous terrain to roads where they can be picked up and transported to the nearest sector office.

Search and rescue missions have made good use of horses because the animals can reach locations that are impenetrable except on foot. "It's amazing what horses can do—climbing steep hills, navigating difficult paths, and staying sure-footed even in the dark," says Agent Rivers.

Horses are also cost effective. It costs less to board, feed, and care for 10 horses a year than to maintain a single 4x4 off-road vehicle. And they last longer; a vehicle may last for two or three years but a horse can be in service for 20 years.

Friends of the environment. The horse patrol has yet another advantage over all other high-tech methods of transport: horses are friendly to the environment. Border Patrol agents work between ports of entry, and in the Southwest this means that much of the land is wilderness—remote, undeveloped, rugged land. And The National Park Service and the Bureau of Land Management want to keep it that way. Motor vehicles, motorized equipment, or any type of mechanical transport cannot be used in these wilderness areas. Agent Jeude says, "In the San Diego sector we patrol in the Tijuana Estuary and it can be a very touchy situation. There are restrictions on vehicles, but the horse patrol can enter these areas without a problem."

Border Patrol Agents

Public agencies aren't the only ones concerned with environmental issues; ranchers are also interested in conserving their rangeland. They don't want 4x4s or ATVs tearing up cactus, leaving tracks on the ground, polluting the air or doing anything else that could lead to environmental degradation.

Sometimes less is more. More powerful engines, bigger tires, computer-assisted navigation, and other such technological trinkets are impressive and useful patrol tools. But they have yet to displace the importance of horses. When it comes to border enforcement and safety, the horses and riders of the mounted patrol can still outmaneuver, outlast, outsmart and give any vehicle or tech-tool a pretty good run.

Thirty-Six Years in the White House
Thomas F. Pendel

Thomas F. Pendel was the doorkeeper at the White House for ten Presidents, serving President Abraham Lincoln through Theodore Roosevelt. Pendel's work was a precursor to the modern role of the Secret Service. Pendel served as a protector to the President and First Lady, their children, friends, guests, and even pets! He wrote a book of memories that told about each of his famous employers. Entitled Thirty-Six Years in the White House, *it was published in 1902.*

Thomas Pendel

Remembering President Abraham Lincoln

In 1861, or 1862, that Metropolitan Police was established by Congress at the Capital, and I made application for and received an appointment on the force. . . .

On November 3, 1864, Sergeant John Cronin, Alfonso Dunn, Andrew Smith, and myself were ordered to report at the First Precinct, in the old City Hall, at one o'clock in the afternoon. We supposed we were to be detailed for detective work in New York City on account of the great riot then on there, especially as we were ordered to report in citizens' clothes, to conceal our revolvers, and to be sure to have them all clean and in good order. We arrived at the City Hall, and then were told where we were to go, which was to the President's Mansion, there to report to Marshal Lanham, at that time United States Marshal of the District of Columbia, and a bosom friend of Abraham Lincoln.

. . . Marshal Lanham took us upstairs and into the President's office, where we were introduced to him and to his two secretaries, Mr. Nicolay and Mr. Hay, the latter now being Secretary of State. We were then instructed to keep a sharp lookout in the different parts of the house, more particularly in the East Room and at the door of the President's office.

. . . Almost every day about ten o' clock I would accompany Mr. Lincoln to the War Department. He was exceedingly anxious about General Sherman's army, which was at that time marching through the South. On one occasion he remarked to me that he felt very uneasy about Sherman's army, since he had not been able to receive any information regarding it for three weeks. In going over to the War Department I used to try to expedite his leaving the White House as much as possible, because people would always hang around and wait to see Mr. Lincoln, and would thrust notes into his hands as he passed and in many ways annoy him. One day just as we got to the front door, after going out of the private corridor, there was a nurse who had been in the East Room with an infant in her arms and a little tot walking by her side. Just as we were about to pass out of the door, she got in front of us. I took hold of the little tot gently, and moved her to one side so that we could get out. The President noticed this action, and rather disapproved of my moving the child to let him pass and said, "That's all right; that's all right." The interpretation I put upon his words was that he would sooner have been annoyed by people thrusting letters into his hands than make a little child move aside for him to pass. When we did get out he started off rapidly. Mr. Lincoln did not seem to be walking very fast, but it kept me hustling to keep up with him; so much so that although I was pretty tall myself, I had a curiosity to know how tall the President was. One day as we were about to leave the White House, I asked the President his height. He replied, "I am just six feet three inches in my stocking feet."

Remembering President Grover Cleveland

President Cleveland was a very plain, matter-of-fact man. On one occasion when I came on duty at midnight, he was in the back end of the upper corridor, trying to find a lamp. I said, "Mr. President, is there anything I can do for you?" And he said, "Yes I am trying to find a lamp." We both went back into the library, and I arranged it for him on his desk, and he went on writing. He was a very hard worker—the hardest working President I ever saw in my life. I used to sit opposite the library door, so that I would be convenient to him whenever he wanted me, and always attended to his wants. It was sometimes three o'clock in the morning when he would retire. Between one and two o'clock one night he called me into his library and said, "Pendel, I wish you would take that mockingbird* down. It annoys me." After I had removed him, the mockingbird got mad and would not sing a bit more.

The President said to me, "Pendel, where did you put him?"

"On Mr. Loeffler's desk," I said.

He said, "You don't think he will catch cold there, do you?"

I said, "Mr President, I don't think he will, but, however, I will move him." I brought him into the inner corridor, and put him behind the screen where he was thoroughly protected. After the President had finished his work in the library, I said, "Mr. President, I have put him behind here, where he will not catch cold."

He then said, "Oh, that is all right, Mr. Pendel."

**The mockingbird was Mrs. Cleveland's pet.*

Record-Breaking Career Ends for San Francisco CBP Canine

Susan Holliday

This article about a U.S. Customs and Border Protection agricultural inspection beagle appeared in the Summer 2012 edition of the CBP magazine Frontline.

Duffy has hung up his work vest and retired. During his nearly six years at San Francisco International Airport as a U.S. Customs and Border Protection agriculture detector dog, the 8-year-old beagle set the port record for the highest number of finds—more than 14,000— that led to the seizure of prohibited agriculture items.

Together, CBP Agriculture Specialist Canine Handler Peter De Souza and Duffy worked more than 4,500 arriving flights. Duffy sniffed more than 4 million pieces of luggage, rooting out a record number of potentially harmful animal or plant agricultural products.

One of Duffy's most surprising finds: two giant African snails. These snails can destroy a variety of plants, including food crops. The snails also may carry a parasite that can infect humans with meningitis. "And we don't even train the dogs to find snails," said De Souza. Although Duffy and his fellow working canines do not train on snails, they develop a scent picture that prompted Duffy to alert his handler that there was something in the bag that he should definitely check out.

Duffy

Duffy made many significant finds of Asian citrus psyllids, fruit flies and their host materials. "One time he pulled me the length of two baggage carousels—about 500 feet—because he smelled a jasmine lei in a woman's handbag," said De Souza. Jasmine is a pathway for psyllids, which can carry citrus greening disease.

De Souza attributes Duffy's success to his high food drive, a common trait for beagles. The handlers reward their canine partners with a treat after every find. "Duffy wanted that treat more than anything," said De Souza.

Duffy retired in early June and will spend his leisure years as De Souza's pet. Agriculture detector dogs live in CBP kennels during their working years and receive ample play and socialization time. The food aromas of a home environment could be confusing to the dogs and could interfere with their work skills. Indeed, during his first days of retirement, De Souza said that Duffy would go to the garbage can and sit, the CBP canine method of alerting to a find. But in just a week, Duffy seemed to learn that he's no longer on the job. He has learned to relax and enjoy his retirement, even passing an apple lying on the ground without giving it particular notice.

De Souza is now training with his next CBP canine partner to continue his agriculture inspections at San Francisco's airport, hoping that the new dog will follow Duffy's sniffing lead.

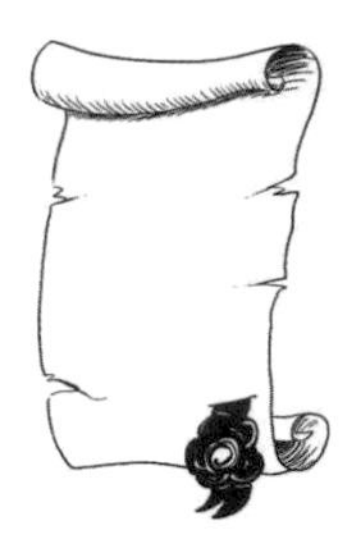

Civics Questions for the Naturalization Test
U.S. Citizenship and Immigration Services

One step in the process of becoming a citizen of the United States is to take a civics test. The questions cover history and government. An officer of the U.S. Citizenship and Immigration Services asks the applicant the questions orally. The applicant studies these 100 questions and answers ahead of time. The officer asks up to 10, and to pass the applicant must answer 6 correctly. How would you do on this test?

AMERICAN GOVERNMENT

A: Principles of American Democracy

1. What is the supreme law of the land? *the Constitution*
2. What does the Constitution do? *sets up the government; defines the government; protects basic rights of Americans*
3. The idea of self-government is in the first three words of the Constitution. What are these words? *We the People*
4. What is an amendment? *a change (to the Constitution); an addition (to the Constitution)*
5. What do we call the first ten amendments to the Constitution? *the Bill of Rights*
6. What is one right or freedom from the First Amendment? *speech; religion; assembly; press; petition the government*
7. How many amendments does the Constitution have? *27*
8. What did the Declaration of Independence do? *announced our independence (from Great Britain), declared our independence (from Great Britain); said that the United States is free (from Great Britain)*
9. What are two rights in the Declaration of Independence? *life; liberty; pursuit of happiness*
10. What is freedom of religion? *You can practice any religion, or not practice a religion.*
11. What is the economic system in the United States? *capitalist economy; market economy*
12. What is the "rule of law"? *Everyone must follow the law. Leaders must obey the law. Government must obey the law. No one is above the law.*

B: System of Government

13. Name one branch or part of the government. *Congress; legislative; President; executive; the courts; judicial*
14. What stops one branch of government from becoming too powerful? *checks and balances; separation of powers*
15. Who is in charge of the executive branch? *the President*
16. Who makes federal laws? *Congress; Senate and House (of Representatives); (U.S. or national) legislature*
17. What are the two parts of the U.S. Congress? *the Senate and House (of Representatives)*
18. How many U.S. Senators are there? *100*
19. We elect a U.S. Senator for how many years? *six (6)*
20. Who is one of your state's U.S. Senators now? *Answers will vary. [District of Columbia residents and residents of U.S. territories should answer that D.C. (or the territory where the applicant lives) has no U.S. Senators.]*
21. The House of Representatives has how many voting members? *435*

22. We elect a U.S. Representative for how many years? *2*
23. Name your U.S. Representative. *Answers will vary. [Residents of territories with nonvoting Delegates or Resident Commissioners may provide the name of that Delegate or Commissioner. Also acceptable is any statement that the territory has no (voting) Representatives in Congress.]*
24. Who does a U.S. Senator represent? *all people of the state*
25. Why do some states have more Representatives than other states? *(because of) the state's population; (because) they have more people; (because) some states have more people*
26. We elect a President for how many years? *4*
27. In what month do we vote for President? *November*
28. What is the name of the President of the United States now?
29. What is the name of the Vice President of the United States now?
30. If the President can no longer serve, who becomes President? *the Vice President*
31. If both the President and the Vice President can no longer serve, who becomes President? *the Speaker of the House*
32. Who is the Commander in Chief of the military? *the President*
33. Who signs bills to become laws? *the President*
34. Who vetoes bills? *the President*
35. What does the President's Cabinet do? *advises the President*
36. What are two Cabinet-level positions? *Secretary of Agriculture; Secretary of Commerce; Secretary of Defense; Secretary of Education; Secretary of Energy; Secretary of Health and Human Services; Secretary of Homeland Security; Secretary of Housing and Urban Development; Secretary of the Interior; Secretary of Labor; Secretary of State; Secretary of Transportation; Secretary of the Treasury; Secretary of Veterans Affairs; Attorney General; Vice President*
37. What does the judicial branch do? *reviews laws; explains laws; resolves disputes (disagreements); decides if a law goes against the Constitution*
38. What is the highest court in the United States? *the Supreme Court*
39. How many justices are on the Supreme Court? *9*
40. Who is the Chief Justice of the United States now?
41. Under our Constitution, some powers belong to the federal government. What is one power of the federal government? *to print money; to declare war; to create an army; to make treaties*
42. Under our Constitution, some powers belong to the states. What is one power of the states? *provide schooling and education; provide protection (police); provide safety (fire departments); give a driver's license; approve zoning and land use*
43. Who is the Governor of your state now? *Answers will vary. [District of Columbia residents should answer that D.C. does not have a Governor.]*
44. What is the capital of your state? *Answers will vary. [District of Columbia residents should answer that D.C. is not a state and does not have a capital. Residents of U.S. territories should name the capital of the territory.]*

Naturalization Ceremony, Portland, OR

45. What are the two major political parties in the United States? *Democratic and Republican*
46. What is the political party of the President now?
47. What is the name of the Speaker of the House of Representatives now?

C: Rights and Responsibilities

48. There are four amendments to the Constitution about who can vote. Describe one of them. *Citizens eighteen (18) and older (can vote). You don't have to pay (a poll tax) to vote. Any citizen can vote. (Women and men can vote.) A male citizen of any race (can vote).*
49. What is one responsibility that is only for United States citizens? *serve on a jury or vote in a federal election*
50. Name one right only for United States citizens. *vote in a federal election or run for federal office*
51. What are two rights of everyone living in the United States? *freedom of expression; freedom of speech; freedom of assembly; freedom to petition the government; freedom of worship; the right to bear arms*
52. What do we show loyalty to when we say the Pledge of Allegiance? *the United States; the flag*
53. What is one promise you make when you become a United States citizen? *give up loyalty to other countries; defend the Constitution and laws of the United States; obey the laws of the United States; serve in the U.S. military (if needed); serve (do important work for) the nation (if needed); be loyal to the United States*
54. How old do citizens have to be to vote for President? *eighteen (18) and older*
55. What are two ways that Americans can participate in their democracy? *vote; join a political party; help with a campaign; join a civic group; join a community group; give an elected official your opinion on an issue; call Senators and Representatives; publicly support or oppose an issue or policy; run for office; write to a newspaper*
56. When is the last day you can send in federal income tax forms? *April 15*
57. When must all men register for the Selective Service? *at age eighteen (18); between eighteen (18) and twenty-six (26)*

Naturalization Ceremony, Grand Canyon

AMERICAN HISTORY

A: Colonial Period and Independence

58. What is one reason colonists came to America? *freedom; political liberty; religious freedom; economic opportunity; practice their religion; escape persecution*
59. Who lived in America before the Europeans arrived? *American Indians or Native Americans*
60. What group of people was taken to America and sold as slaves? *Africans or people from Africa*
61. Why did the colonists fight the British? *because of high taxes (taxation without representation); because the British army stayed in their houses (boarding, quartering); because they didn't have self-government*

62. Who wrote the Declaration of Independence? *(Thomas) Jefferson*
63. When was the Declaration of Independence adopted? *July 4, 1776*
64. There were 13 original states. Name three. *New Hampshire; Massachusetts; Rhode Island; Connecticut; New York; New Jersey; Pennsylvania; Delaware; Maryland; Virginia; North Carolina; South Carolina; Georgia*
65. What happened at the Constitutional Convention? *The Constitution was written. The Founding Fathers wrote the Constitution.*
66. When was the Constitution written? *1787*
67. The Federalist Papers supported the passage of the U.S. Constitution. Name one of the writers. *(James) Madison; (Alexander) Hamilton; (John) Jay; Publius*
68. What is one thing Benjamin Franklin is famous for? *U.S. diplomat; oldest member of the Constitutional Convention; first Postmaster General of the United States; writer of "Poor Richard's Almanac;" started the first free libraries*
69. Who is the "Father of Our Country"? *(George) Washington*
70. Who was the first President? *(George) Washington*

Naturalization Ceremony, Seattle, WA

B: 1800s

71. What territory did the United States buy from France in 1803? *the Louisiana Territory; Louisiana*
72. Name one war fought by the United States in the 1800s. *War of 1812; Mexican-American War; Civil War; Spanish-American War*
73. Name the U.S. war between the North and the South. *the Civil War; the War between the States*
74. Name one problem that led to the Civil War. *slavery; economic reasons; states' rights*
75. What was one important thing that Abraham Lincoln did? *freed the slaves (Emancipation Proclamation); saved (or preserved) the Union; led the United States during the Civil War*
76. What did the Emancipation Proclamation do? *freed the slaves; freed slaves in the Confederacy; freed slaves in the Confederate states; freed slaves in most Southern states*
77. What did Susan B. Anthony do? *fought for women's rights; fought for civil rights*

C: Recent American History and Other Important Historical Information

78. Name one war fought by the United States in the 1900s. *World War I; World War II; Korean War; Vietnam War; (Persian) Gulf War*
79. Who was President during World War I? *(Woodrow) Wilson*
80. Who was President during the Great Depression and World War II? *(Franklin) Roosevelt*
81. Who did the United States fight in World War II? *Japan, Germany, and Italy*
82. Before he was President, Eisenhower was a general. What war was he in? *World War II*
83. During the Cold War, what was the main concern of the United States? *Communism*
84. What movement tried to end racial discrimination? *civil rights (movement)*

85. What did Martin Luther King Jr. do? *fought for civil rights; worked for equality for all Americans*
86. What major event happened on September 11, 2001, in the United States? *Terrorists attacked the United States.*
87. Name one American Indian tribe in the United States. *[USCIS Officers will be supplied with a list of federally recognized American Indian tribes.] Cherokee; Navajo; Sioux; Chippewa; Choctaw; Pueblo; Apache; Iroquois; Creek; Blackfeet; Seminole; Cheyenne; Arawak; Shawnee; Mohegan; Huron; Oneida; Lakota; Crow; Teton; Hopi; Inuit [These are some of the most well-known tribes. There are 565 federally recognized tribes.]*

INTEGRATED CIVICS

A: Geography

88. Name one of the two longest rivers in the United States. *Missouri (River); Mississippi (River)*
89. What ocean is on the West Coast of the United States? *Pacific (Ocean)*
90. What ocean is on the East Coast of the United States? *Atlantic (Ocean)*
91. Name one U.S. territory. *Puerto Rico; U.S. Virgin Islands; American Samoa; Northern Mariana Islands; Guam*
92. Name one state that borders Canada. *Maine; New Hampshire; Vermont; New York; Pennsylvania; Ohio; Michigan; Minnesota; North Dakota; Montana; Idaho; Washington; Alaska*
93. Name one state that borders Mexico. *California; Arizona; New Mexico; Texas*
94. What is the capital of the United States? *Washington, D.C.*
95. Where is the Statue of Liberty? *New York (Harbor); Liberty Island [Also acceptable are New Jersey, near New York City, and on the Hudson (River).]*

B: Symbols

96. Why does the flag have 13 stripes? *because there were 13 original colonies; because the stripes represent the original colonies*
97. Why does the flag have 50 stars? *because there is one star for each state; because each star represents a state; because there are 50 states*
98. What is the name of the national anthem? *The Star-Spangled Banner*

New Citizens at the Kennedy Space Center, FL

C: Holidays

99. When do we celebrate Independence Day? *July 4*
100. Name two national U.S. holidays. *New Year's Day; Martin Luther King Day; President's Day; Memorial Day; Independence Day; Labor Day; Columbus Day; Veterans Day; Thanksgiving; Christmas*

Presidential Proclamation—Fire Prevention Week
Barack Obama

This press release was issued on October 7, 2011, from the Office of the Press Secretary of the White House.

FIRE PREVENTION WEEK, 2011
BY THE PRESIDENT OF THE UNITED STATES OF AMERICA
A PROCLAMATION

Fires, whether caused by people or nature, can have devastating effects. Hundreds of thousands of fires happen in and around American homes every year, killing or injuring thousands of people and causing untold damage to families and communities. This week, we honor the selfless first responders who put themselves on the line to safeguard us all from fire, and we reaffirm the need for Americans to practice fire safety throughout the year.

This year's Fire Prevention Week theme, "Protect Your Family from Fire," encourages all Americans to promote fire prevention awareness both inside and outside the home. Everyone can take significant steps to mitigate the risk of fire, from installing and maintaining smoke alarms on every level of their home to practicing safe cooking behaviors. Families can help protect themselves by designing and practicing an escape plan that includes an outside meeting place with multiple exit paths out of each room. And, with the help of local safety officials, families can work together to protect their neighborhood with a Community Wildfire Protection Plan.

In 2011, Federal firefighting grants have been provided to 16 States to assist with wildfires that have caused destruction to families, farms, and businesses. Those living with the threat of wildfire can safeguard their houses by mowing dry grasses to two inches or less, and by clearing brush, leaves, green grass, and lumber from around their homes. By taking precautionary steps, and by discussing and practicing evacuation plans with our families, we can empower ourselves and our communities with the tools to prevent fires, and to save lives, property, and livestock when fires do occur.

Firefighters Training in Colorado

This week, our Nation honors the dedicated firefighters and other first responders who do the hard, dangerous work of keeping our communities safe from fire. Many have laid down their lives to save our friends and neighbors, and their selfless sacrifice defines the nature of courage. As we pay tribute to their memories, let us resolve to maintain our vigilance and take proactive steps to stop fire emergencies before they begin.

NOW, THEREFORE, I, BARACK OBAMA, President of the United States of America, by virtue of the authority vested in me by the Constitution and the laws of the

United States, do hereby proclaim October 9 through October 15, 2011, as Fire Prevention Week. On Sunday, October 16, 2011, in accordance with Public Law 107-51, the flag of the United States will be flown at half staff on all Federal office buildings in honor of the National Fallen Firefighters Memorial Service. I call on all Americans to participate in this observance with appropriate programs and activities and by renewing their efforts to prevent fires and their tragic consequences.

IN WITNESS WHEREOF, I have hereunto set my hand this seventh day of October, in the year of our Lord two thousand eleven, and of the Independence of the United States of America the two hundred and thirty-sixth.

BARACK OBAMA

Wildfire in Florida

A Marine's Grade-School Dream Is Realized
Federal Bureau of Investigation

Susan Roley Malone and Joanne Pierce Misko were the first two women to become special agents after the FBI changed its males-only policy in 1972. Joanne Pierce Misko was the daughter and sister of police officers and spent ten years as a nun before joining the FBI. She worked as a researcher for two years and served as an agent for twenty-two years. This story about Susan Roley Malone was published by the FBI in 2012.

Susan Roley Malone, the daughter of a Marine pilot stationed outside Washington, D.C., was in eighth grade when her civics teacher assigned a project to research a federal agency and meet some of the people there. This was a plum assignment, since Malone's father was a pilot for the Marine Corps commandant, and the FBI's Training Academy was situated on the Marine base in Quantico.

"The agency that I chose, of course, was the FBI," Malone, 65, said during a recent interview in Kansas City, where the former special agent works as a civilian adviser for the U.S. Army. The young Malone had already read books about the Bureau and seen Jimmy Stewart in the 1959 film drama "The FBI Story." She took a tour of the FBI, which only steeled her resolve to one day join to serve her country. There she met an agent named Bill Stapleton. "He talked to me at length about being an FBI agent," Malone said. "But at the time, the agent position was closed to women."

In college, Malone joined the Marine Corps Reserve. She graduated and was commissioned as a second lieutenant in 1969, serving in California and then Norfolk, Virginia. When FBI Director J. Edgar Hoover died in 1972, she attended his funeral. Within weeks, the longstanding rule barring women from new agent training was repealed.

FBI Academy, 1972. Joanne Pierce is wearing the red dress. Susan Roley is partially visible further back.

"I was encouraged by my friends and my own desires, and I applied," said Malone, who had been contemplating law school. Two months later, she met her roommate, Joanne Pierce Misko, during a new agents swearing-in ceremony at FBI Headquarters.

"Of course, everybody wanted to see who we were," Malone said. "Sometimes I felt like I was an exhibit in a museum because everybody would say, 'Which one are you? Are you the Marine or the nun?'"

Malone's background served her well on the firing range and stamina drills. But it was far from easy. "The FBI takes you from zero," Malone said. "They wanted you to learn the FBI way, so the instruction was very rigorous. We went through all the physical training with our classmates and were held to those same FBI standards."

New agent classes create a bond, and this was no different, even if it was the first class with women. In one case, it was Malone who coached a weaker male swimmer to improve enough to meet a requirement. "I said, 'I'll work with you,' and he said, 'Why would you do that?' I said, 'Look, we are all in this class together. It's a teammate thing. We all have to graduate.' It's something that I learned from my Marine Corps training that I think that FBI does well as a family."

After graduating, Malone was dispatched to the Omaha Division, where she eventually met her husband, Marine Col. George Malone. Her first cases included cattle rustling and train wrecking. "I wondered if my squad supervisor was teasing me," she said. But both were problematic federal crimes, and cattle rustling was big business in a city full of slaughterhouses. Her capture of a deserter made her the first woman in the modern FBI to make an arrest.

FBI Agent in Class

Malone moved next to San Francisco, where she worked on cases that included the Patty Hearst kidnapping and interviewing the Manson family.

Malone, whose home is in Maryland, was an FBI agent for seven years. She left in 1979 to rejoin the Marines and work for the Defense Criminal Investigative Service, the criminal investigative arm of the Office of the Inspector General in the Department of Defense. Over the years, she has worked for the State Department and served in United Nations posts in Iraq, Jordan, and Indonesia. She retired from the Marines as a colonel in 1999 and from DCIS in 2001. Today, she's working with the Army to provide soldiers in Afghanistan and Iraq with first-hand knowledge of what's happening on the ground, having just returned from a year-long deployment in northern Afghanistan. She credits her time in the FBI for much of her success since then.

FBI Agent in Training

"It goes back to my FBI training and investigations and talking to people," Malone said. "The training and the interview techniques and the talent to get the complete story and gather the facts. That training throughout my entire career has held me in good stead and offered me the opportunity to share the gifts of a very special organization—the FBI."

Rain in Summer
Henry Wadsworth Longfellow

Henry Wadsworth Longfellow, born in Portland, Maine, in 1807, is one of America's greatest poets. Following is a portion of his poem "Rain in Summer," published in 1845.

How beautiful is the rain!
After the dust and heat,
In the broad and fiery street,
In the narrow lane,
How beautiful is the rain!

How it clatters along the roofs,
Like the tramp of hoofs
How it gushes and struggles out
From the throat of the overflowing spout!

Across the window-pane
It pours and pours;
And swift and wide,
With a muddy tide,
Like a river down the gutter roars
The rain, the welcome rain!

The sick man from his chamber looks
At the twisted brooks;
He can feel the cool
Breath of each little pool;
His fevered brain
Grows calm again,
And he breathes a blessing on the rain.

From the neighboring school
Come the boys,
With more than their wonted noise
And commotion;
And down the wet streets
Sail their mimic fleets,
Till the treacherous pool
Ingulfs them in its whirling
And turbulent ocean.

In the country, on every side,
Where far and wide,
Like a leopard's tawny and spotted hide,
Stretches the plain,
To the dry grass and the drier grain
How welcome is the rain!

Mr. Chief Justice: The Story of William Howard Taft

Bethany Poore

Late at night, lights shone through the windows of the Taft home, which looked down from Mount Auburn to the city of Cincinnati. On a table, Alphonso spread out the long briefs he had brought home from court to study. At his own desk nearby, his son Will unpacked his school bag to begin his homework. In the quiet after dinner, father and son went to work with their books and papers, pens and ink. After a space of busy quiet, Will politely interrupted his father to ask a question. Soon conversation pleasantly superseded their work. Alphonso read aloud a paragraph from one of the briefs and explained it to his son. Soon he digressed into one of his stories of the history and traditions of the court. One day, Will knew, he would be part of that history like his father. Both pairs of eyes shone with interest as they talked about their favorite subject.

William Howard Taft could not remember when he decided to become a lawyer. Love for the law was in his heart. Taft's father, Alphonso, was a lawyer and judge. Alphonso Taft's life ambition was to serve on the United States Supreme Court. He never attained this position; but along with love and respect for the law, he passed on this ambition to his son.

William Howard Taft's Boyhood Home in Cincinnati, Ohio

On a Saturday afternoon, Will and his brothers were busy with chores. "Come on, hurry and get the weeding done so we can get up a baseball game!" In addition to serious application to their studies, Will's parents held high expectations for hard work and responsibility at home. William Howard Taft was born on September 15, 1857. He was in the middle of five brothers. In 1865, soon after the end of the Civil War, Alphonso and Louise and the five Taft brothers welcomed a baby girl last of all.

The boys stood up and stretched after the garden was cleared of weeds. At last, no more chores and an hour until dinner. They grabbed their baseball gear and rushed off to gather up the neighborhood boys.

"Will, can I play second base this time?"

"Aww, but Will's the best second basemen we've got!"

Between many games of baseball, wrestling, swimming, and fighting to defend the honor of the neighborhood, Will proved himself a rough and ready boy. He was friendly, pleasant and had an easy laugh. He enjoyed himself and people liked him.

Young Taft was an exceptional student, but he had to work hard at it. When he graduated from high school, he was second in his class. There was no question about where he would go next: Yale University in New Haven, Connecticut. It was a family tradition. Alphonso Taft and Will's older brothers Charles and Peter had all graduated with honors from Yale. As a new college student, Will wrote, "a fellow can work hard all the time and still not have perfect marks." He worried a lot about failing to meet his father's expectations.

Yet Taft still enjoyed popularity with his classmates. He yearned to be more involved in athletics, but his time at Yale was mostly given to strict attention to academics. His hard work culminated in taking second place in his graduating class of 132 students. Next was law school. Taft chose to move back home to Cincinnati and attend the Cincinnati Law School. The school's courses involved hearing lectures at the school and getting practical experience by working in a law office. Taft worked in his father's law office and soon took on a part-time job as a reporter with the *Cincinnati Commercial* newspaper. Taft's assignment was covering the city's courts.

Making his daily rounds, young William became a familiar sight in Cincinnati courtrooms. Pen and notepad in hand, he witnessed the law in action. He watched as complex Federal cases were untangled by expert lawyers and judges. He saw courtroom drama as criminal cases unfolded with witnesses, cross-examinations, and lives hanging in the balance. Taft gained a practical education in how the law really worked. He was such an excellent reporter that his editor asked him to take on the job full-time, offering a large salary. Taft enjoyed his part-time reporting, but he was not willing to give up his dream of joining the legal profession. In 1880 he passed the Ohio bar exam, the test required to become a lawyer.

Through his court reporting, Taft became friends with Miller Outcault, one of the county's prosecuting attorneys. The two worked together to expose dishonesty in the county's justice system. Outcault made the charges and Taft wrote a series of articles showing the truth of his friend's claims. One of the men they were accusing was Outcault's boss, county prosecutor Samuel Drew. They managed to convince the public. In the next election, voters ousted Drew and elected Outcault as the new county prosecutor. Outcault appointed William Howard Taft Assistant Prosecutor of Hamilton County. Taft took office in January 1881 at the age of 24.

In 1882 President Chester A. Arthur appointed Alphonso Taft, William's father, Ambassador to Austria. President Arthur also had a surprise appointment for Alphonso's son, William. At 25, Taft received his first Federal appointment: tax collector for the revenue district headquartered in Cincinnati. It was an honor, but Taft soon learned the job was not for him. He hated the endless paperwork and the way he was pressured to fire some workers and hire others simply based on who had done the Republican Party a favor. When he was ordered to fire some of his most trusted workers simply so the places could be given to some who were on the "right side" politically, Taft resigned instead of playing a dishonest game. He learned firsthand that for some, politics were a chance to get ahead rather than a chance to serve their country with integrity. Taft switched to practicing law in Cincinnati and was soon appointed to work again as an attorney for the county government.

In 1886 Taft married Helen Herron, called Nellie, daughter of a Cincinnati attorney. Nellie's and William's parents had known each other for many years. Nellie was intelligent, well-educated, ambitious, and eager for her new husband to advance in his political career. As a young woman, she had visited her father's friend President Rutherford B. Hayes in the White House. She had told Hayes that she wouldn't mind being First Lady someday. Nellie and William Howard Taft had three children, Robert Alphonso, Helen Herron, and Charles Phelps.

Over the next several years, Taft served as a judge on the Ohio Superior Court, as Solicitor General of the United States (the lawyer for the Federal government before the Supreme

William and Helen Taft With Youngest Son Charles

Court), and as U.S. Circuit Judge, the highest level of judges below the Supreme Court.

On a regular workday in January 1900, Taft sat at his desk in his circuit court chambers. He answered a knock on the door, and was handed a telegram from President McKinley: "I would like to see you in Washington on important business within the next few days." Perhaps the time had come–the Supreme Court! Taft traveled to Washington full of wonder and hope. He was completely surprised when he heard the reason for the summons. McKinley wanted him to move to the Philippines, a nation of islands in southeast Asia that the United States had recently acquired in the treaty that ended the Spanish-American War. Taft refused at first. He was opposed to the United States taking over the islands in the first place. McKinley was persistent, and Taft finally decided that if America was there to stay, it was obligated to establish a sound government for the Filipino people. In a very short time, the Taft family found themselves in a boat crossing the Pacific Ocean.

Governing the Philippines was an enormous challenge. While other Americans regarded Filipinos as inferior, Taft considered them brothers. He was determined to change the way other Americans treated them. Taft came to love and respect the Filipino people and as a result he earned their trust. He invited native Filipinos to his home, participated in their parties and festivals, and encouraged their native traditions. He wanted the people to have a voice in the way their country was run, and he placed as many native Filipinos in government positions as he could. Taft worked to make life better in the Philippines. He returned land that had been stolen from native Filipinos, made the tax system more fair, set up city governments, overhauled the court and educational systems, and improved roads and harbors. Many in Washington and in the Army stationed in the Philippines disagreed with Taft's policies. They considered the Philippines a conquered people, but Taft's goal was a better life for the Filipino people. In addition to political turmoil, Taft dealt with serious personal health problems while governing the Philippines.

William and Helen Play Cards On Their Journey to the Philippines

Theodore Roosevelt became President in 1901 after the assassination of President McKinley.

Roosevelt respected and supported the job that Taft was doing. The two developed a close working relationship and friendship.

In the fall of 1902, the Philippines, still struggling to establish stability, were struck by multiple disasters. A cholera epidemic swept through the population and took many lives. A virus killed off many farm and work animals. Drought and windstorms brought the fear of famine and many people lost their jobs. Struggling to govern well in the midst of the storms, Taft received a telegram on October 26, 1902. It was from President Roosevelt. It carried the message that Taft had been waiting to hear all of his life: there was an empty seat on the Supreme Court. "I earnestly desire to appoint you . . ." Taft read it in black and white on the slip of paper in his hand. "I greatly hope you will accept. Would appreciate early reply." Taft, with hand trembling, read the message again. The Supreme Court. The call had come for him to take a place where he most wanted to serve. But what would happen in the Philippines if he left now?

Hard as it was, Taft knew his answer. He could not leave; his duty was to stay and serve. Taft replied to Roosevelt, "Great honor deeply appreciated. Look forward to a time when I can accept such an offer but even if it is certain that it can never be repeated I must now decline." Roosevelt soon asked again, but Taft's resolve was firm. Filipino leaders sent messages to Roosevelt affirming how much Taft was needed in the Philippines.

By the next year, conditions were much better in the Philippines. Taft felt hopeful. His patient work was taking root. He was planning a census which would be followed by a popular election for a Philippine Assembly, giving the people even more voice in their own government. As conditions in the Philippines improved, Taft's own health grew worse. His doctors advised him to return to the United States.

In March of 1903, Taft was handed a letter from President Roosevelt. He slit the envelope and read another offer for a place in the Federal government, this time as Secretary of War. The current Secretary was planning to resign. The letter was typed, but Roosevelt had written a P.S. by hand underneath, "If only there were three of you! Then I would have put one of you on the Supreme Court . . . one of you as Secretary of War . . . and one of you permanently as governor of the Philippines." Taft was touched by his friend's high regard for his abilities. This was not a job he had hoped for, but his doctors were telling him he needed to go home to the United States. He would need something to do if he went back. There was still so much to be done in the Philippines, but perhaps he had laid a good foundation. Perhaps another governor would be able to continue the work he had begun. The thought of working closely with his friend Roosevelt was appealing. In the end, Taft accepted, though he was reluctant to the last to leave his Filipino brothers.

Taft Avenue in Manilla is named after William Howard Taft.

Roosevelt kept Taft busy as Secretary of War. Then in the 1908 election, the highly popular Roosevelt supported his friend Taft as the next President. Taft did not want the job, but with those closest to him, including Roosevelt, his brothers, and his wife strongly urging him, he reluctantly agreed to campaign. He won the election, then spent four miserable years as President. He was deeply hurt to lose his close friendship with Roosevelt during his term in office when Roosevelt publicly criticized his decisions as President.

Taft ran again, but was soundly defeated in the 1912 election. He was full of relief upon leaving the White House. He was shortly after offered a job as professor at his beloved Yale. He spoke and wrote widely, and after four years of criticism and rejection by the American people, he began to enjoy a return of popularity. The new president, Woodrow Wilson, showed his respect for Taft by asking him to lead the committee to build the Lincoln Memorial in Washington, D.C. Wilson also asked him to serve on the War Labor Board during World War I. The Board handled workers in essential wartime jobs. As his roles in civil service continued to expand, Taft always had the Supreme Court in the back of his mind.

In December of 1920, Taft had breakfast at the home of newly-elected Warren G. Harding in Marion, Ohio. Harding would assume the presidency the following spring. They ate their waffles and creamed beef and chatted. Casually, Harding said, "By the way, I want to ask you, would you accept a position on the Supreme Bench, because if you would I'll put you on that Court."

Taft could hardly speak. His long-held hopes soared. But, as he had been surprised by Harding's question, Harding was surprised by his answer, "It has always been my ambition, but I could not accept any place but the Chief Justiceship."

Harding said no more, leaving Taft in anxious suspense.

The then-current Chief Justice was Edward White. While president, Taft himself had placed White on the bench in 1910. By 1920 White was elderly and in bad health. Everyone knew he was likely to resign soon and there was a swirl of talk in the newspapers about who would take his place. White wanted his good friend William Howard Taft to be the next Chief Justice, but it was not up to him to choose.

Taft as Chief Justice

On May 19, 1921, Chief Justice Edward White died. On June 30, Harding nominated William Howard Taft to be the next Chief Justice of the Supreme Court. He sent the nomination to the Senate to be confirmed, then announced his choice to reporters. The Senate confirmed Taft the very same day.

Reporters asked Taft, "Are you pleased with the President's choice of the new Chief Justice?"

Taft's laughed and his eyes shone. "You can judge for yourselves about that."

Taft was fully committed to serving his country as an excellent Chief Justice. He rose early and stayed up late to keep up with his work. His entire schedule rotated around his duties and responsibilities. In addition to presiding over cases, he worked for reform in the entire justice system so that cases could move more quickly through the courts. Taft said, "A rich man can stand the delay and profits by it, but the poor man always suffers." When he first arrived at the Supreme Court, there was an enormous backlog of cases waiting to be heard. The process of working through them was painfully slow, and there were always more coming in. After three years as Chief Justice, he succeeded in convincing Congress to pass laws allowing the Supreme Court the power to decide which cases were important enough for their time and attention. This allowed much greater efficiency in making sure the important cases were heard.

Taft had more changes in mind. The Supreme Court had never had a home of its own. After moving around to several different locations, the Supreme Court had met in the Old Senate Chamber in the Capitol since the Civil War. By Taft's time, Senate committee meetings were crowding into their space. There was not even space to store court records. Taft said, "It really is not fair. In our conference room, the shelves have to be so high that it takes an aeroplane to reach them." Taft worked hard to convince Congress to set aside money to build a Supreme Court building, succeeding at last in 1929 when President Hoover signed the measure.

By then, Taft was growing old and his health was declining, though he continued to give his all to the Court. He reluctantly took a few weeks off to rest and try to get better. He stayed for a week in a Washington hospital, spending most of his time reading detective stories. All letters and court papers were kept away from him. Nellie was the only visitor allowed. Next, he and Nellie went to Asheville, North Carolina, for a vacation. Sadly, the time off did not bring him back to good health. Taft knew the time had come to resign from his beloved Court. His son Robert, then a United States Senator, came to Asheville and talked to his father and his father's doctors. From there, Robert Taft traveled back to Washington to deliver his father's resignation as Chief Justice to President Hoover on February 3, 1930.

Taft was taken back to Washington where he rested at home. His brothers and sons came to visit, and his daughter came to stay. With Nellie nearby, William Howard Taft died on March 8, 1930.

A few weeks before, Taft had received a letter signed by all of his fellow justices of the Supreme Court. The letter addressed him as "Mr. Chief Justice," and read, "We call you Chief Justice still—for we cannot give up the title by which we have known you all these later years and which you have made dear to us. We cannot let you leave us without trying to tell you how dear you have made it. . . . We grieve at your illness, but your spirit has given life an impulse that will abide whether you are with us or away."

Taft's Headstone at Arlington National Cemetery

Lighter Side of Life at the United States Supreme Court

Ruth Bader Ginsburg

Ruth Bader Ginsburg was nominated as an associate justice of the U.S. Supreme Court by President Bill Clinton. She began serving in 1993. In celebration of Law Day in 2009, Ginsburg visited the New England Law School in Boston. She gave the following speech at the Centennial Law Day Banquet.

For these pre-dinner remarks, I have chosen an altogether digestible topic: customs that promote collegiality among the nine Justices of the United States Supreme Court. My aim is to describe not the Court's heavy work, but the lighter side of life in our Marble Palace.

I will comment first on our routine gatherings. They begin with handshakes, 36 of them to be exact. Before each day in Court begins, and before each conference discussion, as we enter the Robing Room or the adjacent Conference Room, we shake hands, each Justice with every other. Every day the Court hears arguments, and every day we meet to discuss cases, we lunch together in the Justices' Dining Room. The room is elegant, but the lunch is not haute cuisine. It comes from the Court's public cafeteria, the same fare available to anyone who visits the Court.

Ruth Bader Ginsburg

We lunch together by choice, not by rule, usually six to eight of us, and more than occasionally all nine. When Justice O'Connor (currently, the only retired Justice) is in town, she often shares the lunch hour with us and enlivens our conversation with reports of her travels in the United States and around the globe.

At the lunch table we may talk about the lawyers' performance in the cases just heard, or a new production in town, perhaps at the D.C. Shakespeare Theatre or the Washington National Opera, or the latest exhibition at the Library of Congress, National Gallery, or Phillips Collection. Sometimes the younger members of the Court speak of their children, the older members, of their grandchildren.

From time to time, we invite a guest to vary the lunch table conversation. Invitees in recent terms have included: former Secretary of State Condoleezza Rice; former President of the Supreme Court of Israel, Aharon Barak; former U.N. Secretary General Kofi Annan; and, most recently, Albie Sachs, Justice of the Constitutional Court of South Africa. [So far, retired Federal Reserve Chairman Alan Greenspan, and former President of the World Bank Jim Wolfensohn, have been our only repeat invitees. (Both have an unusual talent. They can engage in lively conversation and eat lunch at the same time.)]

We celebrate Justices' birthdays with a pre-lunch toast, and a "Happy Birthday" chorus generally led by Justice Scalia, because among us, he is best able to carry a tune. Sometimes the celebration includes a cake baked by my husband, master chef and Georgetown University Law Center tax professor, Martin D. Ginsburg.

Professor Ginsburg is a regular contributor to the lighter side of life at the Supreme Court. Mainly he performs in the kitchen, for the quarterly spouses' lunches held at the Court and, occasionally in past years, at a dinner for the entire Court family — Justices, their spouses, and widows of former Court members. In the beginning, when I was the newest Justice, my dear husband offered aid in lightening my load.

During my first months on the Court I received, week after week, as I still do, literally hundreds of letters—nowadays increasingly fedexes, faxes, and emails—requesting all manner of responses. Brought up under instructions that plates must be cleaned and communications answered, I was drowning in correspondence despite the best efforts of my resourceful secretaries to contain the flood.

Early in 1994, Justice Scalia and I traveled to India for a judicial exchange. In my absence, my spouse tested his conviction that my mail could be handled more efficiently. He visited chambers, checked the incoming correspondence, grouped the requests into a dozen or so categories, and devised an all-purpose response for my secretaries' signature. When I returned, he gave me the form, which to this day, he regards as a model of utility and grace. I will read a few parts of the letter my husband composed. You may judge for yourself its usefulness and grace.

You recently wrote Justice Ginsburg. She would respond personally if she could, but (as Frederick told Mabel in Gilbert & Sullivan's Pirates of Penzance) she is not able. Incoming mail reached flood levels months ago and shows no sign of receding.

To help the Justice stay above water, we have endeavored to explain why she cannot do what you have asked her to do. Please refer to the paragraph below with the caption that best fits your request.

Favorite Recipes. The Justice was expelled from the kitchen nearly three decades ago by her food-loving children. She no longer cooks and the one recipe from her youth, tuna fish casserole, is nobody's favorite.

Photograph. Justice Ginsburg is flattered, indeed amazed, by the number of requests for her photograph. She is now 61 years of age—ah, those were the days!—and understandably keeps no supply.

Are We Related? The birth names of the Justice's parents are Bader and Amster. Many who bear those names have written, giving details of origin and immigration. While the information is engrossing, you and she probably are not related within any reasonable degree of consanguinity. Justice Ginsburg knows, or knew, all of the issue of all in her family fortunate enough to make their way to the U.S.A.

I will spare you my husband's thoughts on Fund-raising, School Projects, Congratulatory Letters, Document Requests, Sundry Invitations, and proceed to one last category:

May I Visit? If you are any of the Justice's four grandchildren and wish to visit, she will be overjoyed. If you are a writer or researcher and want to observe the work of Chambers, the answer is "no." Confidentiality really matters in this workplace.

Justice Ginsburg and President Obama Walk With Other Justices

My secretaries, you will not be surprised to learn, vetoed my husband's letter, and in the ensuing years they have managed to cope with the mail flood through measures more *sympathique*.

Since February 5, the day of my pancreatic cancer surgery, messages of hope and offers of prayer have numbered in the hundreds. I have been obliged to respond by a form letter, but this time, it is one I composed.

Returning to the Court's social life, a typical example of events we host every now and then, mainly for lawyers and judges: We take turns greeting attendees at dinners for newly appointed federal judges, gathered in D.C. for a week of orientation. We also take turns introducing speakers at the Supreme Court Historical Society biannual lecture series.

My most recent ventures for the Historical Society involved, first, an October 27 program at the City Bar Association in New York centered on the work and days of Belva Lockwood, first woman to gain membership in the Supreme Court's Bar. After her 1879 admission, she ran twice for the U.S. Presidency, in 1884 and 1888. Next, in December, I presided at a Historical Society sponsored reenactment of the arguments before the Court in a famous case decided in 1908, *Muller v. Oregon*. The Court's decision in *Muller* broke away from the prevailing laissez-faire philosophy and upheld an Oregon law limiting the hours women could be gainfully employed to 10 per day. *Muller v. Oregon* is also well known for the brief filed on behalf of Oregon by Louis D. Brandeis. That Brandeis brief contained nearly 100 pages of real and supposed facts about social and economic conditions, and only a few pages of standard legal argument.

Four women have served on the Supreme Court. They are pictured here, from left to right: Sandra Day O'Connor, Sonia Sotomayor, Ruth Bader Ginsburg, and Elena Kagan.

An annual pleasant pause. Each May, just after hearings are over and before the intense end of May and early June weeks when the term's remaining opinions must be completed and released, the Court holds a Musicale. That tradition was inaugurated in 1988 by Justice Blackmun, who passed the baton to Justice O'Connor when he retired. For the past seven years, I have attended to arrangements for the Musicales. We have recently added a Fall recital. This term's fall recital artist was Renée Fleming, celebrated Diva at the Metropolitan Opera and other grand opera venues around the globe.

In between sitting weeks, some of us spend a day or two visiting U.S. universities or law schools as I am doing just now, or attending meetings with judges and lawyers across the country. Mid-winter or summer some of us travel abroad to teach, or to learn what we can about legal systems in distant places. For example, in recent recesses, I have taught, lectured, or participated in meetings of jurists in Australia, Austria, China, England, France, India, Ireland, Israel, Italy, Japan, New Zealand, and South Africa.

Work at the U.S. Supreme Court is ever challenging, enormously time consuming, and tremendously satisfying. We are constantly reading, thinking, and trying to write so that at least lawyers and other judges will understand our rulings.

As you may have noticed, we have sharp differences on certain issues — fairly recent examples include affirmative action, public school desegregation, the death penalty, control of electoral campaign financing, access to court by detainees in Guantanamo Bay. But through it all, we remain good friends, people who respect each other, and genuinely enjoy each other's company. In recent terms, we have even managed to agree, unanimously, some 30 to 40 percent of the time. That contrasts with the Court's 5-4 splits, which last term accounted for about 16 percent of the Court's decisions. Our mutual respect is only momentarily touched, in most instances, by our sometimes strong disagreements on what the law is.

All of us appreciate that the institution we serve is far more important than the particular individuals who compose the Court's bench at any given time. And our job, in my view, is the best work a jurist anywhere could have. Our charge is to pursue justice as best we can. The Founding Fathers were wise enough to equip us to do that by according us life tenure (or, as the Constitution says, tenure "during good behavior"), and salaries that cannot be diminished while we hold office.

Our former Chief Justice, William H. Rehnquist, spoke of the role of the judge using a sports metaphor:

> *The Constitution has placed the judiciary in a position similar to that of a referee in a basketball game who is obliged to call a foul against a member of the home team at a critical moment in the game: he will be soundly booed, but he is nonetheless obliged to call it as he saw it, not as the home court crowd wants him to call it.*

The day any judge shirks from that responsibility, Chief Justice Rehnquist counseled, is the day he or she should resign from office. All members of today's Court would concur in that counsel.

With thanks for your patient audience, it is now time to say Bon Appetit!

The Supreme Court Justices, 2010

Plain Bob and a Job

James W. Foley

James W. Foley was born in 1874 and moved with his family to North Dakota in 1878. He began writing while still in his youth. He published several volumes of poetry and served as editor of the Bismarck Tribune *newspaper. He was also involved in politics and worked as private secretary to two North Dakota Governors. His poem "North Dakota Hymn" was made the state song of North Dakota in 1947. "Plain Bob and a Job" appeared in* Tales of the Trail *by James W. Foley, published in 1905. It pays homage to one of the key components of the American economy—the honest worker!*

Bob went lookin' for a job—
Didn't want a situation; didn't ask a lofty station:
Didn't have a special mission for a topnotcher's position;
Didn't have such fine credentials—but he had the real essentials—
Had a head that kept on workin' and two hands that were not shirkin';
Wasn't either shirk or snob;
Wasn't Mister—just plain Bob,
Who was lookin' for a job.

Bob went lookin' for a job;
And he wasn't scared or daunted when he saw a sign—"Men Wanted,"
Walked right in with manner fittin' up to where the Boss was sittin',
And he said: "My name is Bob, and I'm lookin' for a job;
And if you're the Boss that hires 'em, starts 'em working and that fires 'em,
Put my name right down here, Neighbor, as a candidate for labor;
For my name is just plain 'Bob,
And my pulses sort o' throb
For that thing they call a job."

Bob kept askin' for a job,
And the Boss, he says: "What kind?" And Bob answered: "Never mind;
For I ain't a bit partic'ler and I never was a stickler
For proprieties in workin'—if you got some labor lurkin'
Anywhere around about kindly go and trot it out.
It's, a job I want, you see—
Any kind that there may be
Will be good enough for me."

Bob was anxious for a job,
And he said: "Look here, Old Feller—on the first floor, in the cellar,
On the roof or in the attic—I'm a jobster democratic.
And it's all the same, Old Turk, what it is if it is work;
I don't ask for frills upon—I just want a job—I want it!
There's a fever in me rages
For the thing that men call wages,
Put me on the payroll pages!"

Well, sir, Bob he got a job.
But the Boss went 'round all day in a dreamy sort of way;
And he says to me: "By thunder, we have got the world's Eighth Wonder!
Got a feller name of Bob who just asked me for a job—
Never asks when he engages about overtime in wages;
Never asked if he'd get pay by the hour or by the day;
Never asked me if it's airy work and light and sanitary;
Never asked me for my notion of the chances of promotion;
Never asked for the duration of his annual vacation;
Never asked for Saturday half-a-holiday with pay;
Never took me on probation till he tried the situation;
Never asked me if it's sittin' work or standin', or befittin'
Of his birth and inclination—he just filed his application,
Hung his coat up on a knob,
Said his name was just plain Bob—
And went workin' at a job!"

The Real Riches
John G. Saxe

John Godfrey Saxe (1816-1887) was born in Vermont and became a lawyer and successful poet.

Every coin of earthly treasure
We have lavished upon earth
For our simple worldly pleasure
May be reckoned something worth;
For the spending was not losing,
Tho' the purchase were but small;
It has perished with the using.
We have had it,—that is all!

All the gold we leave behind us,
When we turn to dust again,
Tho' our avarice may blind us,
We have gathered quite in vain;
Since we neither can direct it,
By the winds of fortune tossed,
Nor in other worlds expect it;
What we hoarded we have lost.

But each merciful oblation—
Seed of pity wisely sown,
What we gave in self-negation,
We may safely call our own;
For the treasure freely given
Is the treasure that we hoard,
Since the angels keep in heaven,
What is lent unto the Lord.

John Godrey Saxe

Supporting the Library

Do you have a library in your town? Did you ever wonder who pays for it? Every book, magazine, DVD, computer, and piece of furniture cost something! Most libraries receive funding from the city and/or county government. That money comes from taxes paid by individuals and businesses. Most libraries also seek extra money to offer more services than are covered by tax funds. "Friends of the Library" groups are popular. This is a group that believes in the value of the library in their community and supports the library through volunteer work and raising money. It is also common for people to make donations to a library in honor or memory of a loved one. Books purchased from those donations have a bookplate in the front that indicate they were purchased from such a donation. Many libraries have used book sales to raise money. The books for sale are donated by people in the community or withdrawn from the library system. Read the following three excerpts from historic newspapers that discuss different ways of supporting the library—state, local, and individual.

Nebraska's Public Traveling Library
from *Custer County Republican*, Broken Bow, Nebraska, November 7, 1907

The Nebraska Public Library commission was created by the legislature of 1901 and began active work the following November. Its purpose is to encourage the founding of libraries where none exist and the better administration of those already established, to give advice and instruction, when asked, to all libraries and individuals, and to all communities as to the best means of establishing, organizing and administering such libraries.

The commission has a system of traveling libraries. The traveling library contains 40 well-selected books for children and adults and is designed to furnish reading to rural communities which are not large enough to support local libraries. It also may supplement the book collection of the small public libraries whose means are limited. These books are packed in a box and sent to any community upon an application signed by five residents. The library may be kept for three months with a privilege of extending the time, and then exchanged for another. No fee is charged for the use of the books but the borrowers pay all transportation expenses. The libraries may be kept in hotels, stores, schools, residences, or wherever they can be most widely distributed.

The commission also lends out books on special subjects to any study club, literary society, library, or school. The borrower pays for the transportation of the books.

Applications for traveling libraries, or for special loan of books on a particular subject, or request for information on the subject of libraries, should be addressed to the secretary of the commission, Miss Charlotte Templeton, Lincoln, Nebraska.

The Library's Needs
from *The Columbia Evening Missourian*, Columbia, Missouri, September 21, 1921

One of Columbia's most vital institutions stands in grave danger of extinction unless immediate financial aid is given to it.

The Columbia Free Public Library, by the interest shown in it and the use made of it since its inception, has filled a definite need in the community. Its circulation has been rapidly growing. Last month, about 2,500 books were loaned. At present, there are about 7,000 books on its shelves. Most of these were presented to the library. Only a few are added each month, the only funds available for this purpose being fines collected on overdue books.

Previous to this time, the library has been supported by subscriptions from various charitable institutions, civic leagues and individuals. In many cases these donations were made out of funds collected to the institutions for other purposes, and would not have been given had it not been for the pressing need of the library. Too, the funds collected in this manner have not been more than half of what would reasonably be needed to operate a library such as Columbia should have. For this purpose, at least $2,500 should be available.

With such an amount the library could buy 200 or 300 new books each year, which is a very modest number, and could keep its rooms open mornings, evenings, and Sundays. With the present restricted allowance, it is only possible to keep it open from 12 till 5 o'clock in the afternoon.

It can readily be seen that such an insufficient and unstable arrangement cannot continue if Columbia is to have and maintain the sort of library its citizens need. A sufficient appropriation by the city council would enable this deserving and influential institution to continue its good work. Immediate action is necessary.

Rummage Sale
Four Saturday Events to Raise Funds for Library Association
from *The Daily Democrat*, Andarko, Oklahoma, October 8, 1908

The Andarko Library Association will have a "Rummage Sale" next Saturday, October 17. The purpose of the sale is to get new books for the people to read during the long winter evenings. The word "Rummage," in this case, does not mean a worthless lot of articles gathered from dark corners and garrets, but bright good wearing apparel, shoes, coats, pants, dresses, undergarments, top coats, and everything possible, at a figure so cheap, it is almost a gift.

The sale will continue for at least four Saturdays on the pavement in front of the library rooms at the rear of Coombs Brothers' drug store on Fifth Street. Those wanting good stuff to gather cotton in, and something for dress as well will find it there. We want every one in Caddo county to come and see us, whether you are interested or not. Our library is for all the people, all the time.

. . . Come and see us each Saturday for four coming Saturdays at our rooms. We want every one in Caddo county also. Let me tell you a truth: we can't get along without you.

Mrs. J. J. Baird

Children's Room at the Public Library in Berkeley, California

Rich Gold Strike Made Below Douglas

This is a newspaper article about the discovery of a valuable natural resource: gold. The most famous gold strike in American history was the 1848 strike in California which brought "Forty-Niners" flocking. Gold has been found in many of our states. This article appeared in the Bisbee Daily Review *of Bisbee, Arizona, on February 7, 1903.*

Rich Gold Strike Made Below Douglas

Douglas Is Excited

People There Rushing to Scene of New Gold Strike

Edward Sturges, a prospector from a mining district in Mexico, near Douglas, Arizona, reports a tremendous gold strike in the Torres mountains, forty miles from Cos, the terminus of the Nacozari railroad.

Sturges . . . claims to have taken out $150,000 in gold in the last six weeks.

Samples of the ore are said to run as high as 3,600 ounces in gold to the ton. There is great excitement at Douglas and a stampede has begun to the vicinity of the reported strike.

Numerous parties are being organized [in Douglas] to go at once to the scene of the rich gold strike in the Torres mountains.

The entire district in which Sturges made his find is practically unclaimed, and is open to the prospectors who first reach the claims.

Sturges passed through [Douglas] on his way to El Paso, and . . . showed some of the ore he had taken out to friends. It was immensely rich, rivaling even the famous "Lucky Tiger."

Friends of Sturges who were informed by him of the find, made an effort to organize a party and leave the city quietly, but the news leaked out, and now several parties have been organized.

The property is situated in a district, which has been only partially prospected, and several other rich strikes will be probably made in the next few days.

Further reports from the Torres district are awaited [in Douglas] with interest.

Panning for Gold

Change Your Life with Electricity

These four advertisements demonstrate the way electricity changed everyday American life in the early 20th century.

GOODWIN'S WEEKLY 3

FOOT POWER REQUIRED TO RUN A SEWING MACHINE IS LITTLE TO BE SURE, BUT IT IS ENOUGH TO GIVE THE AVERAGE WOMAN A BACKACHE:

A General Electric Motor will drive the machine, allowing undivided attention to be given to the sewing.

The result is better work, more of it, and no backache. The cost of operation averages one cent an hour.

A General Electric Motor can be attached to any standard machine and operated from any electric light socket.

General Electric Sewing Machine Motors carried by most all good Electrical Supply Dealers. If you cannot purchase one locally, kindly drop us a card for further information, which we will gladly furnish.

CAPITAL ELECTRIC CO.

ELECTRIC SHOW DEPARTMENT

19 WEST FIRST SOUTH

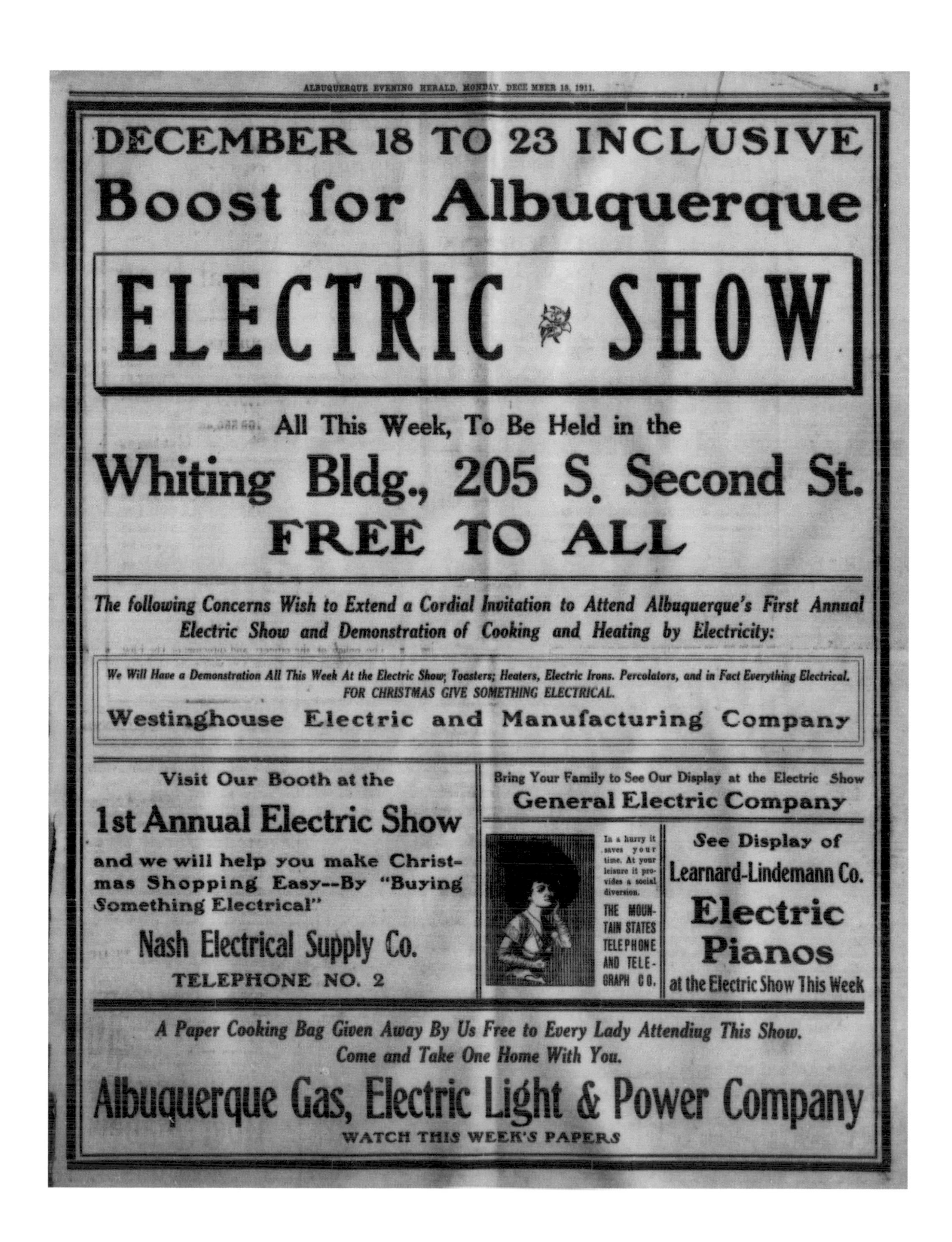

ALBUQUERQUE EVENING HERALD, MONDAY, DECEMBER 18, 1911.

DECEMBER 18 TO 23 INCLUSIVE

Boost for Albuquerque

ELECTRIC SHOW

All This Week, To Be Held in the

Whiting Bldg., 205 S. Second St.

FREE TO ALL

The following Concerns Wish to Extend a Cordial Invitation to Attend Albuquerque's First Annual Electric Show and Demonstration of Cooking and Heating by Electricity:

We Will Have a Demonstration All This Week At the Electric Show; Toasters; Heaters, Electric Irons. Percolators, and in Fact Everything Electrical.
FOR CHRISTMAS GIVE SOMETHING ELECTRICAL.

Westinghouse Electric and Manufacturing Company

Visit Our Booth at the

1st Annual Electric Show

and we will help you make Christmas Shopping Easy--By "Buying Something Electrical"

Nash Electrical Supply Co.

TELEPHONE NO. 2

Bring Your Family to See Our Display at the Electric Show

General Electric Company

In a hurry it saves your time. At your leisure it provides a social diversion.

THE MOUNTAIN STATES TELEPHONE AND TELEGRAPH CO.

See Display of

Learnard-Lindemann Co.

Electric Pianos

at the Electric Show This Week

A Paper Cooking Bag Given Away By Us Free to Every Lady Attending This Show.
Come and Take One Home With You.

Albuquerque Gas, Electric Light & Power Company

WATCH THIS WEEK'S PAPERS

On hot summer days, how a cool breeze does refresh you—when scorching heat makes work an intolerable burden, how a steady waft of fresh air puts new life into you—on sultry, breathless nights, how quickly restful sleep comes with the sweeping breeze of a

GENERAL ELECTRIC COMPANY

G.E. Electric Fan

For homes and small offices the G-E 8-inch Oscillating Fan (the smallest swinging fan made) is exactly right to give the cooling refreshment that all G-E Fans offer—and at a trifling cost. Even the 12-inch and 16-inch G-E Fans use less electricity than an ordinary 16-candle-power light, while the little 8-inch type runs for

Four Hours for only One Cent.

Think of the comfort of the fresh, pure, outdoor air that a G-E Fan draws in, of the sultriness and the cooking odors it drives out, of the banishment of flies who are blown quite away by its sweeping breeze. And then think of the trifling cost for all this comfort.

All G-E Fans are sturdy of frame and scientifically balanced to run with noticeable quietness and smoothness for years. The running parts are self-oiling and enclosed, so that oil-clogged dust cannot soil hands or clothing.

Whichever size or style you prefer, you should insist on the G-E trade-mark, which ensures absolute reliability

Electric shops, stores carrying electrical goods or any lighting company can supply you.

"The Twitch of a Switch"

illustrates many new and inexpensive ways of making electricity save housework and servant trouble. Write for it today.

GENERAL ELECTRIC COMPANY

The World's Largest Electrical Manufacturer

(Dept. 23 C) Schenectady, N. Y.

The Guarantee of Excellence on Goods Electrical

This trade mark insures reliability in anything that generates, transmits or utilizes electricity. It protects you on house-wiring materials, it is on all Edison lamps, and it identifies the most highly perfected electric flatirons, fans, cooking devices, small and large motors and apparatus.

PAGE TWO — MEDFORD MAIL TRIBUNE, MEDFORD, OREGON, THURSDAY, JANUARY 1, 1914.

WE SELL ELECTRIC SERVICE

Start the New Year right and Do Your Work the Electric Way

COOK WITH ELECTRICITY and save time and temper.

IRON WITH ELECTRICITY and save time and fatigue. No time lost going back and forth to change irons.

HEAT WATER WITH ELECTRICITY and insure a constant supply of hot water for all of the household needs.

LIGHT WITH ELECTRICITY; use the improved Tungsten Mazda lamps for best results.

ELECTRIC VACUUM CLEANER keeps your home clean. We have the agency for the latest improved Cleaner; weighs only 9 pounds; has powerful suction, will pick up matches, etc., and gets all the dirt; costs one cent an hour to operate; sells for $30.

USE ELECTRIC MOTORS for all power service to increase production and save labor.

PUMP WATER WITH ELECTRIC MOTOR for irrigating ranches or orchards. Production and not acreage, is the time measure of profit.

Nearly every problem of Lighting, Heating or Power has been solved for Home, Business House, Ranch or Orchard the ELECTRIC WAY

CALIFORNIA-OREGON POWER CO.

MAIN OFFICE, MEDFORD, OREGON

216 W. Main Street — Telephone No. 168

DISTRICT OFFICES AT ASHLAND AND GRANTS PASS

When the Cows Come Home

Agnes E. Mitchell

Agnes E. Mitchell, a minister's wife, wrote this poem while she was living in Louisville, Kentucky. It was published in The Humbler Poets, *an 1899 collection of poetry that appeared in newspapers and magazines between 1870 and 1885.*

With klingle, klangle, klingle,
'Way down the dusty dingle,
The cows are coming home;

Now sweet and clear, now faint and low,
The airy tinklings come and go,
Like chimings from the far-off tower,
Or patterings of an April shower
That makes the daisies grow;
Ko-ling, ko-lang, kolinglelingle
Far down the darkening dingle,
The cows come slowly home.

And old-time friends, and twilight plays,
And starry nights and sunny days,
Come trooping up the misty ways
When the cows come home,
With jingle, jangle, jingle,
Soft tones that sweetly mingle—
The cows are coming home;

Malvine, and Pearl, and Florimel,
DeKamp, Red Rose, and Gretchen Schell.
Queen Bess and Sylph, and Spangled Sue,
Across the fields I hear her "loo-oo"
And clang her silver bell;
Go-ling, go-lang, golingledingle,
With faint, far sounds that mingle,
The cows come slowly home.

And mother-songs of long-gone years,
And baby-joys and childish fears,
And youthful hopes and youthful tears,
When the cows come home.
With ringle, rangle, ringle,
By twos and threes and single,
The cows are coming home.

Through violet air we see the town,
And the summer sun a-sliding down,
And the maple in the hazel glade
Throws down the path a longer shade,
And the hills are growing brown;
To-ring, to-rang, toringleringle,
By threes and fours and single,
The cows come slowly home.

The same sweet sound of wordless psalm,
The same sweet June-day rest and calm,
The same sweet smell of buds and balm,
When the cows come home.
With tinkle, tankle, tinkle,
Through fern and periwinkle,
The cows are coming home.

A-loitering in the checkered stream,
Where the sun-rays glance and gleam,
Clarine, Peach-bloom and Phebe Phillis
Stand knee-deep in the creamy lilies,
In a drowsy dream;
To-link, to-lank, tolinklelinkle,
O'er banks with buttercups a-twinkle,
The cows come slowly home.

And up through memory's deep ravine
Come the brook's old song and its old-time sheen,
And the crescent of the silver queen,
When the cows come home.
With klingle, klangle, klingle,
With loo-oo, and moo-oo and jingle,
The cows are coming home.

And over there on Merlin Hill
Sounds the plaintive cry of the whip-poor-will,
And the dew-drops lie on the tangled vines,
And over the poplars Venus shines,
And over the silent mill.
Ko-ling, ko-lang, kolinglelingle,
With ting-a-ling and jingle,
The cows come slowly home.

Let down the bars; let in the train
Of long-gone songs, and flowers, and rain;
For dear old times come back again,
When the cows come home.

Aim for the Stars: The Story of Shirley Ann Jackson

Bethany Poore

When freshman Shirley Ann Jackson stepped out of the lonely quiet of her dorm room she was surprised to find the hallway outside crowded with young women. Students leaned against the wall, sat cross-legged facing each other, or lay stretched out on their stomachs. Shirley heard the cheerful hum of many conversations happening at once. Textbooks and papers were scattered everywhere on the floor. Pencils whispered across notebook pages slowly solving problems. Foreheads were knitted. Erasers scratched back and forth. Friendly faces shared smiles as lightbulbs of understanding went off.

When Shirley got back from the bathroom, she gathered up the homework from her desk and stepped back to the inviting camaraderie of the hallway. She was excited to know that at her college there were study groups like the ones she had enjoyed in high school. She walked up to a group of girls and asked, "May I join you?"

A girl glanced up at Shirley and said, "Go away."

Stunned, Shirley told them, "Well, I've, I've done half the problems, and I think the answers are right, and I think I know how to do the other half . . ."

Another girl looked coldly up at Shirley. "Didn't you hear her? She said, 'Go away.'"

Shirley turned, walked back into her room, and closed the door. Tears came. Shirley cried quietly by herself for a long while. Then she told herself, well, you still have to finish your physics homework. Sniffling, she got through the set of physics problems.

Why did the girls keep Shirley out of their study group? When she would join a group at a table for lunch, some people would get up even though they weren't finished. If she sat at an empty lunch table, it would tend to stay empty. In her classes, no one would sit in the desks next to hers. Why?

Shirley Ann Jackson was born on August 5, 1946, in Washington, D.C. She was the second of four children. Her family lived in a quiet neighborhood with lots of children to play with. Shirley and her sister and brother went to school, played and learned at home, did chores around the house, and attended Vermont Avenue Baptist Church with their parents. They were a close, loving family.

Shirley's father, George, worked as a supervisor in the postal service. He had wonderful abilities in math, mechanics, and engineering. He was a veteran of World War II and received special honors for devising a safer steering mechanism for an Army vehicle. As a father, he amazed his children with the math problems he could do in his head. He also modeled for them an unending love of learning. He helped Shirley and her younger sister, Gloria, build wooden go-carts to race with other neighborhood children. Shirley had some of her first lessons in physics figuring out which parts and design would make the fastest go-cart on the block.

Shirley's mother, Beatrice, was a social worker. She worked in a home for children with mental handicaps. Beatrice loved books and read to her children every night. She taught each of them to read before they went to kindergarten. Shirley shared her mother's love of books and spent a lot of time at the library. She would check out the maximum number of books to take home and read.

One of Shirley's favorite books was a biography of Benjamin Banneker who lived from 1731 to 1806. He was the son of a former slave and learned clock-making, astronomy, and mathematics. In the early days of the United States, Benjamin Banneker helped survey and plan Shirley's hometown, Washington, D.C. Like her hero, Shirley Ann Jackson was an African-American who refused to believe that prejudice could prevent her from doing great things. George and Beatrice Jackson gave their children the support and encouragement to reach their full potential. George liked to tell his children to "aim for the stars."

Shirley was an exceptionally bright student. Her teachers had to give her extra work so she wouldn't get bored in school. She loved her high school math classes and her teacher, Mrs. Marie Smith. Mrs. Smith was also African American and was an inspiration to Shirley as well as a wonderful teacher. Mrs. Smith was passionate about math as a way of seeing the world and making sense of it. Shirley Jackson shared her special teacher's passion.

One of the principals at Shirley's high school suggested that she go to college at Massachusetts Institute of Technology in Boston, one of the top schools in the world for the sciences. With two major scholarships and financial help from her church and her parents, Shirley arrived at MIT in September 1964. Out of about 900 students in her freshman class, only 43 were women. And there was only one other female African American student.

Shirley excelled in her college classes as she had in school. At MIT, she was able to delve into her favorite subjects and discover new realms of science. But living day by day with the prejudices of students and even teachers meant that MIT was not a warm, welcoming home for Shirley. For strength and support, she had to seek more than what the MIT community was willing to give her. In the quiet of her dorm room, Shirley often read the Bible. She found friendship with African American women from other universities in the area. She spent weekends with their families that lived in Boston. She volunteered in the children's ward of the Boston City Hospital. She tutored high school students in math and science at the YMCA.

As Shirley approached graduation from MIT, she knew she wanted to continue her education in graduate school. She applied to several different universities and was accepted by all of them. In April of 1968, she visited the University of Pennsylvania at the invitation of the graduate school. She saw the campus and met the physics research staff. As Shirley rode to the airport to fly back to Boston, she heard terrible news on the radio: Martin Luther King Jr. had been shot and killed. When Shirley was in high school, King had delivered his most famous speech, "I Have a Dream," in her hometown of Washington D.C. Suddenly, he was gone, and his dream that his children, "will one day live in a nation where they will not be judged by the color

MIT Campus

of their skin but by the content of their character," was left in the hands of those whom he had taught. Shirley was deeply shaken at the news.

By the time Shirley got back to her dorm room at MIT, she had decided where she would attend graduate school. She would stay at MIT to carry on Martin Luther King Jr.'s dream, working to make it a better place for minority students. When she began graduate school in the fall of 1968, she got right to work—studying theoretical physics and taking action to help other young minority scientists have more opportunities and a better experience at MIT.

Shirley Ann Jackson's perseverance paid off. She was the first African American woman to receive a Ph.D. from Massachusetts Institute of Technology. Her parents, sister Gloria, and her high school math teacher, Marie Smith, were there to watch her become Dr. Shirley Ann Jackson.

Shirley Ann Jackson has worked at many important jobs in the field of physics. She has worked for large companies and taught at the university level. In 1985 the governor of New Jersey asked her to be a founding member of the New Jersey Commission on Science and Technology. The purpose of the commission was to increase research and investment in scientific areas that would help the New Jersey economy. She served under three different Governors for a total of ten years. In 1994 President Bill Clinton asked Shirley Ann Jackson to become the first woman and the first African American to chair the Federal government's Nuclear Regulatory Commission. The NRC is responsible to make sure that nuclear power plants across the country are safe and nuclear materials are handled properly. Her knowledge of science and experience in many types of work helped her succeed in this important government position. In 1999 Shirley Ann Jackson became the president of Rensselaer Polytechnic Institute, one of the United States' oldest universities that focuses on science and engineering.

Shirley Ann Jackson at Rensselaer

When Shirley Ann Jackson faced cruel rejection when she asked to study with her classmates, simply because of the color of her skin, she had to choose how she would respond. She could have shown cruelty in return. She could have harbored anger and bitterness. She could have left MIT, saving herself the pain and letting the prejudiced students win. But she believed in another way. When she was a girl, her father taught her, "You can't control everybody else, and you can't control the world and everything that happens, but you can have your greatest control—and certainly your greatest influence—by how you control yourself." Shirley Ann Jackson responded with perseverance. That perseverance opened for Shirley a world of opportunities and a chance to make a difference. She has given many students the gift of knowledge in math and science, developed technologies that impact daily life, made the world safer, and helped give other minority scientists the chance to dream. All because she refused to give up.

The First Long Distance Telephone Call
Thomas A. Watson

Thomas A. Watson (1854-1934) was Alexander Graham Bell's assistant. Together they experimented, struggled, and succeeded in inventing the telephone. On October 17, 1913, Thomas A. Watson gave a speech entitled, "The Birth and Babyhood of the Telephone" at the Third Annual Convention of the Telephone Pioneers of America. As he began his speech, he said, "I shall ask you . . . to be indulgent if I show how proud and glad I am that I was chosen . . . to be the associate of Alexander Graham Bell, to work side by side with him day and night through all these wonderful happenings that have meant so much to the world." In the following portion of the speech, Watson describes the first long distance telephone call, made by Bell in Boston to Watson in Cambridge, Massachusetts. He refers to the newly invented telephone as "the baby."

Progress was rapid, and on October 9, 1876, we got ready to take the baby outdoors for the first time. We got permission from the Walworth Manufacturing Company to use their private [telegraph] wire running from Boston to Cambridge, about two miles long. I went to Cambridge that evening with one of our best telephones, and waited until Bell signaled from the Boston office on the Morse sounder. Then I cut out the sounder and connected in the telephone and listened. Not a murmur came through! Could it be that, although the thing worked all right in the house, it wouldn't work under practical line conditions? I knew that we were using the most complex and delicate electric current that had ever been employed for a practical purpose and that it was extremely "intense," for Bell had talked through a circuit composed of 20 or 30 human beings joined hand to hand. Could it be, I thought, that these high tension vibrations leaking off at each insulator along the line, had vanished completely before they reached the Charles River?

Thomas Watson

That fear passed through my mind as I worked over the instrument, adjusting it and tightening the wires in the binding posts, without improving matters in the least. Then the thought struck me that perhaps there was another Morse sounder in some other room. I traced the wires from the place they entered the building and sure enough I found a relay with a high resistance coil in the circuit. I cut it out with a piece of wire across the binding posts and rushed back to my telephone and listened. That was the trouble. Plainly as one could wish came Bell's "ahoy," "ahoy!" I ahoyed back, and the first long distance telephone conversation began.

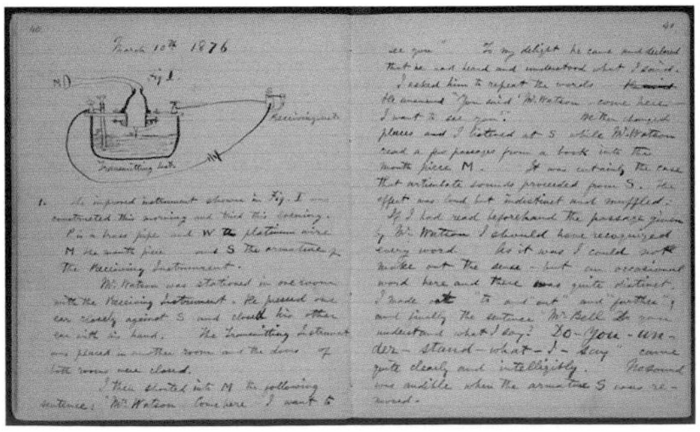

Bell's Laboratory Notebook About the Development of the Telephone

Skeptics had been objecting that the telephone could never compete with the telegraph as its messages would not be accurate. For this reason Bell had arranged that we should make a record of all we said and heard that night, if we succeeded in talking at all. We carried out this plan and the entire conversation was published in parallel columns in the next morning's *Advertiser,* as the latest startling scientific achievement. Infatuated with the joy of talking over an actual telegraph wire, we kept up our conversation until long after midnight. It was a very happy boy that traveled back to Boston in the small hours with the telephone under his arm done up in a newspaper. Bell had taken his record to the newspaper office and was not at the laboratory when I arrived there, but when he came in there ensued a jubilation and war dance that elicited next morning from our landlady, who wasn't at all scientific in her tastes, the remark that we'd have to vacate if we didn't make less noise nights.

Bell (front right) and Watson (behind him) celebrate the 40th anniversary of the telephone at the home of the National Geographic Society.

The House by the Side of the Road

Sam Walter Foss

This is a favorite American poem by New Hampshire native Sam Walter Foss (1858-1911). Foss authored many poems in his lifetime, published in newspapers and magazines and collected into volumes. Foss was a journalist with several Massachusetts newspapers and served as the librarian of the Somerville Public Library of Somerville, Massachusetts, from 1898 until his death.

There are hermit souls that live withdrawn
In the peace of their self-content;
There are souls, like stars, that dwell apart,
In a fellowless firmament;
There are pioneer souls that blaze their paths
Where highways never ran;
But let me live by the side of the road
And be a friend to man.

Let me live in a house by the side of the road,
Where the race of men go by,
The men who are good
  and the men who are bad,
As good and as bad as I.
I would not sit in the scorner's seat,
Or hurl the cynic's ban;
Let me live in a house by the side of the road
And be a friend to man.

I see from my house by the side of the road,
By the side of the highway of life,
The men who press with the ardor of hope,
The men who are faint with the strife.
But I turn not away
  from their smiles nor their tears,
Both parts of an infinite plan;
Let me live in my house
  by the side of the road
And be a friend to man.

I know there are brook-gladdened
  meadows ahead
And mountains of wearisome height;
That the road passes on
  through the long afternoon
And stretches away to the night.
But still I rejoice when the travelers rejoice,
And weep with the strangers that moan.
Nor live in my house by the side of the road
Like a man who dwells alone.

Let me live in my house
  by the side of the road
Where the race of men go by;
They are good, they are bad,
  they are weak, they are strong,
Wise, foolish—so am I.
Then why should I sit in the scorner's seat,
Or hurl the cynic's ban?
Let me live in my house
  by the side of the road
And be a friend to man.

New York Subway Opened

This article about the opening of New York City's famous subway appeared in the Daily Capital Journal *of Salem, Oregon, on October 27, 1904. The New York subway is now managed by the Metropolitan Transportation Authority, a corporation chartered by the state of New York for the public benefit. MTA is a network of buses, subways, and commuter railways that serves a population of 15 million people. MTA's bus fleet is the largest in the nation, and it has more subway and rail cars than all the rest of the nation's subways and commuter rails combined. This mass transit system saves 17 million metric tons of pollutants, which would be emitted if MTA's 2.5 billion annual passenger-trips were taken by car.*

The Rapid Transit Railway, the subway, as it is popularly known, and the most colossal undertaking of its kind in the world's history, was formally opened today with imposing ceremonies. The exercises took place under the point auspices of the Interborough company and the board of aldermen. In City Hall Park, were the great downtown terminal is located, and where the first spadeful of earth was turned, the principal ceremonies of the day took place shortly before noon. The park and city hall were lavishly decorated.

Bishop Potter opened the ceremonies with prayer, and was followed by an address by Alexander E. Orr, president of the Rapid Transit commission, who turned the subway over to the city. Mayor McClellan accepted the trust, and then turned the road over to August Belmont, president of the Interborough Company, who also made a brief address. Archbishop Farley closed the ceremonies.

At 1 o'clock the first train was started over the road, operated by Mayor McClellan in person. Bands of music were stationed at all the principal stops along the route. Included among the passengers on the first train were the city officials, officials of the Interborough Company, a large party of distinguished engineers and other invited guests. Promptly at midnight the road will be opened to the general public. That part of the road that will be operated for the present includes the whole of the main line from City Hall Park to the Harlem River to traffic within a month or so, and also the east side branch to the Bronx.

The great subway today consists of 21 miles of railroad under the city's teeming streets. The actual work of construction has taken just four years and the cost has exceeded $50,000,000. When the entire system is complete it will enable one to travel from the limits of Brooklyn to the northernmost end of Manhattan entirely underground.

A dazzling array of facts and figures tell the story of the building of the mammoth underground road. For instance, more than

3,000,000 cubic yards of dirt and rock were blasted and dug from the streets of the crowded city. To tear away the rock, 900,000 pounds of dynamite were used. Eleven thousand men were employed in the work . . . .

It is estimated that the road will carry 115,000,000 passengers a year. The fare is 5 cents. When the extension to Brooklyn, under the East River, has been completed, it is estimated that the road will carry 200,000,000 passengers a year.

Express trains will run through the subway at the rate of a mile a minute for the benefit of the long hauls from the Bronx to the busiest sections of the city below Fourteenth Street. Local trains will stop at all of the underground stations, every half dozen blocks along the route. The tunnel is ventilated by a system of electric fans, and illuminated the entire route by incandescent lights.

A trip through the great tunnel is all that is necessary to convince one of its entire security. White enameled bricks wall up the sides to a bricked arch overhead. Everything else is of stone and steel and heavy plate glass at the stations to let the light in from the street overhead. It would seem impossible for a disaster to occur where everything is as new and strong and perfect, apparently, as it is within the power of man to contrive. The pneumatic block system is pronounced by experts to be the most wonderful thing of its kind in the world, and it is calculated to make collisions impossible.

The cars have steel bottoms, copper-sheathed sides, and there is very little wood in their construction. The lighting system is entirely separate from the power plant that will move the trains by means of the third rail.

The route of the main line is up Fourth Avenue to Forty-Second Street, then up Broadway until One Hundred and Fourth Street is reached. There it branches into two sections. The first continues straight out Broadway to Kingsbridge, a distance of more than 14 miles from Battery Park. The second section runs east, cutting off a solid rock corner of Central Park, then north through Lenox Avenue and on to the borough of the Bronx.

My Father
Theodore Roosevelt

In this excerpt from Theodore Roosevelt's autobiography, he recalls his father's acts of kindness and service in their community. Roosevelt's description of a man as a "Bull Mooser" refers to the Progressive (or Bull Moose) political party, which Theodore Roosevelt supported at the time he wrote his autobiography.

My father worked hard at his business, for he died when he was forty-six, too early to have retired. He was interested in every social reform movement, and he did an immense amount of practical charitable work himself. He was a big, powerful man, with a leonine face, and his heart filled with gentleness for those who needed help or protection, and with the possibility of much wrath against a bully or an oppressor. . . . When in the city on Thanksgiving or Christmas, my father was very apt to drive my mother and a couple of friends up to the racing park to take lunch. But he was always back in time to go to the dinner at the Newsboys' Lodging-House, and not infrequently also to Miss Sattery's Night School for little Italians.

Theodore Roosevelt Sr.

At a very early age we children were taken with him and were required to help. He was a staunch friend of Charles Loring Brace, and was particularly interested in the Newsboys' Lodging-House and in the night schools and in getting the children off the streets and out on farms in the West. When I was President, the Governor of Alaska under me, Governor Brady, was one of these ex-newsboys who had been sent from New York out West by Mr. Brace and my father.

My father was greatly interested in the societies to prevent cruelty to children and cruelty to animals. On Sundays he had a mission class. On his way to it he used to drop us children at our Sunday-school in Dr. Adams's Presbyterian Church on Madison Square; I remember hearing my aunt, my mother's sister, saying that when he walked along with us children he always reminded her of Greatheart in Bunyan. Under the spur of his example I taught a mission class myself for three years before going to college and for all four years that I was in college. I do not think I made much of a success of it. But the other day on getting out of a taxi in New York the chauffeur spoke to me and told me that he was one of my old Sunday-school pupils. I remembered him well, and was much pleased to find that he was an ardent Bull Mooser!

To Love and Care for Our Neighbor: The Story of Danny Thomas

Bethany Poore

Danny Thomas was in Peoria, Illinois, making another speech to raise money for the children's hospital he planned to build in Memphis, Tennessee. He had spoken to thousands of people, sometimes to hundreds at once, and sometimes in one-on-one conversations. But something happened that made this night stand out from the many others like it. Danny heard a small voice call his name. A young boy looked up to him and said, "Hey, Danny Thomas. I want to help the poor sick kids." The boy handed Danny an envelope with two coins inside, a half dollar and a quarter. Danny learned the boy's name was Billy Johnson. Billy had cerebral palsy and was blind and partially deaf. This generous young boy, who suffered so much himself, made a lasting impression on Danny's heart.

Danny Thomas was born on January 6, 1912, in Deerfield, Michigan. His parents were immigrants from Lebanon. He was the fifth of ten children; nine boys and one girl.

His family lived for a while in an apartment over a bakery owned by a Jewish widow named Mrs. Feldman. After working hard all day baking, selling, and delivering her goods, she would climb upstairs carrying two bags of unsold baked goods for Danny's family. Then she would sit for a while and tell stories. Young Danny absorbed not only the stories she told, but also the art of story-telling. He began telling stories himself. He was alert to all that happened around him and to the personalities of his neighbors of many backgrounds. He used all this real-life material to craft funny stories to entertain his family and friends. He even used story-telling to distract bullies from picking on him at school.

At age eleven, Danny started working part-time at a small theater, but not yet on the stage—he sold candy and soda from the aisles. But he relished being inside a theater every day, fascinated by the succession of professional comedians he saw perform. These men, he realized, were getting paid to tell stories! By the age of twelve, Danny was determined he would have a career in show business.

Danny Thomas in the 1930s

When he grew up, he looked for work in Detroit and finally successfully auditioned for a part on a radio show called "The Happy Hour Club." Soon a beautiful young Italian singer named Rose Marie Mantel joined the show. She and Danny began riding the streetcar together to and from work, and a few years later they began a marriage that lasted fifty-five years.

When Danny and Rose Marie were expecting their first baby, Danny was struggling to find enough work to support his family. The baby was coming very soon, and all Danny had to his name was seven dollars and eighty-five cents. He went to Mass as usual one Sunday and put his customary dollar in the collection box. The priest spoke about money needed for missionaries, and Danny impulsively gave another six dollars. He was stunned when he'd realized what he had done. He prayed, "Look, I've given my last seven bucks. I need it back tenfold because I've got a kid on the way and I have to pay a hospital bill." He went home with eighty-five cents.

The next morning, he got a call offering him a job acting in a skit for a Maytag washing machine sales convention. The pay was seventy-five dollars.

Eventually, Danny Thomas's career flourished. He would become known all over the world as a comedian and actor. He entertained troops in USO shows during World War II. He was a hit in movies and in the new venue of television. He starred in a show called *Make Room for Daddy* that ran for eleven years. He not only built his own successful career, he also helped many other entertainers forward in their own careers. He produced many successful television shows, including *The Dick Van Dyke Show* and *The Andy Griffith Show*. All his life, he continued to be a hit telling stories to live audiences.

Danny Thomas (left) with Jack Benny and Bob Hope

In the early 1950s, after he had become successful and widely known, Danny Thomas embarked on his most important life work. He began a project to build a hospital for children. One of Danny's mentors suggested the location: Memphis, Tennessee. Danny recruited friends and associates, building a base of support for his hospital. He also worked with the mayor of Memphis and local attorneys and businessmen. Soon Danny was traveling across the country to raise money for construction. Rose Marie often accompanied him. Many of their famous Hollywood friends enthusiastically joined the cause. People from all over the United States generously endorsed Danny's dream.

As fund-raising moved along, a Memphis doctor suggested to Danny that this hospital not be a regular children's hospital that treated children from the local area who had all kinds of illness, but a special research facility welcoming children from all over the country. This hospital would both treat children with serious illness and seek cures for those diseases, to save as many lives as possible. The hospital plans moved forward in this direction. By 1957, Danny Thomas and his supporters had raised $1.5 million dollars to build St. Jude Children's Research Hospital.

Fund-raising for construction was going well, but the cost of building would soon be dwarfed by the enormous day-to-day expenses of running the hospital. Danny Thomas was determined that at St. Jude, no family would ever pay for the medical care their children received. Danny had to think of a way to provide for the hospital's on-going support.

Considering this need, Danny remembered some of the last words his father had told him: never forget your heritage. Danny's mother was from the village of Becheri in Lebanon. She moved to Toledo, Ohio, with her parents when she was ten years old. His father emigrated from Becheri to Toledo as a nineteen-year-old bachelor. They met when Danny's mother was thirteen. Like the thousands of immigrants who adopted America as their home, they worked hard to make a living, raised a family, and found the better life they had come seeking.

Danny realized there were thousands of other grateful children of immigrants who had prospered in America. He wondered if the scattered second-generation Lebanese and Syrian immigrants would come together to unite behind a single cause: St. Jude Children's Research Hospital. He sought out Lebanese-Americans and Syrian-Americans in many different towns and cities and shared his dreams for the hospital. He told them that supporting the hospital was a way to repay "this great nation for the freedom it gave our parents and grandparents." Members of Danny's heritage quickly rallied behind him. One hundred representatives met in Chicago in 1957 to form an organization with the sole purpose of raising funds to keep St. Jude Children's Research Hospital operating. Danny Thomas wrote the preamble to the the group's constitution, which reads in part, "One hundred and one years ago, our people began a migration to the blessed shores of these United States of America, seeking the freedoms and opportunities won for us by our founding fathers.

"Therefore: We who are proud of our heritage . . . have formed a non-profit, non-sectarian, charitable corporation titled: ALSAC (American Lebanese Syrian Associated Charities) dedicated to the parable of the Good Samaritan, to love and care for our neighbor, regardless of color or creed. This dedication shall manifest itself in the maintenance of St. Jude Hospital, Memphis, Tennessee, which, in turn, is dedicated to the cure of leukemia and related blood diseases in children, absolutely free. In so doing, we shall serve God and our country and we shall serve the good names of our fathers and mothers who made possible our birth in America, the land of the free."

St. Jude Children's Research Hospital was dedicated on February 4, 1962. Danny Thomas stayed very involved with the hospital for the rest of his life. He continued to donate money and solicit donations from others. He received the Congressional Gold Medal for his work with St. Jude, presented by President Ronald Reagan in a White House ceremony in April 1985, with Danny Thomas's entire family and the St. Jude Board of Directors present. Danny Thomas traveled from the White House directly to St. Jude to share the medal with the people who had helped him receive it.

St. Jude Children's Research Hospital, Memphis, Tennessee

Danny Thomas died on February 6, 1991, two days after celebrating St. Jude's 29th anniversary at the hospital with patients, parents, and staff. Rose Marie died in 2000. They are both buried in the Memorial Garden at St. Jude. Their three children, Marlo, Terre, and Tony, are strong supporters of St. Jude, carrying on their father's dream.

Many children of original members of ALSAC have joined the organization to continue their parents' mission to fully support St. Jude. ALSAC is one of the most successful charities in American history. It carries full responsibility for the operating costs of St. Jude, which treats an average of 7,800 patients a year at a cost of $1.8 million per day. Most of these funds come from millions of private donors. St. Jude is a world-renowned facility that offers excellent treatment to seriously ill children and pioneers successful treatments and cures.

Danny Thomas brought together his own family, families that shared his heritage, and American families of every background behind one world-changing cause. He once said, "I'd rather have a million people give me a dollar than one give me a million. That way you've got a million people involved." Thanks to Danny Thomas, millions of Americans have had the opportunity to be involved in the mission of St. Jude: finding cures and saving children's lives.

Work, Study, Exercise, and Play
Theodore Roosevelt

Theodore Roosevelt wrote these letters while he was President to his son Kermit, who was at a boarding school.

White House, Oct. 2, 1903
Dear Kermit,

I was very glad to get your letter. Am glad you are playing football. I should be very sorry to see either you or Ted devoting most of your attention to athletics, and I haven't got any special ambition to see you shine overmuch in athletics at college, at least (if you go there), because I think it tends to take up too much time; but I do like to feel that you are manly and able to hold your own in rough, hardy sports. I would rather have a boy of mine stand high in his studies than high in athletics, but I could a great deal rather have him show true manliness of character than show either intellectual or physical prowess; and I believe you and Ted both bid fair to develop just such character.

There! you will think this a dreadfully preaching letter! I suppose I have a natural tendency to preach just at present because I am overwhelmed with my work. I enjoy being President, and I like to do the work and have my hand on the lever. But it is very worrying and puzzling, and I have to make up my mind to accept every kind of attack and misrepresentation. It is a great comfort to me to read the life and letters of Abraham Lincoln. I am more and more impressed every day, not only with the man's wonderful power and sagacity, but with his literally endless patience, and at the same time his unflinching resolution.

White House, June 21, 1904
Dear Kermit,

We spent today at the Knoxes'. It is a beautiful farm—just such a one as you could run. Phil Knox, as capable and efficient as he is diminutive, amused Mother and me greatly by the silent way in which he did in first-rate way his full share of all the work.

Tomorrow the National Convention meets, and barring a cataclysm I shall be nominated. There is a great deal of sullen grumbling, but it has taken more the form of resentment against what they think is my dictation as to details than against me personally. They don't dare to oppose me for the nomination and I suppose it is hardly likely the attempt will be made to stampede the Convention for any one. How the election will turn out no man can tell. Of course I hope to be elected, but I realize to the full how very lucky I have been, not only to be President but to have been able to accomplish so much while President, and whatever may be the outcome, I am not only content but very sincerely thankful for all the good fortune I have had. From Panama down I have been able to accomplish certain things which will be of lasting importance in our history. Incidentally, I don't think that any family has ever enjoyed the White House more than we have. I was thinking about it just this morning when Mother and I took breakfast on the portico and afterwards walked about the lovely grounds and looked at the stately historic old house. It is a wonderful privilege to have been here and to have been given the chance to do this work, and I should regard myself as having a small and mean mind if in the event of defeat I felt soured at not having had more instead of being thankful for having had so much.

Kermit Roosevelt and Theodore Roosevelt

White House, November 19, 1905
Dear Kermit,

I sympathize with every word you say in your letter, about *Nicholas Nickleby*, and about novels generally. Normally I only care for a novel if the ending is good, and I quite agree with you that if the hero has to die he ought to die worthily and nobly, so that our sorrow at the tragedy shall be tempered with the joy and pride one always feels when a man does his duty well and bravely. There is quite enough sorrow and shame and suffering and baseness in real life, and there is no need for meeting it unnecessarily in fiction. As Police Commissioner it was my duty to deal with all kinds of squalid misery and hideous and unspeakable infamy, and I should have been worse than a coward if I had shrunk from doing what was necessary; but there would have been no use whatever in my reading novels detailing all this misery and squalor and crime, or at least in reading them as a steady thing. Now and then there is a powerful but sad story which really is interesting and which really does good; but normally the books which do good and the books which healthy people find interesting are those which are not in the least of the sugar-candy variety, but which, while portraying foulness and suffering when they must be portrayed, yet have a joyous as well as a noble side.

We have had a very mild and open fall. I have played tennis a good deal, the French Ambassador being now quite a steady playmate, as he and I play about alike; and I have ridden with Mother a great deal. Last Monday when Mother had gone to New York I had Selous, the great African hunter, to spend the day and night. He is a perfect old dear; just as simple and natural as can be and very interesting. I took him, with Bob Bacon, Gifford Pinchot, Ambassador Meyer and Jim Garfield, for a good scramble and climb in the afternoon, and they all came to dinner afterwards. Before we came down to dinner I got him to spend three-quarters of an hour in telling delightfully exciting lion and hyena stories to Ethel, Archie and Quentin. He told them most vividly and so enthralled the little boys that the next evening I had to tell them a large number myself.

Today is Quentin's birthday and he loved his gifts, perhaps most of all the weest, cunningest live pig you ever saw, presented him by Straus. Phil Stewart and his wife and boy, Wolcott (who is Archie's age), spent a couple of nights here. One afternoon we had hide-and-go-seek, bringing down Mr. Garfield and the Garfield boys, and Archie turning up with the entire football team, who took a day off for the special purpose. We had obstacle races, hide-and-go-seek, blind-man's buff, and everything else; and there were times when I felt that there was a perfect shoal of small boys bursting in every direction up and down stairs, and through and over every conceivable object.

Mother and I still walk around the grounds every day after breakfast. The gardens, of course, are very, very disheveled now, the snap-dragons holding out better than any other flowers.

The Teacher's Dream
William Henry Venable

William Henry Venable (1836-1920) was a native of Ohio. He was a teacher, principal, author, and speaker. He authored twenty-two textbooks and two volumes of poetry. "The Teacher's Dream" is his best-known poem.

The weary teacher sat alone
While twilight gathered on:
And not a sound was heard around,—
The boys and girls were gone.

The weary teacher sat alone;
Unnerved and pale was he;
Bowed 'neath a yoke of care, he spoke
In sad soliloquy:

"Another round, another round
Of labor thrown away,
Another chain of toil and pain
Dragged through a tedious day.

"Of no avail is constant zeal,
Love's sacrifice is lost.
The hopes of morn, so golden, turn,
Each evening, into dross.

"I squander on a barren field
My strength, my life, my all:
The seeds I sow will never grow,—
They perish where they fall."

He sighed, and low upon his hands
His aching brow he pressed;
And o'er his frame ere long there came
A soothing sense of rest.

And then he lifted up his face,
But started back aghast,—
The room, by strange and sudden change,
Assumed proportions vast.

It seemed a Senate-hall, and one
Addressed a listening throng;
Each burning word all bosoms stirred,
Applause rose loud and long.

The 'wildered teacher thought he knew
The speaker's voice and look,
"And for his name," said he, "the same
Is in my record book."

The stately Senate-hall dissolved,
A church rose in its place,
Wherein there stood a man of God,
Dispensing words of grace.

And though he spoke in solemn tone,
And though his hair was gray,
The teacher's thought
was strangely wrought—
"I whipped that boy to-day."

The church, a phantom, vanished soon;
What saw the teacher then?
In classic gloom of alcoved room
An author plied his pen.

"My idlest lad!" the teacher said,
Filled with a new surprise;
"Shall I behold his name enrolled
Among the great and wise?"

The vision of a cottage home
The teacher now descried;
A mother's face illumed the place
Her influence sanctified.

"A miracle! a miracle!
This matron, well I know,
Was but a wild and careless child,
Not half an hour ago.

"And when she to her children speaks
Of duty's golden rule,
Her lips repeat in accents sweet,
My words to her at school."

The scene was changed again, and lo!
The schoolhouse rude and old;
Upon the wall did darkness fall,
The evening air was cold.

"A dream!" the sleeper, waking, said,
Then paced along the floor,
And, whistling slow and soft and low,
He locked the schoolhouse door.

And, walking home, his heart was full
Of peace and trust and praise;
And singing slow and soft and low,
Said, "After many days."

Mt. Hope School in Scioto County, Ohio, was used from 1882 to 1936.

The Open-Hearted and Courageous Way: The Story of Marian Anderson

Bethany Poore

The judges sat alone in the balcony while hundreds of contestants with their teachers and accompanists filled the auditorium below. Click-click, click-click, click-click. With their clicker, the judges moved quickly through the auditions. If the judges were not impressed with what they heard, the loud clicking burst from the balcony, signaling the performer to stop immediately and leave the stage in humiliation.

Marian Anderson sat next to her voice teacher Giuseppe Boghetti in the sea of nervous performers awaiting their turn. She was contestant 44A. At least six times as she waited, she heard other singers begin, "O mio Fernando," the song she had prepared, only to be rudely stopped soon after beginning. Boghetti leaned over to whisper, "Whatever happens, do not let that clicker stop you. They must hear you sing the ending!" The song ended with a difficult trill, perfect for showing off the range and power of Marian's voice.

When "44A" was called, Marian made it onto the stage, closed her eyes, and sang. One part of her mind waited to hear, as she later called it, "the voice of doom upstairs." She knew she could not go on if the judges responded to her performance with the awful click-click, click-click, click-click.

But she sang the song to the end with no interruption from the balcony. A voice from the balcony called down, "Does 44A have another song?" Even her fellow auditioners broke into applause. This would not be the only time in her life that Marian Anderson's voice made people stop and listen.

Marian Anderson won the National Music League contest. The prize was a chance to perform as a soloist with the New York Philharmonic Orchestra at Lewisohn Stadium, a huge outdoor amphitheater in New York City. The concert on August 26, 1925, was attended by 7,500 people, including Marian's entire family and many friends who traveled from Philadelphia to share her triumphant night.

Marian Anderson grew up in a Philadelphia neighborhood with Irish, Italian, and Jewish immigrants and black families that had moved from the South to find jobs. She was born on February 27, 1897, to Anna and John Anderson, who took care of his family by selling ice and coal. Marian had two younger sisters, Alyse and Ethel May. Her family attended the all-black Union Baptist Church, where John Anderson was head usher.

Philadelphia, c.1897

When Marian was twelve years old, her father died after being injured in a work accident. Anna Anderson and her daughters moved in with her in-laws. Anna took in laundry and later found a job cleaning at the Wanamaker's Department Store to support her family. Marian and her sisters helped by running errands and delivering laundry. They scrubbed their neighbors' front steps to earn five or ten cents.

At the age of six, Marian joined the junior choir at church, where her Aunt Mary sang in the senior choir. Aunt Mary began to take young Marian to local events and fund-raisers. Marian would perform a song or two and earn twenty-five or fifty cents. Aunt Mary had flyers printed with the advertisement, "Come and hear the baby contralto, ten years old."

While still a girl, Marian was invited to join the hundred-member People's Chorus, drawn from the choirs of black churches all over Philadelphia. The director had Marian stand on a chair to sing her solos. When she was old enough, she joined the senior choir at Union Baptist Church, while continuing to sing in the junior choir. She also continued to sing at public events, and her fees rose to one, two, and eventually five dollars. Invitations kept coming. Marian began to dream of a career doing what she had always loved best: singing.

When a well-known tenor named Roland Hayes first heard Marian Anderson sing, he immediately recognized her gift and urged her to get professional training. The Anderson family did not have money for voice lessons, but their church family committed to paying the tuition to the music school Marian wanted to attend.

Marian lined up with other prospective students to enroll in the school. When her turn came, the woman at the desk looked right past her. One by one she helped those behind Marian in line. Only when everyone else had been helped did she acknowledge Marian with, "What do you want?" When Marian asked for an application form, the lady answered icily, "We don't take colored." Marian was shocked. The woman's cruelty made her feel physically sick. Crushed, she asked herself, "Can't I sing? Can't I be a singer because I'm colored?"

Through a family friend, Marian met a well-known black soprano named Mary Saunders Patterson. She lived only a few blocks away and gave Marian voice lessons free of charge. She next studied with Agnes Reifsnyder, and then Giuseppe Boghetti. At first Boghetti declared that he was too busy and wanted no new student. Finally he was reluctantly persuaded to hear her sing one song. After hearing her sing "Deep River" he enthusiastically took her on as a student. Again, since the Anderson family had no extra money for voice lessons, the Union Baptist Church held a benefit concert to support their faithful choir member and soloist. Marian studied with Boghetti for several years.

Meanwhile, Marian continued to grow in demand as a performer. Her circuit grew to concerts out of town and out of state. She teamed up with a pianist named Billy King. Together they performed at black churches and colleges, theaters, and concert halls. They evenly split $100 for each appearance. Over time, as she saved what she could, Marian was able to help her mother buy a house across the street from her grandparents' house. For the first time since her father died when Marian was twelve years old, her family had their own home.

Eventually, Marian was earning enough that she persuaded her mother to quit her job at Wanamaker's Department Store. Marian remembered, "One of the things that made me happiest in my life was that I could tell Mother, who worked hard every day, that she didn't have to work anymore." She called her mother's supervisor herself.

Marian spent a great deal of time in Europe in the 1930s, performing and developing her vocal technique. She was a dazzling success. She traveled to all corners of the continent, performing in nearly every major city. People flocked to hear this beautiful young American woman with a marvelous, unforgettable voice. A famous conductor named Arturo Toscanini told her, "A voice like yours is heard once in a hundred years."

She returned to the United States with a strong reputation as a performer. Her career was in full swing, and she performed in all parts of the country. Americans who lived far from concert halls were able to hear her sing by way of radio broadcasts. She held audiences spellbound with her moving, powerful performances of classical songs and negro spirituals.

Marian Anderson was invited to sing at the White House for President and Mrs. Franklin D. Roosevelt in 1936. As she continued her annual concert tours, demand for tickets increased. Concerts in Washington, D.C., sponsored by the local Howard University, were a regular part of her concert tour. Year by year, Howard University had to change to larger venues to accommodate public demand to hear Marian Anderson.

Washington D.C.'s largest auditorium is Constitution Hall, built in 1929 as part of the headquarters of the Daughters of the American Revolution (DAR). The DAR is a patriotic organization of women who have at least one ancestor who participated in the Revolutionary War. Constitution Hall was used for DAR events and rented out for major performances. When Howard University applied for use of the hall for their annual Marian Anderson concert, they received a firm no. In 1932, the DAR had enacted a policy that only white performers were eligible to perform in Constitution Hall. The university decided to challenge the DAR. They were joined by other national leaders who stood for Marian Anderson and against prejudice. Among them was first lady Eleanor Roosevelt, a member of the DAR. She resigned from the organization in protest of their policy and their treatment of Marian Anderson. Her firm public stand was big news across the United States.

February 26, 1939.

My dear Mrs. Henry M. Robert, Jr.:

I am afraid that I have never been a very useful member of the Daughters of the American Revolution, so I know it will make very little difference to you whether I resign, or whether I continue to be a member of your organization.

However, I am in complete disagreement with the attitude taken in refusing Constitution Hall to a great artist. You have set an example which seems to me unfortunate, and I feel obliged to send in to you my resignation. You had an opportunity to lead in an enlightened way and it seems to me that your organization has failed.

I realize that many people will not agree with me, but feeling as I do this seems to me the only proper procedure to follow.

Very sincerely yours,

A Draft of Eleanor Roosevelt's Resignation Letter to the DAR

Marian Anderson's supporters were not only interested in protesting discrimination. They refused to let racism prevail and decided to take positive action. If the DAR would not give her space to perform, they would find another venue. Walter White, secretary of the NAACP (National Association for the Advancement of Colored People) and Marian Anderson's manager, Sol Hurok, discussed the idea of a free public outdoor concert at the Lincoln Memorial. Walter White spoke to Oscar Chapman, the assistant secretary of the Interior, since the Lincoln Memorial was under the jurisdiction of the Department of the Interior. Chapman went to his boss, Interior Secretary Harold L. Ickes. Ickes in turn went to his boss, President Franklin D. Roosevelt. What was his opinion? "I don't care if she sings from the top of the Washington Monument," the President declared, "as long as she sings."

Marian Anderson continued her concert tour and, as usual, left all concert arrangements to her manager. She was only vaguely aware of the controversy unfolding in Washington. On her way to a concert hall in San Francisco, she passed a newsstand where a newspaper headline announcing Eleanor Roosevelt's resignation from the DAR caught her eye. She was shocked that the dispute over her Washington concert had gone so far. Soon reporters everywhere she went were asking for her opinions on the controversy. She shied away from making public comments. By no choice of her own, Marian Anderson had become the center of the storm. When she was asked to give the concert at the Lincoln Memorial, it was not a quick or easy decision for her. She was not an activist, understanding she was not, as she put it, "designed for hand-to-hand combat." She felt compassion for the people at fault, graciously believing that their actions came from a lack of understanding. In the end, Marian Anderson decided to sing because she realized she had become a symbol, a representative of her people. As much as she disliked confrontation, her conscience told her she must sing. With Marian in agreement, the concert was announced for Easter Sunday, April 9, 1939.

Staging the "Freedom Concert" was an enormous feat, bringing together local and Federal officials on all levels and many volunteers. Police were enlisted to handle the expected enormous crowd. Programs were designed and printed. Sound technicians brought in microphones and amplifiers. Newspapers assigned reporters to cover the event. Boy Scouts were recruited to hand out programs. Eleanor Roosevelt and other supporters convinced radio stations to air a nationwide broadcast of the concert. Workers carried a grand piano up the steps of the Lincoln Memorial and set up a carpeted platform to seat 200 distinguished guests.

Marian Anderson left Philadelphia with her mother and sisters early Easter Sunday on the train to Washington. The former governor of Pennsylvania, Gifford Pinchot, lived in Washington and had invited them to stay in his home. Shortly before the 5:00 p.m. concert, Marian and her accompanist, Kosti Vehanen, were taken by limousine with motorcycle escort to the Lincoln Memorial. They were escorted to a small room beside the statue of Lincoln. There they met Interior Secretary Ickes, who talked through the program with them. And then, already, it was time for the concert to begin.

New York Congresswoman Caroline Day and Assistant Secretary Oscar Chapman led Marian Anderson to her seat on the platform, where she joined her mother and sisters, government officials, and many prominent supporters. Harold L. Ickes introduced her to the crowd with a speech about racial equality and an expression of thanks to Marian Anderson.

Marian Anderson's accompanist remembered later, "She looked regal and dignified as she came forward with slow steps." She walked to the large cluster of microphones positioned in the curve of the piano. She wrote later, "There seemed to be people as far as the eye could see. The crowd stretched in a great semicircle from the Lincoln Memorial around the reflecting pool on to the shaft of the Washington Monument. I had a feeling that a great wave of good will poured out from these people, almost engulfing me." As Kosti Vehanen played the opening notes, Marian Anderson looked at 75,000 hushed, expectant faces. Closing her eyes, she began, "My country 'tis of thee, Sweet land of liberty, To thee we sing."

When America stopped to listen to Marian Anderson sing on the steps of the Lincoln Memorial, it took a step toward freedom and equality. Even the Daughters of the American Revolution learned something from what happened that Easter Sunday. A few years after the controversy, World War II brought the country together in a united cause. The DAR organized a series of fundraising concerts for war relief to be held at Constitution Hall. They asked Marian Anderson to give the first concert. In her newspaper column "My Day," Eleanor Roosevelt wrote, "Last night I attended the Marian Anderson concert, given for Chinese relief. As every seat was filled in Constitution Hall, I am quite sure

Marian Anderson sings at the Lincoln Memorial.

Secretary Harold Ickes congratulates Marian Anderson after her performance at the Lincoln Memorial.

it was a successful financial undertaking. Miss Anderson's program was beautiful and she was certainly most enthusiastically received. It was a significant evening not only from the artistic point of view but from the social point of view."

Marian Anderson continued her singing career, continuing to touch a worldwide audience. In the 1950s, she toured as a goodwill ambassador with the U.S. State Department and served as a delegate to the United Nations. In 1957, she sang at the inauguration of president Dwight D. Eisenhower and in 1961 at the inauguration of John F. Kennedy. Marian Anderson concluded her professional singing career with a farewell tour in 1964–1965. For the site of the first concert on the tour, she chose Constitution Hall in Washington, D.C. When reporters asked about her feelings toward the organization, Marian Anderson said, "I forgave the DAR many years ago. You lose a lot of time hating people."

Eleanor Roosevelt and Marian Anderson in Japan, 1953

After she retired from touring professionally, Marian Anderson continued to serve in her community, support young musicians, and to sing. Her sister Ethel's son, James DePriest, became an accomplished orchestral conductor. He and Marian Anderson performed together several times. On July 4, 1976, America's 200th birthday, she sang at the Independence Day celebration in her hometown of Philadelphia. She lived her later years on her farm in Danbury, Connecticut. She died on April 8, 1993.

A few years later, in an interview celebrating the 100th anniversary of Marian Anderson's birth, James DePriest said of his Aunt Marian, "I think we all fight the battles that need to be fought in different ways, and she had hoped the dignity of her personhood would be an example that would break many barriers as, indeed, was the case."

On January 27, 2005, the United States Postal Service issued a Marian Anderson stamp to commemorate her contributions to music and her country. The United States Postal Service asked the Daughters of the American Revolution to host the ceremony to introduce the stamp. The stamp was unveiled at Constitution Hall in Washington, D.C. by DAR President General Presley Wagoner, Deputy Postmaster General John Nolan, and Marian Anderson's nephew James DePriest.

Marian Anderson's autobiography, *My Lord, What a Morning*, published in 1956, concludes, "There are many persons ready to do what is right because in their hearts they know it is right. But they hesitate, waiting for the other fellow to make the first move—and he, in turn, waits for you. The minute a person whose word means a great deal dares to take the open-hearted and courageous way, many others follow. Not everyone can be turned aside from meanness and hatred, but the great majority of Americans is heading in that direction. I have a great belief in the future of my people and my country."

Vermont's Old Constitution House

Windsor Tavern, owned by Elijah West, on Main Street in the town of Windsor, Vermont, was the site of many discussions about the formation of "The Free and Independent State of Vermont." On July 8, 1777, delegates adopted Vermont's first state constitution there. Fourteen years later Vermont joined the United States as the 14th state. Windsor Tavern functioned as a tavern until 1848 and was subsequently used as a store and manufacturing facility. Around 1870 it was moved to a side street and used as an apartment house and then a warehouse. In 1901 people began efforts to preserve the tavern, which became known as Old Constitution House. Supporters formed the Old Constitution House Association in 1911. The Association had raised enough money by 1914 to begin the restoration. The Old Constitution House Association managed a museum and public tea room in the house until 1961, when it transferred the house and its collections to the state of Vermont. The Old Constitution House is now part of the Vermont Division for Historic Preservation system of historic sites. The following article appeared in the Burlington Weekly Free Press *on April 11, 1912.*

Old Constitution House
Organization Effected to Preserve Historic Structure in Windsor
Bulletin, Just Issued, Says that Object Should Appeal to All Vermonters—What It Is Hoped to Accomplish.

The first bulletin of the recently organized "Old Constitution House Association" has just been issued.

The objects of the association are to acquire either by purchase or gift, in trust or otherwise, the building situated in the village and town of Windsor, commonly known as the "Old Constitution House," to acquire a site in the said town of Windsor upon which to place said building, to restore, maintain and preserve said structure as a historic relic in the said town of Windsor, and to devote the same to literary, historical and social uses and purposes under the management and control of said association, and in general to stimulate and foster a knowledge of the history of and patriotic feeling for the government and institutions of the State of Vermont.

Old Constitution House

Sherman Evarts of Windsor, who has had the laboring oar in organizing the association, has been elected president and there is a distinguished list of 14 vice-presidents, including two United States senators and five ex-governors. There are three classes of members, life, sustaining and annual. Life members are liable for no payments beyond the membership fee of $25. Sustaining members pay $5 annually and annual members $1 each year. President Taft has become a life member. F.B. Tracy of Windsor is the treasurer of the association.

Following are some extracts from the bulletin:

"The success of the association depends, obviously, upon a large and widely distributed membership. Its object should appeal to all Vermonters. If the membership consisted of 200 life members, 1,000 annual members and 500 sustaining members, this historic building could be maintained always with the dignity its character deserves. These numbers are by no means impossible of attainment, if those interested in the purpose of the association will cooperate as they are able towards its fulfillment.

"The present management has reason to be encouraged by the results of less than three months' efforts in bringing the matter of rescuing the "Constitution House" to the attention of the public. With continued and more systematic efforts in the same direction it may be possible to move the building upon a permanent site next July, one hundred and thirty-five years after the transactions took place which have made it famous."

The Purest Guardians of a National Shrine
John A. Washington

George Washington's great-grandnephew, John A. Washington, then owner of Mount Vernon, wrote this letter to Ann Pamela Cunningham of the Mount Vernon Ladies' Association in 1858, to communicate his willingness to sell the property to the Association.

Mount Vernon, March 13th, 1858
To A "Southern Matron"
Madam

Your letter of March 12th has been received in which you inform me that the bill providing for the purchase of Mount Vernon by Virginia, has been defeated in the House of Delegates—and in the name and on behalf of the Mount Vernon Association you renew your offer to purchase this place.

Heretofore I have only been willing to dispose of Mount Vernon to the United States or to Virginia as I believed that in the hands of one or the other it would be better protected and preserved than in the possession of any individual or association. The events of the past seven years however, seem to indicate that neither Virginia nor the United States wish to acquire the place.

Under the circumstances, and believing that after the two highest powers in our country the Women of the land will probably be the safest as they will certainly be the purest guardians of a national shrine, I am willing so far to comply with your request as to await for a seasonably limited period of time the propositions you may wish to make to me on behalf of the Association over which you preside. And I assure you that unless these proposals are inconsistent with what I believe to be my duties upon the occasion I shall be inclined to give them the most favorable consideration.

With assurances of the highest respect
I have the honor to be your obedient servant,
John A. Washington

Mount Vernon

North Head Lighthouse Officially Transferred to Washington State Parks

Washington State Parks and Recreation Commission

The Washington State Parks and Recreation Commission issued this press release on November 19, 2012.

The Washington State Parks and Recreation Commission announces the official transfer of ownership of the North Head Lighthouse to State Parks from the United States Coast Guard (USCG).

North Head Lighthouse at Cape Disappointment State Park in Pacific County recently was transferred to the ownership of State Parks after a nearly 19-year process between the USCG and State Parks. Congress approved the transfer of the lighthouse in 1993, however, lead-based paint contaminated soil around the lighthouse prevented the title transfer from occurring. Federal law requires any federal agency transferring real property out of federal ownership to be certified that all remedial action to protect human health and the environment has been taken. With soil cleanup and the transfer completed, State Parks now will be working to restore the 114-year-old lighthouse with the support of the Keepers of the North Head Lighthouse.

"The North Head Lighthouse is an icon and historical landmark. We are very thankful to now be the official caretakers and owners of this national treasure. And we look forward to the continued support and partnership of our friends' groups," said State Parks Director Don Hoch.

The Washington State Department of Ecology and State Parks proposed a plan to facilitate the cleanup. The plan was approved and work began in October 2011 to remove the lead-based paint contaminated soil. While the agencies worked through the clean-up and transfer process, the USCG and State Parks entered a lease agreement allowing State Parks to maintain and perform minor restoration work on the lighthouse. In 2009, the Keepers of the North Head Lighthouse formed and partnered with the Friends of the Columbia River Gateway and State Parks to restore the North Head Lighthouse. With funding tight for state parks, volunteers were interested in raising public awareness about the lighthouse and spearheading efforts to repair it. The Keepers of the North Head Lighthouse began raising funds and in-kind donations for lighthouse repair work through direct donations, merchandise sales, events and Lighthouse Environmental Program (LEP) grants in 2010 and 2011. With the title transfer official, the Keepers will to continue to apply for LEP funds to support future restoration efforts.

On May 16, 1898, the North Head Lighthouse was put into service as the primary navigational aid at the mouth of the Columbia River. The Cape Disappointment Lighthouse had served this function since 1856; however, ships continued to run aground at the "Graveyard of the Pacific." Due to the sheer number of shipwrecks, it was determined a second lighthouse was needed on the northwestern spur of Cape Disappointment, commonly referred to as North Head. With all of the original buildings associated with the station still standing, the North Head Lighthouse is the most intact lighthouse reservation in the Pacific Northwest.

The North Head Lighthouse is open for tours from May to September. Tours of the lighthouse lantern room are provided by State Parks volunteers. Hours for lantern room tours vary seasonally. Tour admission is $2.50 per adult and free for ages 7 to 17. . . .

Cape Disappointment State Park is a 1,882-acre camping park on the Long Beach Peninsula, fronted by the Pacific Ocean and lying along the Columbia River. The park offers two miles of ocean beach, two lighthouses, hiking trails and the Lewis and Clark Interpretive Center. As part of a larger art installation, the park also features the Confluence Project amphitheater, designed by world-renowned architect and artist, Maya Lin. . . .

The Commission manages a diverse system of more than 100 state parks and recreation programs, including long-distance trails, boating safety and winter recreation. The 99-year-old park system will celebrate its 100th anniversary in 2013.

North Head Lighthouse

Thoughts on Education
John Marshall

John Marshall, one of the few Americans to serve in all three branches of government, wrote the following letter to his grandson. He made a mistake dating the letter; it was written on December 7, 1834, near the end of his long tenure as Chief Justice of the United States Supreme Court.

Richmond, November 7th, 1834

My Dear Grandson,

I had yesterday the pleasure of receiving your letter of the 29th of November, and am quite pleased with the course of study you are pursuing. Proficiency in Greek and Latin is indispensable to an accomplished scholar, and may be of great real advantage in our progress through human life. Cicero deserves to be studied still more for his talents than for the improvement in language to be derived from reading him. He was unquestionably, with the single exception of Demosthenes, the greatest orator among the ancients. He was too a profound philosopher. His "*de officiis*" is among the most valuable treatises I have ever seen in the Latin language.

History is among the most essential departments of knowledge; and, to an American, the histories of England and of the United States are most instructive. Every man ought to be intimately acquainted with the history of his own country. Those of England and of the United States are so closely connected that the former seems to be introductory to the latter. They form one whole. Hume, as far as he goes, to the revolution of 1688, is generally thought the best Historian of England. Others have continued his narrative to a late period, and it will be necessary to read them also.

John Marshall

There is no exercise of the mind from which more valuable improvement is to be drawn than from composition. In every situation of life the result of early practice will be valuable. Both in speaking and writing, the early habit of arranging our thoughts with regularity, so as to point them to the object to be proved, will be of great advantage. In both, clearness and precision are most essential qualities. The man who by seeking embellishment hazards confusion, is greatly mistaken in what constitutes good writing. The meaning ought never to be mistaken. Indeed the readers should never be obliged to search for it. The writer should always express himself so clearly as to make it impossible to misunderstand him. He should be comprehended without an effort.

The first step towards writing and speaking clearly is to think clearly. Let the subject be perfectly understood, and a man will soon find words to convey his meaning to others. Blair, whose lectures are greatly and justly admired, advises a practice well worthy of being observed. It is to take a page of some approved writer and read it over repeatedly until the matter, not the words, be fully impressed on the mind. Then write, in your own language, the same matter. A comparison of the one with the other will enable you to remark and correct your own defects. This course may be pursued after having made some progress in composition. In the commencement, the student ought carefully to reperuse what he has written, correct, in the first instance, every error of orthography and grammar. A mistake in either is unpardonable. Afterwards revise and improve the language.

I am pleased with both your pieces of composition. The subjects are well chosen and of the deepest interest. Happiness is pursued by all, though too many mistake the road by which the greatest good is to be successfully followed. Its abode is not always in the palace or the cottage. Its residence is the human heart, and its inseparable companion is a quiet conscience. Of this, Religion is the surest and safest foundation. The individual who turns his thoughts frequently to an omnipotent omniscient and all perfect being, who feels his dependence on, and his infinite obligations to that being will avoid that course of life which must harrow up the conscience.

My love to your mother and the family,
Your affectionate Grandfather,
J. Marshall

Makers of the Flag
Franklin K. Lane

Franklin K. Lane was Secretary of the Interior under Woodrow Wilson. He was born on Prince Edward Island, Canada, in 1864 and moved to California with his family when he was still a boy. He became involved in civic life in many different ways in his adopted country of the United States. It was during his term as Secretary of the Interior that the National Park Service was created. He delivered this speech on June 14, 1914, to the approximately 5,000 employees of the Department of the Interior. He used the flag as a symbol to represent our country.

This morning, as I passed into the Land Office, The Flag dropped me a most cordial salutation, and from its rippling folds I heard it say: "Good morning, Mr. Flag Maker."

"I beg your pardon, Old Glory," I said, "aren't you mistaken? I am not the president of the United States, nor a member of Congress, nor even a general in the army. I am only a government clerk."

"I greet you again, Mr. Flag Maker," replied the gay voice, "I know you well. You are the man who worked in the swelter of yesterday straightening out the tangle of that farmer's homestead in Idaho, or perhaps you found the mistake in that Indian contract in Oklahoma, or helped to clear that patent for the hopeful inventor in New York, or pushed the opening of that new ditch in Colorado, or made that mine in Illinois more safe, or brought relief to the old soldier in Wyoming. No matter; whichever one of these beneficent individuals you may happen to be, I give you greeting, Mr. Flag Maker."

Franklin K. Lane

I was about to pass on, when The Flag stopped me with these words: "Yesterday the president spoke a word that made happier the future of ten million [laborers] in Mexico; but that act looms no larger on the flag than the struggle which the boy in Georgia is making to win the Corn Club prize this summer.

"Yesterday the Congress spoke a word which will open the door of Alaska; but a mother in Michigan worked from sunrise until far into the night, to give her boy an education. She, too, is making the flag.

"Yesterday we made a new law to prevent financial panics, and yesterday, maybe, a school teacher in Ohio taught his first letters to a boy who will one day write a song that will give cheer to the millions of our race. We are all making the flag."

"But," I said impatiently, "these people were only working."

Then came a great shout from The Flag:

"THE WORK that we do is the making of the flag." I am not the flag; not at all. I am but its shadow.

I am whatever you make me, nothing more.

I am your belief in yourself, your dream of what a people may become.

I live a changing life, a life of moods and passions, of heartbreaks and tired muscles.

Sometimes I am strong with pride, when men do an honest work, fitting the rails together truly.

Sometimes I droop, for then purpose has gone from me, and cynically I play the coward.

Sometimes I am loud, garish and full of that ego that blasts judgment.

But always I am all that you hope to be, and have the courage to try for.

I am song and fear, struggle and panic, and ennobling hope.

I am the day's work of the weakest man, and the largest dream of the most daring.

I am the Constitution and the courts, statutes and the statute makers, soldier and dreadnaught, drayman and street sweep, cook, counselor, and clerk.

I am the battle of yesterday, and the mistake of tomorrow.

I am the mystery of the men who do without knowing why.

I am the clutch of an idea, and the reasoned purpose of resolution.

I am no more than what you believe me to be and I am all that you believe I can be.

I am what you make me, nothing more.

I swing before your eyes as a bright gleam of color, a symbol of yourself, the pictured suggestion of that big thing which makes this Nation. My stars and my stripes are your dream and your labors. They are bright with cheer, brilliant with courage, firm with faith, because you have made them so out of your hearts. For you are the makers of the flag and it is well that you glory in the making."

Sources

Books

A Colored Man's Reminiscences of James Madison, Paul Jennings
As I Remember: Recollections of American Society during the Nineteenth Century, Marian Gouverneur
The Complete Poetical Works of Henry Wadsworth Longfellow, Henry Wadsworth Longfellow
Dreams in Homespun, Sam Walter Foss
Have Faith in Massachusetts: A Collection of Speeches and Messages, Calvin Coolidge
The Humbler Poets, Slason Thompson, ed.
Immigration and Americanization, Philip Davis, ed.
Letters to His Children, Theodore Roosevelt
Life Among the Piutes: Their Wrongs and Claims, Sarah Winnemucca Hopkins
The Life and Letters of Charles Bulfinch, Architect, Ellen Susan Bulfinch
Miracle in the Hills by Mary Sloop, Used by permission. Copyright 1953, McGraw-Hill Book Company, Inc. Reprinted with permission from The Crossnore School, current copyright holder of the book.
Personal Memoirs of U.S. Grant, Ulysses S. Grant
Poems Teachers Ask For
Poems Teachers Ask For, Book 2
Poems, John Hay
The Political and Economic Doctrines of John Marshall, John Marshall
Saga of the Oak, and Other Poems, William Henry Venable
Scouting for Girls, 1920
The Sunny Side of Diplomatic Life 1875-1912, L. De Hegermann-Lindencrone
Tales of the Trail, James W. Foley
*Theodore Roosevelt: An Autobiography,*Theodore Roosevelt
Thirty-Six Years in the White House, Thomas F. Pendel
The Writings of Samuel Adams, Volume 4 1778-1802, Harry Alonzo Cushing, ed.

Other Publications

Albuquerque Evening Herald, Albuquerque, New Mexico
"The Birth and Babyhood of the Telephone," 1913 speech by Thomas A. Watson
Bisbee Daily Review, Bisbee, Arizona

Burlington Weekly Free Press, Burlington, Vermont
The Citizen, Berea, Kentucky
The Columbia Evening Missourian, Columbia, Missouri
Custer County Republican, Broken Bow, Nebraska
Customs and Border Protection Today, a publication of Customs and Border Protection, Department of Homeland Security
Daily Capital Journal, Salem, Oregon
The Daily Democrat, Anadarko, Oklahoma
Daily Evening Bulletin, Maysville, Kentucky
Daily Globe, St. Paul, Minnesota
The Evening Missourian, Columbia, Missouri
Frontline, a publication of Customs and Border Protection, Department of Homeland Security
Goodwin's Weekly, Salt Lake City, Utah
The Indianapolis News, Indianapolis, Indiana
"Makers of the Flag," 1914 speech by Franklin K. Lane
Medford Mail Tribune, Medford, Oregon
The Morning Star and Catholic Messenger, New Orleans, Louisiana
The National Tribune, Washington, D.C.
New York Tribune, New York, New York
New York World, New York, New York
Omaha Daily Bee, Omaha, Nebraska
The St. Johns Herald, St. Johns, Apache County, Arizona Territory
St. Paul Daily Globe, St. Paul, Minnesota
The San Francisco Call, San Francisco, California
Times and Democrat, Orangeburg, South Carolina
The Youth's Companion

Other Sources

American Presidency Project at the University of California at Santa Barbara
Ashbrook Center at Ashland University
Calvin Coolidge Memorial Foundation
Catholic University of America
Digital History, The University of Houston
Federal Bureau of Investigation
The Fells Historic Estate and Gardens
Kansas Historical Society
Library of Congress
Lincoln Home National Historic Site, National Park Service
Montpelier Foundation
Mount Vernon Ladies' Association
National Archives and Records Administration
Public Broadcasting Service
Speaker of the House John Boehner
State of California
State of Louisiana
State of Maine

State of Montana
State of Nevada
State of Ohio
United States Capitol Visitor's Center
United States Citizenship and Immigration Services
United States Department of Defense
United States Department of the Interior - Bureau of Indian Affairs
United States Election Assistance Commission
United States Fish and Wildlife Service
United States House of Representatives
United States Senate
United States Supreme Court
University of North Carolina at Chapel Hill
Washington State Parks and Recreation Commission
The White House
The White House Historical Association

"Lighter Side of Life at the United States Supreme Court" by Ruth Bader Ginsburg gratefully used by special permission of the United States Supreme Court.

Image Credits

Numbers indicate the page numbers of images. The meanings of the letters t, m, b, l, and r are as follows: t - top of page; m - middle; b - bottom; l - left; r - right.

Images marked CC BY 2.0 are licensed through the Creative Commons Attribution 2.0 Generic License. For more information, visit http://creativecommons.org/licenses/by/2.0/deed.en

Images marked CC BY 3.0 are licensed through the Creative Commons Attribution 3.0 Unported License. For more information, visit http://creativecommons.org/licenses/by/3.0/deed.en

aa7ae (Flickr, CC BY 2.0), 16b
Andreas Matern/amatern (Flickr, CC BY 2.0), 156
Andrew Magill/AMagill (Flickr, CC BY 2.0), 119
Architect of the Capitol, 64, 94, 99
Arvind Govindaraj (Flickr, CC BY 2.0), 44
Bruce Tuten (Flickr, CC BY 2.0), 171
Christian Reed (Flickr, CC BY 2.0), 115
Cliff1066™ (Flickr, CC BY 2.0), 7, 71tl/tm/tr
Collection of the Supreme Court of the United States (Steve Petteway), 130, 132, 133
D.H. Parks (Flickr, CC BY 2.0), 39
Don O'Brien/dok1 (Flickr, CC BY 2.0), 161
DrKenneth (CC BY 3.0), 146b
Elvert Xavier Barnes Photography (Flickr, CC BY 2.0), 134b, 135
Federal Bureau of Investigation, 121, 122
Franklin D. Roosevelt Presidential Library and Museum, Hyde Park, New York, 82t, 164
George Bush Presidential Library, 18 (Eric Draper)
Gerald R. Ford Library, 55 (David Hume Kennerly)
Grand Canyon NPS (Flickr, CC BY 2.0, 116 (Michael Quinn)
IrishFireside (Flickr, CC BY 2.0), 50
Jim Bowen/jimbowen0306 (Flickr, CC BY 2.0), 45b, 46, 93
joebeone (Flickr, CC BY 2.0), 38t
JupiterImages, ii, iii, iv, v, vi (and these same images throughout the book), 1, 2, 9, 22, 123, 150
Library of Congress, 3, 4, 6, 8, 14, 15, 16t, 20, 20t, 23, 24, 25, 26, 29, 30, 31, 32, 33, 34, 35, 45t, 47, 49, 52b, 54, 57, 59, 60, 68, 70, 71bl/bm, 72tr, 73, 74, 75b, 76t, 77l, 78, 80b, 83t, 84, 89, 90, 91t, 92, 101, 102, 111, 126, 128, 136, 138, 139, 140 (University of Utah, Marriott Library), 141 (University of New Mexico), 142 (University of California, Riverside), 143 (University of Oregon Libraries), 148, 149, 151, 152, 159, 162, 166t, 174
Carol M. Highsmith's America, 62, 169
Mary Evelyn McCurdy, cover
Mayor McGinn (Flickr, CC BY 2.0), 117 (Jen Nance)
MiguelVieira (Flickr, CC BY 2.0), 21b
NASA, 72bm, 118 (Jim Grossmann)
nathanborror (Flickr, CC BY 2.0), 61t
National Archives, 5, 12, 36, 37, 58, 85, 91b, 165, 166b
National Park Service, 66
rwgeaston (Flickr, CC BY 2.0), 17
seanmfreese (Flickr, CC BY 2.0), 38b
Sheryl Long (Flickr, CC BY 2.0), 43
SouthCoastToday.com, 75t
State of Nevada, 96
stevebott (Flickr, CC BY 2.0), 28
Susan Sermoneta/Susan NYC (Flickr, CC BY 2.0), 105, 106
Ta Duc/DucDigital (Flickr, CC BY 2.0), 127
Teresa Williams/tearbear (Flickr, CC BY 2.0), 134t
TimOller (Flickr, CC BY 2.0), 13
U.S. Air Force, 82b
U.S. Army Research, Development and Engineering Command/RDECOM (Flickr, CC BY 2.0), 147
U.S. Customs and Border Protection, 108 (Historical Collections Del Rio Sector), 110 (James Tourtellotte), 113
U.S. Department of Labor (Flickr, CC BY 2.0), 118
U.S. Department of the Interior, 104 (Tami A. Heilemann-Office of Communications)
U.S. Fish and Wildlife Service, 120 (Josh O'Connor)
U.S. Navy, 77r
United States Mint, 53
United States Senate, 72tl
uvuphotos (Flickr, CC BY 2.0), 175
White House, 131 (Pete Souza)
Wikimedia Commons, 10, 11, 40, 52t, 61b, 71, 72tm/bl/br, 76b, 79, 83, 95, 98, 103, 107, 124, 129, 146t, 153, 154, 155, 160, 167 (Adair Mulligan), 172

INDEX

Also Available from Notgrass Company

America the Beautiful by Charlene Notgrass

America the Beautiful is a one-year American history, geography, and literature course. It combines the flexibility and richness of a unit study with the simplicity of a textbook-based approach to history. Ages 10-14.

The *Walking In* Series by Mary Evelyn McCurdy

Each workbook is a 30-lesson study of what the Bible says about a particular topic such as faith, peace, and truth. Ages 7-12.

A Record of the Learning Lifestyle by Charlene Notgrass

This simple and effective record-keeping system helps you focus on the most important things and feel good about what you are accomplishing. All ages.

Exploring World History and *Exploring America* by Ray Notgrass

Each of these courses allows your child to earn one year of credit in history, English (literature and composition), and Bible. Engaging history lessons combined with primary sources provide a rich understanding of the past. High school.

Exploring Government and *Exploring Economics* by Ray Notgrass

These one-semester studies give your child a historical perspective on and a contemporary understanding of the subjects covered. High school.

For more information about our homeschool curriculum and resources, call 1-800-211-8793 or visit www.notgrass.com.